LANDSCAPES OF
EXCLUSION

LALH

LANDSCAPES OF EXCLUSION

STATE PARKS AND JIM CROW
IN THE AMERICAN SOUTH

WILLIAM E. O'BRIEN

LIBRARY OF AMERICAN LANDSCAPE HISTORY   AMHERST, MASSACHUSETTS

To Elizabeth and Eugene
&
Wairimũ and Mũmbi

Library of American Landscape History
P.O. Box 1323
Amherst, MA 01004
www.lalh.org

Library of Congress Control Number: 2021947082
ISBN: 978-1-952620-35-5

Designed by Jonathan D. Lippincott
Set in Goudy Old Style

Distributed by
National Book Network
nbnbooks.com

Frontispiece: Campers at Crabtree Creek RDA in 1943. Courtesy State Archives of North Carolina.

The Library of Congress has cataloged the hardcover edition as follows:
Names: O'Brien, William E., 1963– author.
Title: Landscapes of Exclusion : state parks and Jim Crow in the American South
/ William E. O'Brien.
Description: Amherst : University of Massachusetts Press, in association
with Library of American Landscape History, 2015. | Series: Desiging the
American park | Includes bibliographical references and index.
Identifiers: LCCN 2015027970 | ISBN 9781625341556 (cloth : alk. paper)
Subjects: LCSH: Souther States—Race relations—History—20th century. |
Racism—Sothern States—History—20th century. | Parks—Southern States—
History—20th century. | African Americans—Southern States—History—
20th century.
Classification: LCC F220.A1 O27 2015 | DDC 305.800975—dc23
LC record available at http://lccn.loc.gov/2015027970

Publication of the paperback edition of

Landscapes of Exclusion

is supported by the Nancy R. Turner Fund.

CONTENTS

FOREWORD BY ETHAN CARR, FASLA

Park design is a unique form of cultural expression, reflecting many themes of social, cultural, and environmental history, only some of which are explicitly articulated by park supporters and officials. With this first comprehensive history of state park planning in the South, William O'Brien illuminates the deep influence of racism in park design. One of the most understudied and difficult chapters of this history, as O'Brien observes in this important book, involved the collision of what many describe as "America's best idea"—parks—with one of its worst—Jim Crow. *Landscapes of Exclusion* is an outstanding contribution not only to park design history but to larger narratives of the roles and meanings of public landscapes in American life.

O'Brien's discussion of the struggle to desegregate southern state parks is also a major contribution to legal and social history. Like schools, state parks became the focus of major challenges to the legal precedent of *Plessy v. Ferguson*. The struggle to desegregate schools is far better known, but as O'Brien shows, legal strategists at the NAACP and elsewhere identified public parks as the "Achilles' Heel" of the Jim Crow system. Duplicating a truly "equal" segregated park system in southern states would entail enormous expense. Scenic areas and popular recreation destinations were often already set aside as parks. Even if the political will existed to do so, the creation of a second state park system of equivalent quality would not be possible. By the 1950s, any legal rationale for segregating public park systems was collapsing, and the conflict over equal access to state parks was a front line of the civil rights movement.

The lessons and implications of this book contribute to a broader recognition of the impact of racial ideologies on park design throughout the twentieth century—and to this day. O'Brien's conclusions bear on current attitudes and policies as much as they revise historical understanding, while his preface to the paperback edition traces the recent efforts of thoughtful park administrators who seek to understand the reasons for the lack of diversity among park visitors and address the deeply embedded racism at its root.

PREFACE TO THE PAPERBACK EDITION

It has been six years since *Landscapes of Exclusion* was published. I express my ongoing gratitude to the Library of American Landscape History for investing its resources, energy, and effort into this important project. I remain grateful as well to Sarah L. Turner and the California Community Fund, who provided generous support for the original publication, and to the Foundation for Landscape Studies for a David R. Coffin Publication Grant. Funding was also supplied by the FAU Foundation, which provides support to the Harriet L. Wilkes Honors College, its students and faculty.

I am also grateful to the award committees of the Foundation for Landscape Studies and the American Association for State and Local History for recognizing this book's value and contribution. *Landscapes of Exclusion* is counted among a growing number of works that link parks to themes of environmental jus-

tice, in this case illustrating how racial inequality under Jim Crow was etched into American state park landscapes. In the concluding chapter, I discuss the issue of remembrance and ask whether and how the memories of racial segregation might be addressed going forward in these landscapes of the American South.

In this new preface, I reflect on recent trends in park administration regarding race and memory and consider to what extent optimism remains warranted about addressing the past in a more honest and inclusive way. I have been encouraged by the overwhelmingly positive response from employees of state parks and park systems who have seen the book's practical value to their work. In helping bring to light the hidden history of the separate and unequal design of southern state parks, it was my sincere hope to inspire such effort. Those and other attempts to reclaim memories of

racial injustice provide some of the hopeful-
ness needed to move forward. Indeed, the book
emerged as part a broader trend of reconsider-
ing familiar historical narratives, including the
"heritage" claims about many southern memorials and monuments and unspoken assumptions about whom parks, particularly scenic
reserves, are designed for.

Park staff and officials in a number of states
have reached out to express their enthusiasm
in supporting this effort in their own work.
In Tennessee, for instance, agency staff have
enhanced existing interpretive programs and
have pursued historic designations for Booker
T. Washington and T. O. Fuller State Parks.
In Virginia's Twin Lakes State Park (which
includes the former Prince Edward State Park),
the staff have updated interpretive displays and
added educational lessons about the segregation history of its two lakes and the Black workers of the Civilian Conservation Corps who
constructed their dams. An effort in Maryland
is uncovering material to aid interpretation at
Sandy Point State Park, which was featured in
the federal lawsuit that led to the end of legal
public park segregation in 1955.

Among these encouraging actions, I want to
highlight efforts at Texas Parks & Wildlife. Its
recent additions include interpretative signage
at its sole state park with segregated design,
Tyler State Park. Remarkably, the agency has
gone even further, adding signage in other
parks that recognize the Texas state park system's racial exclusion policy under Jim Crow.
At Tyler, the agency has erected an interpretative marker at a hiking trail that asks visitors to
reflect on the path that lies before them. Titled
"Road to Equality," it reveals that the trail was
a repurposed truck road that became the segregated entrance to the park's African American
section. Visitors are asked to contemplate the
experience of discrimination in public facilities
their taxes had paid for: "Imagine paying for
something and not being able to use it due to
the color of your skin." The marker includes
an image and description of Supreme Court
Justice Thurgood Marshall, who at the time of
the photo was an NAACP attorney involved
in a lawsuit about the park. It also includes a
remarkable 1950s-era image of the segregated
park facilities, displaying the stark contrast
between the well-developed white amenities
with the meager ones available to Black visitors. The marker ends with a positive declaration: "Today, Tyler State Park is proud to invite
everyone to enjoy the outdoors."

Beyond Tyler, particularly inspiring is the
recognition in other Texas parks of the policy
of outright racial exclusion. Bastrop and Garner State Parks, which themselves under Jim
Crow had allowed no Black access at all, include
interpretive displays pointing out that historical
fact. At Bastrop, a sign titled "Path to Justice"
declares that today the park "is here for all, but
it wasn't always welcoming to everyone." Under
the heading "No Admittance," it recalls that
under Jim Crow, African Americans "were simply excluded" from all parks in the area.

The trend toward retelling stories of race
has also impacted the Florida Park Service.
In 2016, the John U. Lloyd State Park, located
in Hollywood, was renamed the Dr. Von D.
Mizell–Eula Johnson State Park, after the civil
rights activists credited with organizing "wade-

ins" as acts of civil disobedience aimed at white-only Broward County beaches. Their names and story displace that of a long-time county attorney who purportedly worked to enforce Black exclusion from its beaches and resisted desegregation. Another renaming is being considered as well. After the one hundredth anniversary of the Ocoee Election Day Massacre of 1920, the Florida Park Service convened a committee to consider renaming opportunities at state parks in the Ocoee vicinity, not far from Orlando. Identified as the deadliest election day in American history, the massacre was perpetrated by a white mob in retaliation for the defiant exercise of Black voting rights. An unknown number of Black residents were murdered, with estimates as high as sixty, including the public lynching of Julius "July" Perry. The Black section of Ocoee was burned to the ground and its residents fled the area, vacating properties that were appropriated by whites. The outcome of this renaming initiative was pending at the time of this writing.

While this forward movement is encouraging, the path forward is not always clear, and we will see how these trends will unfold in the face of backlash politics. These steps that connect parks, race, and memory are important to making such spaces more relevant to diverse communities. Seeing one's history acknowledged helps transform scenic parks from exclusionary "white spaces" into more inviting places where all feel recognized and welcome. Those pressing for this change are numerous civic organizations, particularly among Black Americans, that have emerged to address minority underrepresentation in park visitation. The National Park Service, partly motivated by national demographic trends regarding race and ethnicity (a factor closely tied to contemporary racial backlash), has also been promoting such efforts through media campaigns, research, interpretation, and hiring.

There is still much work to do in rewriting the racial narratives that have shaped our present. For instance, there remains in Tennessee a state park named for Nathan Bedford Forrest, infamous as both a Confederate general and as the first Grand Wizard of the Ku Klux Klan. Despite the backlash politics that attempts to postpone change, I can imagine a time in the not-too-distant future when this name, too, will disappear from the landscape, like so many other monuments to the Confederacy. Perhaps the park will be renamed in recognition of a state or local leader in the fight for civil rights or in memory of a tragic episode of racial injustice. Time will tell.

LANDSCAPES OF EXCLUSION

INTRODUCTION

On July 4, 1968, in rural east Georgia, a busload of mixed-race Upward Bound students and staff from Paine College, a historically Black college in Augusta, rolled into Magnolia Springs State Park, located just north of Millen. They had driven forty-five miles to hold a picnic, perhaps unaware that their outing coincided with the annual Miss Magnolia Springs Contest. Attendees of that event, sponsored by the Millen Jaycees and Jaycettes, were surely not expecting this busload of visitors. The arrival of fifty African Americans and five whites from the college brought the contest festivities to a halt. When Black students walked onto the dance floor, a park staff member locked up the jukebox. Witnesses from the group said they were then pressured by the staff and by the taunts and physical threats of white park-goers to leave the formerly "white only" state park. They were told they should take their picnic instead to Lincoln State Park, located in the city of Millen just five miles away. Only a few years earlier, prior to court-ordered desegregation of state parks across the South, the park named for Abraham Lincoln had been one of Georgia's small collection of what the park agency called "state parks for Negroes."[1]

By 1968, however, parks had been officially desegregated through a combination of lawsuits, brought mainly by lawyers affiliated with the National Association for the Advancement of Colored People (NAACP), by federal courts that ruled in their favor, by civil rights protest, and ultimately by passage and enforcement of the 1964 Civil Rights Act. The Independence Day encounter of the Upward Bound group at Magnolia Springs State Park was an instance of enduring white resistance to the desegregation of southern state park systems.

This volume takes a comprehensive look at

the untold story of racial exclusion and segregation in southern state parks, from before their creation to the aftermath of desegregation.[2] At the start of the twentieth century, as the rules of Jim Crow, both customary and statutory, were becoming entrenched in the South, there were also rising hopes across the country of preserving scenic landscapes on a grand scale. Born of an earlier movement that produced the magnificent municipal landscape parks in major U.S. cities, including New York's Central Park, the emerging state park movement carried its naturalistic design principles to more rural and remote areas, creating scenic reservations that Americans have embraced for generations since. These two historical themes of racial subjugation and park development—the latter a feature of what has been called "America's best idea" and the former representing its worst—intersected most prominently in the state park landscapes of the South.[3] This book examines the creation and operation of the relatively few state parks in the region that allowed African American access, emphasizing how racism and discrimination were etched into the geography and design of the region's scenic landscapes.

Exclusion from park access was just one of the many indignities faced by African Americans living under Jim Crow. Named for a nineteenth-century minstrel character, this brutal system of white supremacy applied to all facets of southern life and fundamentally sought to deny any sense of equality between Black and white. The historian Leon F. Litwack explains that "to maintain and underscore its absolute supremacy, the white South systematically dis-

franchised black men, imposed rigid patterns of racial segregation, manipulated the judicial system, and sustained extraordinary levels of violence and brutality."[4] The system was designed, he continues, "to impress on black men and women their political and economic powerlessness and vulnerability—and, most critically, to diminish both their self-esteem and their social aspirations."[5] White supremacy was maintained in part by making inequality visibly apparent, as was evident in the exclusion of African Americans from most state parks, and white indifference to such circumstances was the norm.

State parks hold a special but underappreciated place in American landscape history. National parks are more widely celebrated in the American imagination as visible symbols of democracy, yet state parks were also envisioned to fulfill egalitarian ideals of access for all citizens, and today they see more than twice the annual number of visitors to national parks.[6] The purported therapeutic value of direct contact with scenic landscapes was a key justification for establishing systems of well-distributed state parks. The view was expressed, for instance, by the biologist and park advocate Stanley Coulter in a 1925 speech at Clifty Falls State Park in Indiana: "In a noisy world . . . we lose grip upon ourselves, and feel the strain so keenly that we realize we must break under it unless we find relief. And this nature brings, for it gives us of its infinite life-giving silences. Creative silences, when we find ourselves again, give new values to life and effort and win a new courage for the work still before us."[7] That "new courage" would be instilled by establishing parks that were more easily accessible than the national parks, thus helping Americans throughout the nation alleviate the mounting stresses of everyday life.

State parks have existed since the 1864 creation of Yosemite Park in California. By the end of the century they included well-known sites such as the Niagara Falls and Adirondack reservations in New York, and relatively lesser known ones such as Itasca State Park at the headwaters of the Mississippi River in Minnesota. As the concept of landscape preservation gained in popularity, the effort to provide state parks took a more systematic turn through the creation of the National Conference on State Parks in 1921. The slogan "a state park every 100 miles" emerged out of its first annual meeting in Des Moines, Iowa, thus expressing the goal of situating a state park within a fifty-mile drive of all citizens.[8] In the words of conference organizers, the parks would "provide health-giving playgrounds for each and every man, woman and child."[9]

For decades the idea of locating parks within a fifty-mile radius of all citizens served as a marker of success for individual states, and

Catwalk through cypress swamp at Florida's Highlands Hammock State Park, 1930s. Courtesy National Archives, College Park.

substantial progress toward attaining the goal was made nationwide from the 1920s to the 1960s. The New Deal had ushered in a major boom in state park construction, and after a hiatus during World War II, park development resumed with the economic prosperity and increase in family travel during the decades that followed. In his 1962 work, *The State Parks: Their Meaning in American Life*, the writer and educator Freeman Tilden confirmed the successes of the state park movement, echoing earlier pronouncements that such parks were designed to provide scenic and recreational opportunities "within easy access of all the citizens of every state and territory."[10]

Along with the rest of the nation, states of the American South, including the eleven states of the old Confederacy, the border states of Maryland, West Virginia, and Kentucky, and also Oklahoma, expressed an early enthusiasm for state parks. Progress lagged in the region, however, relative to other parts of the country. By the early 1920s the only scenic parks were Mount Mitchell State Park in North Carolina's Appalachian region, Maryland's Patapsco Forest Reserve outside Baltimore, Royal Palm State Park in Florida's Everglades, and a few historical sites in other states. Relative poverty constrained the southern states, and many had no agency to oversee park development. These limitations were dramatically removed during the Great Depression with the influx of federal dollars, planning, and labor that came with the New Deal.

National Park Service director Stephen Mather had used his personal wealth and political connections to formalize the state park movement in 1921 under the auspices of the National Conference on State Parks. Enlisting the participation of important park advocates, conservationists, and landscape architects, Mather was a major driving force in the movement from its inception until his death in 1930.[11] In addition to promoting public access to rural parks, he envisioned the creation of state park systems partly as a means of protecting significant landscapes that were not considered spectacular enough for national park status.[12] His profound influence on the movement contributed to the close collaborative partnerships between the Park Service and the states that would last until World War II.

The Park Service directed New Deal state park planning generally, and agency staff implemented their designs through labor provided most notably by the Civilian Conservation Corps (CCC) and Works Progress Administration (WPA).[13] Many of the new parks were located on lands acquired through donation or purchase from state, county, and municipal governments and private interests. Others were situated on federal land controlled by agencies including the Resettlement Administration (RA), the Department of Agriculture (USDA), and the Tennessee Valley Authority (TVA). Typically, the recreation facilities developed on these federal lands were turned over to the states to be administered as state parks.

With this federal help, hundreds of state parks were constructed nationwide, including around 150 in the South, by the time the CCC was disbanded in 1942. The foreword to a 1940 guide to South Carolina's state parks expressed the purported general ideal of the access these parks were to provide: "For every person in South Carolina—the young, the old, the rich, the poor, the sportsman, the mother of a family, the laborer, the farmer, the college professor, and all others—there is a State park within approximately fifty miles of home, where picnic shelters provide for a day's outing, where sanitary bathing facilities may be found, or well equipped cabins accommodate guests for a longer vacation."[14]

But throughout the South "every person" did not include African Americans, who were excluded from nearly all of the new parks. By 1940 only seven widely scattered state park facilities were available to Black southerners. These segregated parks were located in only five of the fifteen states in the region. They were late to appear relative to the parks for whites—most progress occurred after 1937, whereas state park construction for whites commenced in 1933—and were limited in the scenic and recreational amenities they offered. Moreover, given the economic and social constraints on African American travel at the time, for most, these relatively few parks were hardly accessible in any practical sense.

The public recreation needs of African Americans—in state parks, municipal parks, and playgrounds—succumbed to indifference among white officials in the region. In 1944 the Swedish social scientist Gunnar Myrdal observed, "The Southern whites are unconcerned about how Negroes use their leisure time, as long as they are kept out of the whites' parks and beaches."[15] J. Austin Burkhart noted that by 1952 the lack of concern had not much changed; he wrote in *The Crisis*, the magazine of the NAACP, that it was as if the need among African Americans for recreation and relaxation was dismissed among whites by pointing and stating, "Yonder sits the rocking chair."[16]

The discrimination faced in all areas of life by African Americans living under Jim Crow was extreme, although incremental changes would begin during the New Deal. By the late 1930s, pressed by African American advocacy organizations and especially the NAACP, the doctrine of "separate but equal," established since the 1896 *Plessy v. Ferguson* decision of the U.S. Supreme Court, was beginning to undergo greater scrutiny by the judicial and executive branches of the federal government. States finally began to feel some pressure to extend park access to African Americans, both as a moral consideration and in order to satisfy the law.[17] By 1935 the National Park Service had begun encouraging states to provide some park access to African Americans, but white recalcitrance translated into limited success.

Amid the region-wide proliferation of parks for exclusively white use, most southern states emerged from the New Deal with no state parks available to African Americans. Moreover, the efforts of the Park Service presumed the constitutionality of "separate but equal," and thus the collaborative park planning by the state and federal agencies accommodated Jim Crow restrictions. No state—even those that made significant early efforts to duplicate facilities, such as Tennessee and South Carolina and by the 1950s Georgia and Florida—even attempted to provide recreational land or physical accommodations and amenities equal to those whites enjoyed. Maps produced

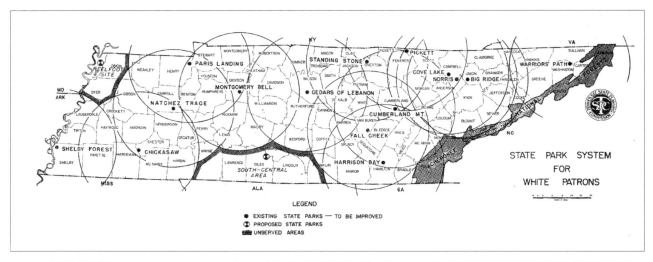

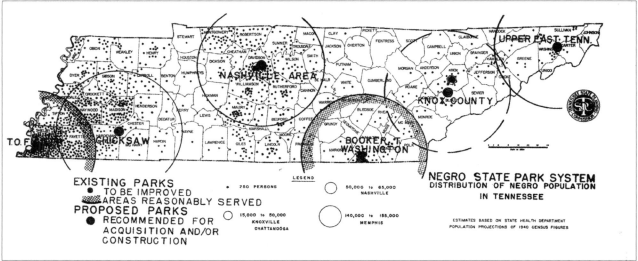

The Tennessee Division of State Parks' 1952 plan for expanding its "white" and "Negro" park systems. Courtesy Tennessee State Library and Archives.

by the Tennessee Division of State Parks in 1952, for example, presented separate "white" and "Negro" park systems. The "white system" illustrates that the state had largely succeeded in providing a park within fifty miles of all white residents. In contrast, the "Negro system" included only T. O. Fuller State Park in Memphis and Booker T. Washington State Park near Chattanooga. Moreover, the maps show that planners envisioned African American access remaining unequal, foreseeing just three additional "Negro" facilities. (None were constructed prior to the desegregation of Tennessee's state parks in 1962.) As the historian Robert R. Weyeneth observed, "As public policy, duplication represented a feeble nod in the direction of providing 'separate but equal' facilities that were emphatically separate and never equal."[18] Across the South, white visitors had exclusive access to a broader array of state parks, including choices near home, and to the best scenery, larger land areas through which to roam, the most interesting and special historical artifacts, and the best-developed recreational facilities and accommodations.

The states' limited attempts to provide space for African Americans took two forms: a "Negro area" either as part of an original "dual-use" design or added to an already existing state park that accommodated whites, or a separate park site, often in proximity to a park for whites. During the decades of segregated state parks from the 1930s through the early 1960s, half of the forty sites that were ultimately made accessible to African Americans consisted of entirely separate parks; the other half were the dual-use type. Both types commonly occupied a relatively small fraction of land area, never included the highest-quality locations, and typically offered relatively rudimentary physical facilities. Their construction and maintenance were often characterized by delay and neglect, and a significant number of envisioned facilities never went beyond the planning stage, stalled by problems with funding or with locating sites that would not attract protest from local white residents.

Among the dual-use parks, the African American sections were nearly always much smaller than the main, white areas and were normally provided with day-use facilities only. To maintain racial separation, these areas typically had separate access roads and were set apart from the rest of the park by both distance and landscape features that formed buffers between the Black and white sections. The most common buffers were tracts of forest and expanses of water, such as lakes or ponds.

Joe Wheeler State Park Negro Area, near Rogersville, Alabama, 1953. Photo by C. E. McCord. Courtesy National Archives, Morrow, Georgia.

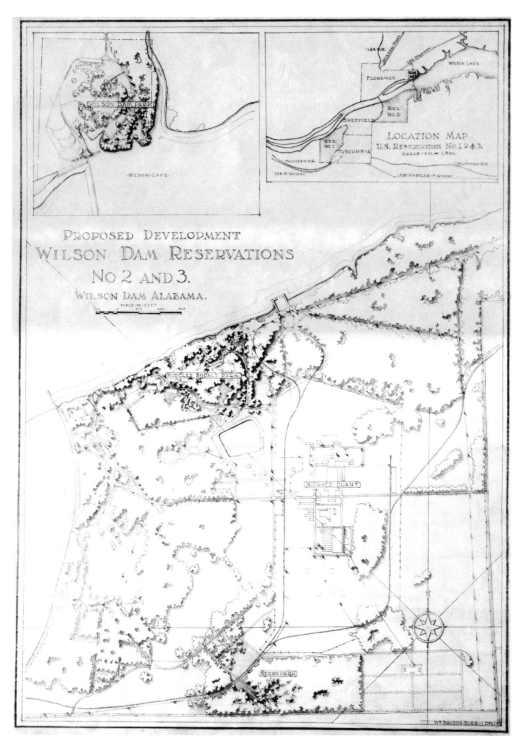

Master plan for the Wilson Dam Reservations in Muscle Shoals, Alabama. Courtesy National Archives, College Park.

A prototype of the dual-use park was a demonstration project developed in 1935 by the TVA, the Park Service, and the CCC in northwestern Alabama, at the site of Wilson Dam. A master plan displays segregated spaces that included "Muscle Shoals Park" for whites along the bank of the Tennessee River and a smaller area called "Negro Park" on the south edge of the property. The separate spaces are buffered by the maximum possible distance, while the hundred-acre Negro Park is sited, as if adding cliché to injury, on the other side of railroad tracks. The separate access road leads to a lone picnic area in a patch of forest. In contrast, the elaborate road network in the four-hundred-acre Muscle Shoals Park incorporates amenities such as overnight cabins, a nature study museum, a lookout tower, rustic footbridges and guardrails, and ornamental plantings, allowing white visitors multiple opportunities to enjoy the space in varied settings. Visitors to

the white park also had access to views of the Tennessee River from the "precipitous bluff" at the water's edge—the prime location—while any possible sightline to the water from Negro Park contended with distance as well as a nitrate production plant situated between the two sites. Prior to construction the site of Negro Park was regarded as a dumping ground and considered "not much more than a mosquito-breeding spot—a menace to health."[19] The park reportedly saw only light traffic, owing mainly to its limited day-use-only status.[20]

Georgia's Magnolia Springs and Lincoln State Parks, where this introduction began, illustrate as well the inequities in the design of separate state parks. Located five miles north of Millen, Magnolia Springs was established during the New Deal, designed by National Park Service planners and constructed with CCC labor. Georgia's state park agency, itself in existence only since 1931, operated Mag-

Postcard of the Magnolia Springs recreation site in the early 1930s, prior to its development as a state park. Courtesy Georgia Archives, Vanishing Georgia Collection, jnk095.

nolia Springs, which was restricted to whites from its 1939 opening. The forested tract of one thousand rural acres was average size for a state park and showcased underground springs as its most compelling feature. Because of its springs, the site had long attracted visitors from around the area and included recreation facilities even before the New Deal. The location also offered a historical connection to the Civil War— the archaeological remnants of Camp Lawton, the largest Confederate Civil War prison for Union soldiers, which was liberated during General William Tecumseh Sherman's "March to the Sea" in late 1864. Translating the unique site into a state park, the Park Service designed a road network that wound its way to picnic areas, dining halls, and overnight camping, as well as a twenty-eight-acre lake for swimming and fishing.

Five miles down the road was Lincoln State

Magnolia Springs State Park in the 1950s. Stell Photo Service. Courtesy Georgia Archives, Small Print Collection, brw192.

Park, sited on land acquired through donation in 1955 by the Georgia Department of State Parks, Historic Sites and Monuments. At fifty-two acres, the area reserved for African Americans comprised one-twentieth the area of Magnolia Springs. Additionally, and contrary to the ideal of a rural reservation or retreat, Lincoln State Park was located within the city limits of Millen itself, just a few blocks west of its main intersection. As was typical of state parks reserved for African Americans, it was limited to day-use activities, which included access to a picnic area, swimming pool, and areas for hiking.[21] There was nothing remarkable about the site in terms of scenery, recreational potential, history, or even topography. By all appearances Lincoln State Park was a pleasant city park.

Given the challenges of locating any high-quality sites for African American use that would not run into white objections, park agencies around the South were led either to give up their searches entirely or to settle for virtually any parcel of donated land that could pass the test of local approval. The small Lincoln State Park parcel, located in a preponderantly African American section of Millen, was deemed acceptable despite its commonplace features. From the state's perspective, applying the label "state park" to such subpar sites could at least serve as a fig leaf to cover the inequity problems they faced as legal challenges to "separate but equal" commenced during the postwar years.

Noting the exclusively white access to the highest-quality state park locations, Norfolk's *Journal and Guide*, a prominent African American newspaper, pointed out in 1950 that "the scenic beauties of the seashore or the grandeur of the mountains, which may be seen in the various state parks . . . cannot be moved to [a] colored state park."[22] *New South*, the journal of the Atlanta-based Southern Regional Council (SRC), concurred, remarking that even though legislatures might approve African American state parks on sea or lake shores or in the mountains, the problem of access to unique scenic features remained: "A state's highest waterfall, deepest or only gorge, and its oldest Indian mounds obviously cannot be duplicated. The white parks generally developed first, and they have acquired most of the spots of unusual natural beauty, the extraordinary natural phenomena, and the historical relics of the state."[23] Highlighting the problem of access, the lighthouse at South Carolina's Hunting Island State Park was visible from the African American beach at the park's north end. But this unique and historic feature was off limits to African American park visitors, who were restricted to their segregated area. As one historian declared, "no black person dared to stray across the line."[24]

The pervasiveness of racial discrimination at state parks made them a powerful focal point in postwar legal attempts to dismantle Jim Crow. Writing in the *Virginia Law Review* in 1954, Robert M. McKay remarked that even compared to more widely discussed arenas of segregation like schools or transportation, "the actual fact is that the differences are more pronounced in this field [parks and recreation] than in any other area in which distinctions based on race persist."[25] McKay

The lighthouse at South Carolina's Hunting Island State Park viewed from the formerly segregated African American beach. Photo by the author, 2012.

relied on data from a survey of southern state parks conducted in 1952 and 1953 by the SRC. By that time, the number of state parks for African Americans had increased from 7 in 1940 to 18, but despite these additions, the gulf between Black and white state park access remained vast: the survey counted 180 state parks reserved for white use (the actual number was significantly higher as several states did not respond).[26]

Further, data from the nine states respond-

ing to the survey suggested that although African Americans comprised 22 percent of the population in these states, they had access to only 6 percent of the state parks. Most dramatic was the disparity in accessible land area. McKay calculated that in these nine states 986,184 acres of park land were available to whites but only 8,879 acres to African Americans, a mere 0.9 percent of the total.[27] (Burkhart had pointed out in his 1952 article in *The Crisis* that Tennessee's two state parks designated for African Americans comprised 1,350 acres, while just one of the thirteen parks for whites held 42,000 acres.)[28]

The obvious region-wide inequity left state park systems open to constitutional challenges that commenced in the years after World War II. This postwar litigation effort was led by the NAACP's Legal Defense Fund, which by 1948 had in all legal actions set its sights on achieving desegregation rather than equalization.[29] The federal court system had by then grown generally more attentive to concerns about inequality in separate provisions. During the 1950s and early 1960s, federal judges, including the justices of the U.S. Supreme Court, heard state park cases, and their rulings created reverberations throughout the South.

Initially park agencies responded by crafting a more or less unified, region-wide "equalization" strategy that emphasized increasing the number of African American state park facilities. Their strategy, however, would ultimately fail. In addition to increasing federal judicial support for desegregation by the early 1950s, state legislatures remained reluctant to fund expensive park duplication efforts.[30] Indeed, no state would pursue actual equalization. At most, some attempts were made to appease the courts by creating a few additional facilities for African Americans. But such plans were often thwarted by local white residents who, backed by their political leaders, routinely continued to reject the construction of "Negro" state park facilities near their homes and communities. By 1955, despite a region-wide increase in the overall number of facilities, eight of the southern states had managed to maintain only one

park that allowed African American visitors. Only the park agencies of Georgia, Florida, and South Carolina had succeeded in constructing more than three. Louisiana was the last to commence the effort, building its first of three in 1956 as a segregated section of Lake Bistineau State Park, near Shreveport. Arkansas, which had opened Watson State Park for African Americans near Pine Bluff in 1938 but closed it in 1944, had none at all.[31]

The precedent set by the U.S. Supreme Court's landmark *Brown v. Board of Education* decision in 1954, which pronounced that "separate educational institutions are inherently unequal," would guide subsequent rulings on state parks as well, in favor of the NAACP. These rulings were met with a mixed response. Oklahoma and the border states of Maryland, West Virginia, and Kentucky integrated their park systems by 1955 or soon after. Other states of the South participated in a massive resistance campaign against federal court demands for desegregation, with some governors and legislatures threatening to close parks or lease them to private interests.

Beyond the legal arena, the strengthening civil rights movement would add acts of civil disobedience to African American protests against white-exclusive state parks. The dual pressure of legal battles and protests culminated in the 1963 U.S. Supreme Court ruling in *Watson v. City of Memphis*, which called for immediate desegregation of public parks, and passage of the 1964 Civil Rights Act, which ultimately forced the end of Jim Crow. By mid-decade, all of the South's state park systems were officially desegregated—although de facto

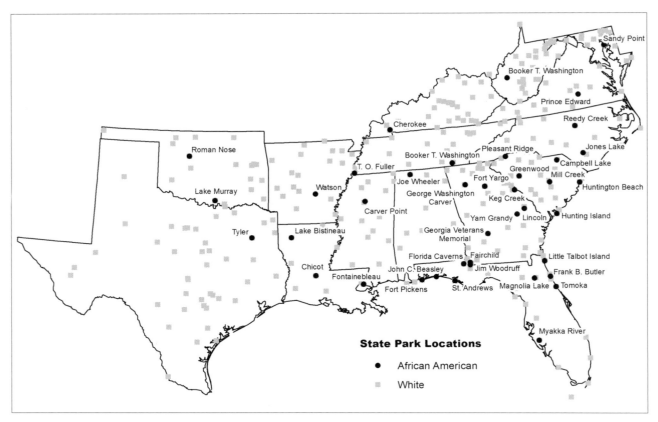

Locations of state parks in the South highlighting facilities made available to African Americans between 1937 and 1962. Map by the author.

park segregation remained in many places for years to come.

Southern state park systems were born into a Jim Crow culture, reflecting its racism and discriminatory values and giving visible, spatial form to its demands for racial exclusion and separation. These values have been durably imprinted across southern landscapes, and are still apparent to anyone who cares to see. An influential proponent of parks, Col. Richard Lieber of the Indiana state park service, idealized state park spaces as having "outstanding scenic or wilderness character," and offering "significant historical, archaeological, ecological, [and] geological . . . values."[32] But in the South both scenic landscape preservation and design and the provision of recreational resources were enlisted also as tools for delineating and enforcing the values of Jim Crow. Park boundaries, gates, roads, and other features inscribed physical indications of who was entitled to enjoy the scenery and accommodations and who was to be excluded; of who was to be allocated more recreational space, and who would get less—or nothing at all.

More than a generation after the dismantling of Jim Crow, many physical inscriptions remain as ghostly presences on contemporary state park landscapes. Lonely entry roads leading to an isolated section of Georgia's Fort Yargo State Park, Louisiana's Chicot State Park, and South Carolina's Lake Greenwood State Park, among others, remain today as unremarked reminders of this segregated past. There has been little eagerness among southern state park services to inform today's visiting public about this history. Few have erected markers or provided interpretive materials of any kind recalling the events that shaped these park landscapes. It is possible, though, that a shift toward greater recognition of this past will follow contemporary trends of increased memorialization of America's racialized history. In their book *Civil Rights Memorials and the Geography of Memory*, Owen J. Dwyer and Derek H. Alderman proclaim: "The future can, in part, be traced back to what is remembered and forgotten on the cultural landscape."[33] One purpose of this book is to encourage a wider commemoration.

ONE

JIM CROW RECREATION

Several years after Frederick Law Olmsted and Calvert Vaux won the 1858 design competition to create Central Park, Olmsted accepted a job in California's Sierra Mountains managing the Mariposa Mining Company. Living not far from Yosemite Valley, Olmsted took his family on a camping trip to the site in 1864 and was profoundly inspired by its scenic beauty. During that year, Congress was considering a bill that would designate Yosemite as a publicly owned park to be protected "for public use, resort, and recreation" and administered by the state of California.[1] On its approval, Governor Frederick F. Low appointed Olmsted as chairman of the commission that would manage and develop the site.[2] Olmsted's proposed design for Yosemite, with its carefully constructed views, trails, and other features, promoted his idea that scenic parks were picturesque works of art, an approach that formed a bridge be-

tween British naturalistic style and an emerging American preservation movement.[3] His vision of park design, which embraced both scenic preservation and enhanced visitor access and experience, would eventually find expression in rural reservations around the nation and would fundamentally shape American expectations about the visual character of a scenic park.[4]

Olmsted's work at Yosemite, the nation's first state park, came as the United States was emerging from the horrors of civil war and coincided with the national transition from antebellum to Reconstruction America. Presented at this historic moment, Olmsted's 1865 report on Yosemite, the scholar Richard Grusin suggests, can be viewed in larger terms as an attempt to participate "in the re-creation of American national identity,"[5] to reorient the primary axis of American identity away from a North-South direction, which had culminated in national conflict centered on cleavages of slavery and race, and toward an East-West alignment that embraced a future of national expansion, manifest destiny, and reunification.[6] Yosemite would emerge as a revered emblem of scenic nationalism, particularly after achieving national park status in 1890.[7] American fascination with the West and its spectacular scenery would give rise to a new phase in the park movement, and eventually national and state parks would become important markers of American identity.

The possibility of reorienting the nation away from its racialized North-South division was thwarted, however, by postwar trends. Racial discord and animosity would only intensify in the decades following the Civil War. As the desire to preserve America's most spectacular scenic landscapes grew, hostility among southern whites toward freed African Americans spread throughout the nation, added to nativist antagonism aimed at a new wave of immigrants to the United States. Appeals to racial stereotypes, reinforced by white fears of "race suicide" near the turn of the twentieth century, led to the definition early on of scenic parks as white space. The coincidence of these trends was the foundation for the nationwide exclusion of African Americans from most public parks through the 1920s.

State Park Differences

After Yosemite was established in 1864, two decades passed before other state parks were created and a state park movement developed. Olmsted and his associates played a vital role in its growth, translating their naturalistic municipal landscape parks in America's cities into the rustic design that came to characterize both national and state parks. (Fig. 1.1) Beginning in 1885, after twenty years of lobbying, Olmsted transformed Niagara Falls from an overly commercialized reminder of the excesses of privatization into the picturesque Niagara Reservation. The Adirondack Forest Preserve was also created in 1885, and stringent "forever wild" protections were added by New York's legislature in 1894. More scenic state parks were created in much of the country during the 1890s and into the next century.

By then the label "state park" was being used more commonly.[8] Examples emerged with increased regularity as states constructed facilities mainly in the Northeast, Midwest, and West—Minnesota's Itasca State Park (1891), New York and New Jersey's jointly administered Palisades Interstate Park (1900), Michigan's Mackinac Island State Park (1895), and California's Big Redwoods Basin State Park (1902), among others in Connecticut, Pennsylvania, and Massachusetts. In the Pacific Northwest, Washington and Idaho began adding parks in the 1910s; Oregon produced its first in 1920.[9] Wisconsin had three parks by 1917, and the landscape architect and planner John Nolen had included blueprints for others in his 1908 report *State Parks for Wisconsin*. Then in 1921, with the formation of the National Conference on State Parks, the movement became focused on systematic park expansion nationwide. In that year, "twenty-nine states . . . had no state parks at all."[10] The

Fig. 1.1. Postcard of a rustic cabin at Oklahoma's Robbers Cave State Park, designed by the Park Service and constructed by the CCC. Photo by Jeff Griffin. Courtesy Caroline Brown Collection, Oklahoma Historical Society Research Division.

pace of state park creation would increase steadily thereafter, but with little money allocated by states in the 1920s, the full realization of construction goals would have to await the large-scale financial and institutional support of the New Deal.

After the turn of the century, automobile ownership became a major factor in the rise of tourism, and scenic rural parks became increasingly popular destinations.[11] This mobility encouraged park development and was presumed in the state park movement's goal of providing a park within a fifty-mile drive of every state resident. As the landscape historian Ethan Carr points out, the naturalistic design

of these parks and the selective inclusion of recreational amenities helped shape the experience of generations of park visitors: "When early-20th-century tourists arrived at county or state reservations, they expected to find parks that encompassed the natural scenery they had come to admire, that had roads and trails to make the scenery accessible, and that often featured lodges, campgrounds, and facilities for various outdoor activities."[12] National parks were significantly more restrictive, disallowing recreational facilities that ran counter to a "back to nature" concept. State parks, by contrast, were created with greater flexibility and range in scenic quality, landscape modification such as constructed lakes, and recreational facilities that often included playgrounds, tennis courts, baseball fields, and even golf courses. The significant diversity that emerged among state parks in design and amenities was controversial in the early twentieth century and has remained so.[13] Acceptance of this divergence in the quality of state parks, however, would later influence the design and construction of the segregated state park spaces for African Americans in the South.

During the 1920s, as the state park movement attempted to develop a more coherent message, tensions emerged over just how closely such parks should maintain fidelity to a naturalistic ideal. Early differences among proponents often emphasized the challenges of making parks accessible while maintaining standards of scenic quality. Frederick Law Olmsted Jr.'s widely influential 1929 survey of California state parks expressed a desire to make state parks "equitably accessible" to residents in all areas of the state but cautioned that site quality could be diminished by too strict adherence to goals of nearby access. Olmsted argued for preserving sites that were "distinctive and notable" to the point of attracting visitors from all around the state and not just those from nearby locations.[14]

An emphasis on scenic quality and fidelity to nature, as opposed to accessibility and recreational amenities, was also advocated by James L. Greenleaf in his address to the National Conference on State Parks in 1925. A landscape architect and board member of the conference, Greenleaf referred to "development" as "a dangerous term to use." Skeptical of the idea of locating a state park every hundred miles, Greenleaf argued that the motivation for such construction "is not the preservation of scenery but the urge of motor travel," and that movement away from scenic ideals would lead to the "vulgarizing" of state parks. Such a direction would encourage the establishment of "motor camps" rather than truly scenic reservations worthy of the state park label. Greenleaf proposed that the slogan "a state park every 100 miles" be adjusted to "a State Park wherever Nature smiles; a motor camp every 100 miles."[15]

On the other hand, the landscape architect Harold Caparn and Jay Downer, a civil engineer, endorsed diversity among state parks, which they believed should include not only nature preserves but also historical monuments, battlefields, and other significant markers of state identity. Also, by the 1920s the progressive playground park movement in the nation's cities had greatly influenced discussions of the recreational purpose of parks and the types of facilities that should be available. Caparn and Downer argued that "a State Park may be planned with the characteristics of a National, State, county or city park and yet be a State Park."[16] Not wedded to an ideal, they believed that questions of design and development depended on context.

Differences of opinion persisted over the types of recreation facilities allowable as well as the size of the site and quality of scenic resources. In 1962 Freeman Tilden, an author of influential works on the national and state parks, reflected on these early debates over park ideals and on the widely divergent outcomes over time. He answered the question "What is a state park?" with a half-joking response: "A state park is any area of any size set aside for any type of recreation purpose, or as a historical memorial, or to preserve scenery or a natural curiosity, and *called* a state park."[17] Tilden's facetious definition captures the reality that, in practice, scenic quality was not a fundamental consideration in state park development.

Acceptance of diversity in quality, design, and function would become a significant factor during the eventual creation of state parks for African Americans in the South after the mid-1930s. Idealized rural reservations, such as Minnesota's Itasca State Park or even the naturalized Niagara Reservation, would share the designation of "state park" with small and relatively unremarkable parks, which were sometimes located in or near urban areas and included few scenic resources. In the South, the state and federal agencies that built the state park facilities for African Americans would take full advantage of being able to label virtually any publicly owned site a "state park." Usually small in size and poor in scenic quality and other amenities, the facilities provided for African Americans could be called state parks under Tilden's flexible definition and thus be counted as legitimate units in park systems that supported claims of adherence to the "separate but equal" doctrine.

Despite the creation of the National Conference on State Parks, through the end of the 1920s little state park development occurred in the Southeast, especially of scenic rural reserves. Early parks in the South commemorated historical events, such as the Texas independence struggle and the Civil War. In 1899, for instance, the state of Florida created a commission and purchased land to erect a monument at Olustee Battlefield which marked an 1864 Confederate victory. The site is considered to be "the first state-acquired lands still within the park system."[18] In 1883 the state of Texas purchased the Alamo as well as the cemetery and battlefield associated with Sam Houston's defeat of Santa Ana's army at San Jacinto, which became San Jacinto State Park in 1907. Additional battlefield and other sites significant to Texas's independence history were preserved by the 1920s, including what became Gonzales, Goliad, and Kings State Parks.[19] (Fig. 1.2)

Few early state-administered parks in the South were devoted to the preservation of scenic features. One of them was Patapsco Forest Reserve in Maryland, which was referred to as a park as early as 1911. Another was North Carolina's Mount Mitchell State Park, created in 1915.[20] Royal Palm State Park in the Florida Everglades was developed the following year, though it was never administered as state-controlled land and was later incorporated into Everglades National Park.[21] In Arkansas, the acquisition of Petit Jean State Park, located on Petit Jean Mountain along the Arkansas River, was authorized by the state legislature in 1923 after Stephen Mather, as director of the National Park Service, recommended that the location be preserved for that purpose.[22] Like most southern parks, however, development of

Fig. 1.2. Survivors of the Battle of Olustee at the 1912 dedication of the battlefield monument in Florida's first state-owned park. Courtesy State Archives of Florida.

Fig 1.3. Postcard showing Mount Mitchell, site of Mount Mitchell State Park in western North Carolina, 1938. Courtesy North Carolina Collection, Lewis Round Wilson Special Collections Library, UNC at Chapel Hill.

COPYRIGHT 1938
WALTER M. CLINE
CHATTANOOGA, TENN.

MT. MITCHELL – ALTITUDE 6684 FEET
HIGHEST POINT IN EASTERN AMERICA
FROM BUCK CREEK GAP, N.C.

the site would wait on the allocation of New Deal funding and labor. (Fig. 1.3)

The historian Thomas Cox speculates that the South's late start in producing state parks of the scenic variety was due to "poverty, traditions of limited government, the weakness of transcendentalism (thanks in part to its ties to abolition), and the pastoral-plantation ideal that extolled the country estate rather than unsullied nature."[23] Mark Hersey adds that preservationism in general lagged there owing to the absence of landscapes that would have been recognized as wilderness in comparison to the spectacular examples in the West.[24] Before the establishment of Louisiana's park system, the conservationist Caroline Dormon of the Louisiana State Parks Association wrote about the state's scenic features that would justify such development, lamenting that "many natives of Louisiana are not yet aware of the beauty of their own state."[25] Nonetheless, factions

within nearly every state had at least aspired to preserve scenic locations as the nationwide state park movement took shape. A handful of southern states, such as Texas, Florida, and Virginia, had created agencies for the purposes of planning and land acquisition in the decade preceding the New Deal.[26] Other states, including West Virginia, Louisiana, Mississippi, and South Carolina, delayed the creation of park agencies until the beginning of the New Deal, when it became necessary to facilitate collaboration with the Park Service and other federal agencies.[27]

After this slow start, the arrival of federal funds and labor in the South accelerated state park construction. In 1927 Alabama created its Commission on Forestry, which oversaw the construction of a 421-acre parcel called Talladega County State Park by 1930.[28] Three years later, construction had expanded to eleven sites, and by 1935 there were twenty-two state park land acquisitions.[29] In Alabama and elsewhere, however, this rapid improvement in park access had ignored the South's large African American populations, which were excluded from all facilities until late in the New Deal. Adhering to the Jim Crow system that ruled southern race relations, the exclusive access for whites was a designed feature of the region's budding state park systems.

The Rise of Jim Crow

The Union victory in the Civil War and subsequent adoption of the Thirteenth Amendment formally abolishing slavery had ensured the permanence of President Lincoln's 1863 Emancipation Proclamation and raised hopes that emancipation would mean freedom for all African Americans to participate in the full benefits of citizenship. The better lives that freed slaves had envisioned at war's end seemed attainable with the onset of Reconstruction, which provided new political, social, and economic opportunities for African Americans in the region and sought to transform the entrenched racial hierarchies of the South. From the start, however, most white southerners resented what they perceived as a federal imposition on their autonomy and an assault on their way of life. They worked to undermine Reconstruction at every step, inflicting a campaign of intimidation and violence aimed particularly at Black southerners. Leon F. Litwack recounts the fear among whites that Black success would permanently disrupt their system of racial supremacy: "Whites employed terror, intimidation, and violence to doom Reconstruction, not because blacks had demonstrated incompetence but because they were rapidly learning the uses of political power, not because of evidence of black failure but the far more alarming evidence of black success." While apparent in social and economic affairs, successes were particularly evident in politics, including gains in voting rights and the election of African Americans to political office. Litwack continues, "This was clearly unacceptable to a people who deemed themselves racially superior and who resisted any evidence to the contrary."[30]

In the face of continuous resistance, northern support waned steadily after 1874 and Reconstruction ended with the Compromise of 1877, which removed federal military protection for African Americans in the South. The result was a reversion to the rule of southern whites and a resurgence of measures designed to reestablish the old racial order. Expressed through both custom and law, the emergent system of racial separation and subordination called "Jim Crow" would rapidly spread through all areas of southern life. Racial segregation was a key feature of the system. As Litwack explains, "What the white South did was to segregate the races by law and enforced custom in practically every conceivable situation in which whites and blacks might come into social contact: from public transportation to public parks, from the workplace to hospitals, asylums, and orphanages, from the homes for the aged, the blind, deaf, and dumb, to the prisons, from saloons to churches."[31]

The expanding railways in the postwar

South were among the first sites of segregation law, although the rail companies were often reluctant enforcers. Not wanting the added expense of policing southern race relations, some of these companies searched for ways to evade compliance.[32] Seeking in 1892 to nullify a new Louisiana law requiring segregated rail cars, a local group of Black, Creole, and white people called the Committee of Citizens colluded with the East Louisiana Railroad to test the statute by arranging for its violation. Homer Plessy, a legally "Negro" man who was seven-eighths Caucasian, was chosen as an ideal plaintiff. He attempted to enter a white-only car on the train and was promptly arrested.[33]

Before the U.S. Supreme Court in 1896, Plessy's lawyers in the case known as *Plessy v. Ferguson* argued that the segregation law violated the Constitution's Fourteenth Amendment, suggesting that statutory racial separation defined African Americans as inferior. The court, by a 7-to-1 vote, rejected the argument, establishing the "separate but equal" doctrine that would legitimize Jim Crow laws and customs for much of the next century. But there was little effort to enforce the "equal" provision, and both inferior facilities and outright exclusion would remain the norm for Black southerners until after the civil rights victories of the 1960s ended official segregation restrictions.

Economic transformation in the New South after the Civil War, which included significant migration of African Americans from rural farms into southern cities and towns, generated a particular anxiety for whites. Many grew increasingly concerned about the economic implications and also felt that "corrupting" urban influences would encourage the emergence of the so-called New Negro, who was ever more willing to question his or her station in life. Southern whites countered by promoting an idealized image of the "Old Negro." In *Making Whiteness*, Grace Elizabeth Hale recounts the emergence of a romantic, Old South nostalgia among white, middle-class southerners. Calling it "the funhouse mirror of New South progress," she points out that this nostalgia by 1900 was freed from actual events and clear memories regarding the days of slavery, generating in their place an idealization of race relations between southern whites and their slaves. As Hale states, "The making of modern southern whiteness began, then, within a time and space imagined as a racially innocent plantation pastorale, where whites and blacks loved and depended upon each other."[34] This image of harmonious race relations in the South, where all knew and accepted their place in society, was promoted by white southerners up to and beyond the demise of Jim Crow more than sixty years later.[35] But whites were unable to prevent the emergence of the New Negro, and by the end of the nineteenth century this trend, in Litwack's words, elevated "the presence of the Negro and the exercise of his [or her] constitutional rights to the level of crisis" in southern society.[36]

Preventing moves toward greater equality translated into intensified white hostility and denial of any social standing for African Americans in the South. The preferred remedy for the "problem" of the emerging New Negro was to subordinate African Americans as a laboring class, "doomed to provide labor and service to whites, while otherwise keeping to their separate and inferior place."[37] African Americans were routinely denied due process in the region's court systems and terror tactics were used to enforce compliance with their subordination. Lynching, a practice of summary execution without trial, became the iconic form of racial terrorism, while mob violence conducted by whites against Black communities was also common. If violence and intimidation were significant means of enforcement, deprivation and discrimination were the bedrock of racial subordination. Denial of amenities, such as public parks, that were on par with those available to whites was aimed at halting the development of greater confidence among African Americans. This white imperative to remind Black southerners of their presumed inferior place in society laid the foundation for the vast inequality in access experienced by Black southerners as state and municipal parks were constructed in the region. (Fig. 1.4)

Among southern state park systems this discrimination was achieved not by law per se, but nearly always through enforced custom.[38] Reviewing the basis for public park segregation, the legal scholar Robert M. McKay in 1954 noted no systematic pattern of legal seg-

Fig. 1.4. The scene of the white mob massacre in 1921 that came to be known as the Tulsa race riot. Courtesy Oklahoma Historical Society Research Division.

regation of southern recreation facilities: "It is apparent . . . that the statutory provisions are not the significant restraining factor."[39] For instance, characterizing its policy as "tradition," North Carolina's Board of Conservation and Development in 1957 verbalized the custom-based approach to park segregation that guided most states in the region: "The committee does not take the position that there is any law or administrative rule or policy which excludes Negroes from the use of certain of our State Parks. . . . During the years some of our parks have traditionally been used by white citizens and others have traditionally been used by Negro citizens."[40] In some states, the nonstatutory nature of the rules allowed for a degree of discretion by individual park managers who understood the degree of local white tolerance; for example, in some circumstances certain individual African Americans might be permitted to fish at a lake in a white-only state park.[41] Most of the time, however, such customary rules were enforced as if they carried the weight of law.

The few specific laws that were eventually passed in certain states are notable for their appearance after World War II, when legal challenges to segregated state parks were beginning to be brought before federal courts. By 1950 Virginia law mandated segregation more broadly in "any public hall, theatre, opera house, motion picture show or any place of public entertainment or public assemblage."[42] Texas and South Carolina mandated the segregation of their state park facilities by the early 1950s; Louisiana would do the same in 1956. These late attempts at formalizing segregation rules, however, were little more than last-gasp efforts to stem the tide of desegregation.

Wilderness and Fears of Racial Degeneration

Beyond the South, the nationwide rise of the preservation movement and the construction of parks coincided with the descent to the nadir of race relations in the United States. Inspired by transcendentalist writings and Romantic landscape art, the preservation movement was promoted by elites including eastern industrialists, intellectuals, artists, and planners who lauded the spiritual and character-building value of contact with nature. But by the first decades of the twentieth century access to wilderness and scenic parks was also presented in racialized tones as providing both a respite for relatively affluent white Americans and a means of maintaining the prevailing racial order. This creation of scenic parks as white spaces mirrors the general exclusion of African Americans from such recreational opportunities in those years.

The *Plessy* ruling by the Supreme Court, while ostensibly addressing southern affairs, reflected what by then had become entrenched racial presumptions nationwide. Such views were aided by scientific racism, which presented white superiority as rooted in biology. In particular, the period from circa 1890 to the early 1930s witnessed intensely expressed hostility toward racial minorities and the nativist rejection of immigrants from China, Japan, the Philippines, and countries of central and southern Europe. American anxieties about race in the late nineteenth and early twentieth centuries included careful policing of the boundaries of who did and did not "belong," stoking fears among many white Americans about the potential for national racial decline.

Regarding African Americans, white concern in the North soon shifted from relative indifference to open hostility as Black southerners moved in ever-greater numbers to the northern and midwestern urban industrial centers during the Great Migration in the early decades of the twentieth century. When African Americans sought manufacturing jobs, they were ghettoized in the cities, and white northerners subjected them to discriminatory practices in both public and private spheres. As a sign that Jim Crow might even creep northward, racial segregation was made official policy in 1913 under President Woodrow Wilson, a Virginian, who oversaw the extension of segregation rules to federal offices in Washington, D.C. Some northern states entertained proposals for installing Jim Crow measures, prompting the *Charlotte Observer* to note in 1913 that "the country has fairly come to be of one mind upon the so-called negro problem."[43]

More generally, as the cities of the nation grew in population and became less and less healthful, the need to preserve wilderness came to be seen as increasingly important. John Muir famously described this need in terms of mental health: "Thousands of tired, nerve-shaken, over-civilized people are beginning to find out that going to the mountains is going home; that wildness is a necessity; and that mountain parks and reservations are useful not only as fountains of timber and irrigating rivers, but

as fountains of life."[44] Theodore Roosevelt shared Muir's enthusiasm for wilderness. Roderick Frazier Nash writes that Roosevelt was "delighted that his country had taken the lead in establishing wilderness preserves and urged 'every believer in manliness . . . every lover of nature, every man who appreciates the majesty and beauty of the wilderness and of wild life' to give them full support."[45]

Preservationists articulated the profound racism that characterized the era. Roosevelt expressed his belief that the presence of African Americans in the United States was a "terrible problem" that had no true solution. The historian Gary Gerstle recounts that Roosevelt, lamenting that Africans had ever been brought to America, "always regarded the Negro as an indelible black mark on the white nation, . . . a constant reminder of America's racial imperfection."[46] The environmental historian Carolyn Merchant notes that John Muir also had demonstrated the prevailing "cultural prejudices against blacks," pointing to his descriptions of the African Americans he encountered in the South in his account of his 1867 thousand-mile walk to the Gulf of Mexico: "Although he described some as 'well trained,' 'extremely polite,' and very 'civil,' he viewed most as lazy and noisy. He wrote that 'the Negroes are easy-going and merry, making a great deal of noise and doing little work. One energetic white man, working with a will, would easily pick as much cotton as half a dozen Sambos and Sallies.'"[47]

Amplifying prejudice and stereotype, white anxieties were also expressed in notions about Anglo-Saxon "race suicide." The closing of the American frontier, documented by the 1890 census, raised fears that the nation's "rugged" character, shaped through struggle with "wild" nature and Indians on the frontier, was endangered by a modernizing trend, which presented the threat of "over-civilization." Compounded by nativist fears and racial hostilities, the idea of preserving scenic landscapes became widely viewed among many whites as essential for guaranteeing racial preservation. Roosevelt's admonitions, for instance, were based in concerns about a declining "American race" which had been strengthened through encounters with North American landscapes. The historian Thomas Dyer relates how the results of the 1890 census, which revealed declining birth rates among whites and increases in nonwhite populations, marked for Roosevelt "the beginning of a twenty-eight-year obsession with the maintenance and preservation of the racial integrity of old-stock Americans and indeed all members of the 'English-speaking race.'"[48]

For the geographer Denis Cosgrove, concern about immigration was "more significant than the closing of the frontier in the minds of most Anglo-Americans in the 1890s." Attraction to wilderness lands was expressed in relation to immigration and urbanization as an escape of sorts: "The open spaces of the West were as far removed geographically, culturally, and experientially from the crowded immigrant cities of New York, Philadelphia, Pittsburgh, or Chicago as they could be."[49] Merchant elaborates: "Dark, smoke-filled cities contrasted with the purity of mountain air and the clarity of whitewater rivers, waterfalls, and lakes. Sublime nature was white and benign, available to white tourists; cities were portrayed as black and malign, the home of the unclean and the undesirable."[50] The spectacular national parks of the West, such as Yosemite, Yellowstone, and Glacier, were increasingly viewed as an escape for those white Americans who could afford the trip.

A significant notion among wilderness advocates was that social and demographic trends were leading to racial degeneration. The historian Stephen R. Fox remarks that while the wealthy backers of the wilderness movement viewed such spaces as retreats from modern stress and urban living, suggesting "a nostalgia turning back to recover an imagined, idealized past," their views also tied this sentimentality to gendered and racialized fears. Wilderness provided "a safety valve for nativist worries over the new immigrants and their high birthrates. Immersed in the wilderness, the gentry hoped to recover the lost manly virtues—courage, self-reliance, physical strength and dexterity— and so to avoid the specter of 'race suicide.'"[51]

The surety of Anglo-Saxon destiny, which had grown in the United States since the mid-nineteenth century, was thus cast into doubt by the start of the twentieth. Scientific theories attempted both to confirm and to explain white superiority as well as the potential for racial decline.[52] Explanations for this potential decline included ideas borrowed from the French naturalist Jean-Baptiste Lamarck, who early in the nineteenth century had argued that environmental influences on the behavior and character of living animals could be inherited by descendants, suggesting that encounters with natural elements might lead to enhancement or decline in a species.[53] Charles Darwin's work later in the century would lead biologists to reject Lamarck's view, emphasizing genetic inheritance in its place.

Despite the Darwinian shift in science, the Lamarckian strain persevered among American scientific racists, who, as the political scientist Kimberly K. Smith points out, "would nevertheless persist in describing the process of race formation as a dynamic interaction between an internal vital power and the external environment."[54] Race theorists fixated on the defunct concept of "vitalism" to suggest that environmental challenges faced in northern Europe and now on the frontier of North America resulted in an inherited racial superiority among members of those groups. Those of northern European stock displayed greater "vigor" and "vitality" as a result, allowing them to further develop and grow as civilizations relative to the "lesser" races, which were presumed to be in decline. Smith writes, "Many racists in fact clung to Lamarckianism precisely because it made the vital force central to racial development: it suggested that those races that respond to their environment with vigor (that is, that have more of this vital force) will be rewarded by seeing the traits acquired by such efforts passed on to their offspring."[55]

Anxieties about the disappearing frontier fomented concerns that American civilization was perhaps *too* successful. In a modern America of relative comfort and urban living, those of northern European stock—including the WASPs who laid claim to the nation—saw their futures jeopardized by the softening effects of over-civilization as they faced competition from immigrants who were viewed as better adapted to urban life. Attempting to avoid what the conservationist and eugenicist Madison Grant in 1916 called "the passing of the great race," Roosevelt and other preservationists argued for protecting wilderness as a means of maintaining the needed "vigor."[56] Grant had argued that current modern trends such as urbanization, as Smith relates, "favored Mediterraneans in the struggle for survival—leading to the 'fading of the Nordic type.' Preserving rural and wild places would give Nordic types the environment they needed to flourish, thus giving them a competitive advantage over the other races flooding into the United States."[57] Visiting scenic parks and wilderness areas was therefore central to the strategy of maintaining the self-perceived white racial superiority.

By the late 1920s, such appeals to racial fitness would be tied to the public health benefits of state park access. At the 1927 meeting of the National Conference on State Parks at Bear Mountain in Palisades Interstate Park, W. A. Stinchcomb of the Cleveland Metropolitan Park District expressed the need to establish state parks near large cities. Connecting park development to racial health, he echoed Grant's concern about racial decline. Stinchcomb stated that growth in leisure time and mobility resulting from automobile ownership "has increased the urge to get out into the country and has stimulated the movement looking to the establishment of metropolitan park systems and the creation of State and National parks." He also implored (presumably white) Americans to utilize parks to maintain vitality. Stinchcomb argued that if leisure time is spent building moral, mental, and physical strength, then "America is safe, but if this idle time is frittered away to pursuits tending to break down the moral fiber, to weaken the mentality, and to soften and weaken the physical fiber of our people, then America will go the way of other races and other civilizations which have decayed."[58] Stinchcomb by implication discounted the need to consider access to park facilities for those of "other races," as he put it.

By the late 1920s the influence of scientific racism was waning. The view that racial characteristics and achievements are rooted in biology was being gradually replaced by a cultural view of race introduced by the anthropologist Franz Boas, which was also embraced and promoted by African American intellectuals, including W. E. B. Du Bois. Denying the biological notions of a fixed racial hierarchy, these cultural perspectives offered intellectual room to present the case for social justice and equality. Approaching justice in park access was a slow process, however, as facilities available to African Americans emerged only gradually, first in northern cities and then later (and minimally) in parks in the South.

Emerging Parks and Racial Stereotypes

The push to make parks available to African Americans came first to the nation's northern cities near the end of the Progressive Era. By the late nineteenth century, urban reformers including Jacob Riis and Jane Addams had implemented a campaign in the North to make cities cleaner, safer, and more livable. The development of playground parks was an element of these progressive reforms, promoting exercise and healthier environments for children and adults. The Parks and Recreation Association (PRA) was created in 1906 to encourage their construction. Park availability remained restricted to white urban residents, however, until after World War I, when the numbers of African Americans arriving in the urban North became too large to ignore.[59] These first steps toward providing playground parks in cities would lead eventually to African American access to rural reserves such as state parks, including in the South.

By 1920 the PRA added a Bureau of Colored Work, directed by Ernest Attwell—a graduate of the Tuskegee Institute—to help ensure more adequate park provision for African Americans. His efforts shaped the first significant, systematic efforts to improve African American recreational access. As the recreation scholar James Murphy recounts: "This service was one of the few early efforts undertaken by a national agency to help ameliorate the deficient leisure opportunities for a subordinate racial group."[60] Attwell himself noted the status of African American park access at the beginning of his tenure in 1920 by stating that "until lately we have not heard much of his need for recreation."[61]

Despite what he characterized as the "keen desire" for playground recreation facilities among African Americans, Attwell pointed to their severely limited access. Citing a PRA survey of American cities, he estimated "that about three per cent of all the playgrounds now operated in America, beckon colored inhabitants to participate in the activities incident to their use."[62] The rate of municipal park access grew steadily through the 1920s, though significant inequality remained, particularly in the South. But despite the significant impacts of the Bureau of Colored Work, the recreational facilities and programs created by the PRA did not challenge prevailing racial norms. Murphy explains that "in most cases they were maintained on a 'separate but equal' basis or as was prescribed by the prevailing federal and local statutes."[63] This pattern held true in the formally segregated South as well as in the unofficially segregated North. Such unofficial segregation measures would decline in the North during the 1930s and 1940s, while segregated recreation in the South persisted throughout the Jim Crow years.

Furthermore, the common justification for providing such facilities was negative, grounded in stereotypes of Black pathology, aimed at addressing elements of the nation's so-called Negro problem, such as crime and juvenile delinquency. Introducing a speaker at the Twelfth Recreation Congress, held in Asheville, North Carolina, in October 1925, chairman Robert Lassiter pointed out that, in the context of the northward migration trend, urban recreation would help African American communities address the difficulties they faced: "The problem whether they make good citizens in the new community lies with the community. With proper attention to recreational facilities, they will make you good citizens. Improper attention to that, and neglect and abuse of it, will make a criminal population."[64] Ernest Attwell echoed Lassiter's sentiment in 1926. Calling Lassiter's assertion a challenge that should garner public and private contributions to such efforts, Attwell agreed that access to recreation facilities would lead to social improvement. Using more uplifting terms than Lassiter's, he pointed to "the great good that will result to America and civilization when recreational activities bring colored people together in happy, wholesome relationships, develop the social instinct, promote good-will, and create a higher type of Negro citizenship."[65]

Correcting perceived pathology would remain a primary justification for providing African American recreation facilities. After World War II, as the southern state park agencies faced serious legal challenges to inequality in their segregated park systems, such arguments were used in attempts to sway park officials and state legislatures toward improving African American access. At the 1950 annual meeting of the Association of Southeastern State Park Directors, held in Albemarle, North Carolina, a session titled "State Parks for Our Negro Citizens" included invited speaker Dr. J. L. Reddix, president of Jackson State College. Reddix called for a significant expansion in African American park facilities, arguing before his white audience that alleviating crime, delinquency, and family troubles were important reasons to provide such recreational outlets. He explained that "adequate park facilities tend toward lowering crime among all of the people. A boy that has a good home, a good school, and adequate recreation, is not likely to become a criminal. Most delinquency can be traced to broken homes and inadequate recreation."[66]

As persuasive as such arguments may have been to white decision makers, park provision for African Americans in the South materialized very slowly. By the end of the 1920s, exclusion and discrimination in city parks remained a serious problem, with no access allowed in the few state parks constructed during that decade. In 1928, the sociologist Forrest Washington published the results of a survey of facilities available to African Americans in southern and northern cities, documenting the availability of both public parks and private, social service–oriented recreation settings. The private opportunities included camps run by organizations such as the Boy Scouts, Girl Scouts, and Camp Fire Girls.

Commenting on southern facilities in particular, Washington noted that in "both public and private, it is hardly necessary to state that no mixing of the races will be found. The only interesting fact to look for . . . is whether or not any accommodations at all—even segregated—are provided for Negroes." The survey responses from seventeen southern cities suggested that all but four had made some provision for segregated public parks for African Americans, although Washington points out that "the amount of acreage allotted for Negroes is usually far below their proportion of the population."[67]

With no official Jim Crow policies in place, none of the forty northern cities surveyed claimed segregation in any of their public municipal parks. However, regarding summer camping experiences among private social service providers, facilities for Boy Scouts and Camp Fire Girls were subject to segregation of some sort, such as alternating Black and white use of facilities, although none fully excluded

African Americans. In the South, such private facilities were to a much greater degree exclusive to whites. Fourteen of the seventeen cities reported that Boy Scout facilities were available to whites only, and fifteen cities had exclusively white Camp Fire Girls facilities.[68]

These results underscored the fact that access to recreational space in general remained seriously limited for African Americans. In 1930, the sociologist Charles S. Johnson of Fisk University confirmed this status in terms similar to Washington's, noting that in "most communities" nationwide the recreation needs of African Americans "are utterly ignored, or only just being considered." Addressing recreation beyond the bigger cities, he pointed to the virtual unavailability of recreational facilities for small, urban African American communities of ten thousand or fewer as well as for African Americans living in rural areas and small towns: "These are the greatest sufferers for lack of any program."[69]

With landscape preservation associated strongly with the concerns of upper- and middle-class white Americans, the presumption developed that African Americans were simply not interested in visiting rural reservations like national and state parks. Both state and federal officials rationalized their failure to provide equitable public recreation opportunities with economic arguments about African American poverty as well as social stereotypes about Black attitudes toward nature and wilderness.[70]

Investigating American race relations in the late 1930s and early 1940s, Gunnar Myrdal relayed the common explanation in the South for the lack of provision, at once paternalistic and punitive: "The observer is frequently told by white Southerners that, since Negroes are so poor and pay virtually no taxes, they are actually not entitled to get more public services than the whites care to give them."[71] Further, it was presumed that such facilities would go underutilized, thus rendering significant expenditures unwise. Additional stereotypes rationalized outright exclusion. As Jearold Winston Holland explains in *Black Recreation: A Historical Perspective*: "some whites described black recreation as purposeless. . . . These whites could not conceive that blacks knew how to engage 'properly' in recreation and leisure." Deprivation was justified by appeals to contradictory stereotypes of, on the one hand, laboring African Americans with no time for recreation and, on the other, of "carefree" Black people whose lives were already spent "taking it easy" or utilizing "their free time loafing, boasting, telling exaggerated stories, singing and dancing."[72]

In *TVA and Black Americans*, Nancy L. Grant describes how stereotyping and discriminatory economics and their design implications were reflected in the recreational demonstration sites built by the Tennessee Valley Authority during the New Deal (many of these sites were later transferred for administration as state parks).[73] Like the state parks, the TVA recreational facilities were designed by National Park Service architects and constructed with the aid of other federal New Deal agencies. Ultimately few in number, the facilities for African Americans reflected a double stan-

dard that presumed the construction of white facilities while forcing those for Black citizens to pass an economic test. (Fig. 1.5)

Despite official nondiscrimination policies, these federal efforts in the South complied with the prohibitions on race-mixing demanded by Jim Crow. Grant explains: "In conformity with local practices, TVA planners as a matter of course drew up plans for separate recreational facilities. Yet while plans for a white recreational facility were drawn up for almost every reservoir, plans for Black recreational facilities were delayed until economic feasibility studies were made." She continues, "The construction of a separate black facility was considered an additional cost outlay, and surveys had given regional planners the impression that blacks were less inclined than whites to use recreational facilities. TVA therefore frequently turned down proposals for Negro parks on the grounds that not enough blacks would use the facilities."[74]

Those few TVA facilities constructed by the Park Service for African Americans were the products of what Grant calls "the practice of planning around a stereotype."[75] Quoting a 1940 memo addressing the characteristics of TVA's Wilson Dam "Negro Park" at Muscle Shoals, Alabama, she shows how "planners recommended only day-outing facilities because the 'accent should be on facilities that will satisfy the gregarious nature of the Negro rather than on those designed to promote close associations with nature; in other words, "lively" as against "contemplative." '"[76]

This approach was replicated in segregated state park facilities throughout the South, whether designed by the Park Service before

Fig. I.5. Booker T. Washington State Park, 1950. Courtesy Tennessee State Library and Archives.

World War II or by the state agencies in the years after. Under Jim Crow, African Americans were offered mainly day-use opportunities with only minimal (and often delayed) construction of camping areas and cabins, and even then, only in particular parks. Smaller parcels were presumed as adequate to cater to the "lively" socialization expected of African American visitors, while the "contemplative" stereotype of white park visitors would justify larger parcels with more spectacular scenery to facilitate hiking, camping, and nature appreciation. African American park users were presumed to require little more than a picnic area, a place to swim and fish, and perhaps a ball field.

The historian Colin Fisher has noted that far from expressing a disinterest in natural spaces,

Black writers since early in the century mirrored white preservationists' calls to use leisure to enjoy time in the outdoors.[77] For instance, in 1914 Dr. A. Wilberforce Williams, the health columnist for the *Chicago Defender*, remarked on the "ever increasing demand . . . for us to get out, and away from the city—to get close to nature—to commune with the running brooks, trees, and singing birds, and all growing vegetation—to get far away from the heat, the dust, the hurry, the bustling marts, and streets of the overcrowded, jostling municipality and find some cool, shady spot to camp where one may find rest for mind and body with nature's purest food, water, and air."[78]

In his 1920 essay "Of Beauty and Death," W. E. B. Du Bois describes his experience of the aesthetic spectacle he encountered on a visit to Bar Harbor, Maine, which shares Mount Desert Island with Acadia National Park:

There mountains hurl themselves against the stars and at their feet lie black and leaden seas. Above float clouds—white, gray, and inken, while the clear, impalpable air springs and sparkles like new wine. Last night we floated on the calm bosom of the sea in the southernmost haven of Mount Desert. The water flamed and sparkled. The sun had gone, but above the crooked back of cumulus clouds, dark and pink with radiance, and on the other sky aloft to the eastward piled the gorgeous-curtained mists of evening. The radiance faded and a shadowy velvet veiled the mountains, a humid depth of gloom behind which lurked all the mysteries of life and death, while above, the clouds hung ashen and dull; lights twinkled and flashed along the shore, boats glided in the twilight, and the little puffing of motors droned away. Then was the hour to talk of life and the meaning of life, while above gleamed silently, suddenly, star on star.[79]

Du Bois expressed his affinity for this land and seascape in poetic terms that rival John Muir's descriptions of Yosemite. But his point in the essay, as Kimberly Smith emphasizes in her discussion of it, was to "explain why he doesn't spend more time in such inspiring places."[80] Du Bois followed this eloquent description of the Maine coast by asking: "Why do not those who are scarred in the world's battle and hurt by its hardiness travel to these places of beauty and drown themselves in the utter joy of life?"[81] For African Americans, arriving at such awe-inspiring sites implied the necessity of travel and thus the likelihood of racialized, hostile encounters. The thought of taking the train to such a location, for instance, as Du Bois put it, would more likely "depress" than excite. He asked, "Did you ever see a 'Jim-Crow' waiting-room? There are always exceptions . . . but usually there is no heat in winter and no air in summer; with undisturbed loafers and train hands and broken, disreputable settees; to buy a ticket is torture; you stand and stand and wait and wait until every white person at the 'other window' is waited on. . . . The agent browbeats and contradicts you, hurries and confuses the ignorant, gives many persons the wrong change, compels some to purchase their tickets on the train at a higher price, and sends you and me out on the platform, burning with indignation and hatred!"[82]

Those embarking by car would potentially face similar indignities when attempting to visit national and state parks. From the mid-1930s on, the period during which segregated state parks began to appear in the South, African American drivers might hope to navigate potentially hostile territory by relying on information about accommodations and other travel advice in *The Negro Motorist Green Book*, published from 1936 to 1964. Many potential travelers, however, would opt to forego a possibly humiliating and even dangerous trip and simply develop safer recreation activities nearer to home. In that manner, African Americans from many communities developed durable patterns of recreation, passed down through generations, that tended to exclude the often more distant scenic reservations.[83] Travel difficulties discouraged African American park visitation, which in turn lent credibility to the expectation of low use and further excuse not to provide facilities for African Americans.

Despite the presumption that they did not need or desire parks and recreational facilities, there was in fact no shortage of African Americans seeking such opportunities. Forrest Washington pointed out in his study that many African Americans took it upon themselves to create private recreation retreats, including exclusive rural resorts in places such as Buckroe, Virginia, Idlewild, Michigan, and Gulfview,

Mississippi. "Perhaps the most heartening development," he commented, "is the fact that the Negro is refusing to allow himself to become discouraged because of the failure of the white man to provide adequate, wholesome recreation for him. He is gradually developing better forms of recreation for himself."[84]

African Americans, as taxpaying citizens, nonetheless also continued to pursue access to public parks and recreation. Advocacy for their provision came from various sources, including the Girl Scouts and Boy Scouts of America, the Camp Fire Girls and 4-H clubs, editors of the Black press, Negro chambers of commerce, clergy and church groups, chapters of the NAACP, and from ordinary citizens simply hoping to locate a relaxing place for a family outing. For instance, two of the region's earliest state facilities to allow African American access, Oklahoma's Roman Nose State Park and Lake Murray State Park, were constructed following considerable effort by Roscoe Dunjee, editor of Oklahoma City's *Black Dispatch*. Likewise, Stanley A. Harris, director of Inter-Racial Activities at the New York office of the Boy Scouts of America, expressed in 1938 what proved to be a common plea: "I certainly do wish that you could greatly extend facilities for Negroes to camp. There is almost no place in the country where they can camp and, with all the vast amount of acreage there is in some of the reservations, surely some part of it could be set aside for Negroes."[85]

Gains would be painfully slow in coming. For African Americans, even rest and relaxation was a social justice issue involving struggle. As such, recreation would eventually become a significant venue for pressing civil rights concerns both through the courts and in public protest. In the following chapters, I trace the development and use of specific state park spaces for African Americans and the legal and protest challenges that confronted the segregated and unequal status of southern park systems. Central to the events that unfolded was the constitutionality of the "separate but equal" doctrine.

TWO

THE NEW DEAL AND
EARLY STATE PARKS IN THE SOUTH

The National Park Service was created in 1916 by an act of Congress to administer the expanding national park system and was first directed by Stephen T. Mather, a tireless promoter of scenic parks. After the establishment of Yellowstone as the first national park in 1872, parks added to the system were administered as separate entities, and their protection and policing remained tenuous. The new Park Service would help to ensure that national park spaces would be preserved and protected rather than utilized for their natural resources or damaged by uncontrolled use.[1]

By the time of Mather's appointment, the national park system included some of the most spectacular landscapes of the American West, and the Park Service soon received many requests from congressmen around the country to preserve scenic places in their states. Mather considered most proposed sites to be of not high enough quality for national park status, but he saw an opportunity to use such spaces to build on the emerging trend of state park development. He began working toward creating a more formal state park movement and organized the first meeting of the National Conference on State Parks, held in Des Moines, Iowa, in January 1921. Embracing the rise of automobile ownership as a boon for vacation travel, Mather told the delegates, "I believe we should have comfortable camps all over the country, so that the motorist could camp each night in a good scenic spot, preferably a state park."[2] The close association initiated by Mather between the National Park Service and state park development in the 1920s would continue through the 1930s under subsequent Park Service directors Horace Albright and Arno Cammerer as the programs of the New Deal helped realize Mather's vision.

Following the 1929 stock market crash, the worldwide Great Depression was characterized by major declines in industrial productivity, agricultural prices, and international trade. The crisis had left millions of Americans destitute and unemployed, including African Americans, who were already the most disadvantaged group in the country.[3] The inauguration of Franklin Delano Roosevelt as president in 1933 was immediately followed by his administration's implementation of the New Deal, a label that identified a range of federal programs aimed at economic stimulation and relief for the poor. Among the emergency relief programs were some that promoted resource conservation and the construction of parks and recreational facilities.

The most significant of these programs was the Civilian Conservation Corps, which employed hundreds of thousands of unemployed young men, providing a stipend, food, and housing in exchange for labor that developed parklands throughout the country.[4] This development included national, state, and municipal parks as well as recreational demonstration projects that converted overused, or "submarginal," agricultural land into new Recreational Demonstration Areas (RDAs). The Park Service directed park planning and development work, and from 1933 to 1940 it received $200 million for projects funded through New Deal programs, including the CCC.[5] Regarding state parks specifically, the result of the Park Service–CCC collaboration was that progress in the field was "carried forward fifteen to twenty years ahead of schedule [than] had regular manpower and appropriations been relied upon."[6]

Between the creation of the CCC in 1933 and its dissolution in 1942, the partnership between the federal and state agencies constructed a reported 711 state parks and 46 federal recreational demonstration projects, most of which were later designated as state parks.[7] In addition to the CCC, the Park Service received labor, funding, and land from new agencies that included the Federal Emergency Relief Administration (FERA), the Resettlement Administration, the WPA, and TVA, while the WPA's National Youth Administration (NYA) and USDA's Soil Conservation Service would play more minor roles. (Fig. 2.1)

State park planning work after 1933 was directed at the Park Service by the landscape architect Conrad Wirth, himself a future director of the agency. As assistant director in charge of the Branch of Land Planning, Wirth selected Herbert Evison, a former executive secretary of the National Conference on State Parks, to assist him. Wirth instituted an effective cooperative process with the states through which the Park Service would, in Ethan Carr's words, "provide extensive planning and design assistance—without suggesting that local authorities were being bypassed or overruled by a federal bureau."[8] The ability of Wirth and his staff to navigate delicate local and state political terrain helped greatly to ensure the general pattern of success in state park development. At the same time, the federal power to allocate funds and CCC camps provided leverage over the states, which assisted the Park Service in maintaining consistency in park design.[9]

The New Deal had also helped to propel important changes in American race relations, although they were ultimately slow and slight in improving economic and social conditions for African Americans, including park access.[10] Gunnar Myrdal remarked in his study on the limited improvements in park access made during the era. In the South in particular he noted that "not only beaches and playgrounds, but also public parks, are often entirely closed to Negroes, except for Negro nurses watching white children."[11] He recognized that federal efforts in the 1930s had generated "considerable improvements" in access, though, as he put it, "so far, only a small part of the distance be-

tween 'nothing at all' and 'full adequacy' has been covered."[12]

In the hostile racial climate of the Jim Crow South, the park movement's ideal of providing "access for all" did not encompass the recreational needs of the region's African American population. The Park Service initiated consideration of these needs during the New Deal, but, while significant, its efforts ultimately had little impact on closing the enormous gap in access, as Myrdal found. Since the start of the New Deal in 1933, the number of state parks for southern whites had expanded dramati-

Fig. 2.1. President Franklin Delano Roosevelt visiting a CCC camp at Big Meadows on August 12, 1933, during the construction of Shenandoah National Park. *Seated from left to right:* Maj. Gen. Paul B. Malone, Commander of the 3rd Corps Area; Louis McHenry Howe, Secretary to the President; Harold Ickes, Secretary of the Interior; Robert Fechner, Director of Emergency Conservation Work; the President; Henry A. Wallace, Secretary of Agriculture; and Rexford Tugwell, Administrator of the Resettlement Administration. Courtesy National Archives, College Park.

cally—by the time the United States entered World War II in 1941, about 150 had been constructed. In contrast, in 1941 only nine state parks in just five southern states permitted segregated African American access. Additionally, the Park Service had constructed segregated group camps for African American youth in only four southern RDAs between 1938 and 1940, although such facilities were originally envisioned in ten of the sites.

Of the fifteen southern states, African American access to state parks during the New Deal was limited to Arkansas, North Carolina, Oklahoma, South Carolina, and Tennessee. The organized group camps in the RDAs were located in Kentucky, North Carolina, and Virginia, although only one of these—the segregated camp at Crabtree Creek RDA near Raleigh—would eventually become a state park facility for African Americans.[13] Before the end of the New Deal, the Park Service attempted to foster further consideration in the South. The congressionally mandated Park, Parkway, and Recreational-Area Studies, carried out by state planning commissions in collaboration with the Park Service, highlighted the need for additional state parks that allowed African American access. But the Park Service and the states took little action on these proposals as World War II approached and New Deal park funding dried up.

The successful provision for African Americans amid the general park construction boom in the region was limited by contradictory Park Service policies. On the one hand, the agency

articulated an official policy of nondiscrimination and had worked in the South with all apparent sincerity to construct state park and RDA sites for African Americans. Park Service concern about the issue is evident in Herbert Evison's response to a 1940 inquiry on the topic: "I should like to assure you that the National Park Service is tremendously interested in the problem of providing reasonably adequate facilities for Negro recreation, as evidenced by many developments of the past three or four years throughout the South."[14] But the potential for success was undermined by the agency's policy of accommodating what it called "local custom" regarding race and thereby avoiding confrontations with white expectations of both racial segregation and inequality. The Park Service typically yielded to local white protests against site proposals for African American facilities, which significantly hindered planning and construction even of projects on federal lands. The expansion of African American facilities was also thwarted by the insistence at the agency's highest level that planners provide evidence that they would be used sufficiently to justify the expense of construction.[15]

Given these constraints, Evison's reference to "many developments" was a clear overstatement. Moreover, his use of the phrase "reasonably adequate" suggests that neither the federal nor the state agencies had envisioned full recreational equality. Adherence to "separate but equal" ought to have meant the duplication of facilities for Black and white at each state park site, but no federal or state park official had advocated for this standard. Playing by the South's rules, the Park Service settled for Af-

Fig. 2.2. An African American scouting group at Camp Whispering Pines in the Crabtree Creek Recreational Demonstration Area, 1943. Courtesy State Archives of North Carolina.

rican American facilities that were far fewer in number, smaller in size, and limited in amenities relative to parks for whites.

Nonetheless, although outcomes fell far short of Park Service goals, the New Deal effort initiated important changes in southern approaches to race and recreation. The work of the Park Service, encouraged by the pressure and support of African American interest groups, planted the seed of consideration in the region's state park agencies. With changing social expectations and demands, state offi-

cials were subsequently more inclined to act on the acknowledgment that African Americans needed and deserved access to parks. Such effort toward provision would vary by state, often considerably, yet the concern would become part of the states' planning considerations after federal financial support ended with World War II. (Fig. 2.2)

The conflicting policies of the Park Service reflected a wider federal ambivalence regarding race, which arose in part from a concern in the Roosevelt administration not to offend key Democratic constituencies in Congress. While sympathetic to African American causes, the administration feared, as the historian Raymond Wolters noted, that "any challenge to white racism would alienate the South and thus endanger the administration's entire program for economic recovery."[16] The resulting racial inequality was evident not only in vastly unequal park provision but also in access to jobs, relief, and other benefits of various New Deal programs. Still, that the administration took a sympathetic stance on race was clearly evident, for instance, in Roosevelt's appointment of Harold Ickes as secretary of the interior in 1933. A former president of the Chicago chapter of the NAACP who employed a racially diverse staff, Ickes oversaw the activities of the National Park Service. Other appointments at New Deal agencies linked to park and recreational development reinforced this atmosphere of support. Mary McCloud Bethune, a renowned African American voice for education and civil rights who was included in Roosevelt's informal group of policy advisers known as the "Black Cabinet," was director of the Division of Negro Affairs within the National Youth Administration; Aubrey Williams, an influential white liberal from Alabama, directed the NYA.[17] Williams's friend Harry Hopkins was appointed by Roosevelt in 1934 to head FERA, and in 1935 Hopkins was chosen to direct the WPA, where he employed a staff of African American advisers.[18]

A significant result of Hopkins's effort was that "the share of FERA and WPA benefits go-ing to Negroes exceeded their proportion of the general population."[19] Roscoe Dunjee, the editor of Oklahoma City's Black Dispatch, applauded the positive employment record of the WPA, stating that the agency "has swallowed up so many Negroes in gainful endeavor that plantation owners, who pay starvation wages, rebel against this type of government relief."[20] Will Alexander, a white southern liberal and former head of the Council for Interracial Cooperation, was appointed in 1937 to lead the USDA's Farm Security Administration (successor to the Resettlement Administration).[21]

New Deal agencies were affected by racist tendencies as well, however. Roosevelt appointed Robert Fechner, a segregationist from Tennessee, to head the CCC. While the agency employed around 200,000 African Americans during its lifespan, Fechner worked to enforce the racial segregation of CCC camps even in states outside the South.[22] Furthermore, despite a specific ban on discrimination in the agency, African Americans experienced hiring bias in the CCC, particularly in the early years, and Fechner resisted hiring African Americans in administrative roles.[23] Nonetheless, the CCC's ultimately positive record in employing African Americans earned the agency praise in the Black press.[24]

The Agricultural Adjustment Administration (AAA) and National Recovery Administration (NRA) were also racially biased in their practices.[25] The NRA provided support to measures that improved worker wages and hours, aimed to stimulate the economy; the AAA sought to raise farm prices by controlling production, disbursing payments to farmers who limited cultivation.[26] African Americans experienced significant discrimination in both programs. As Wolters remarked, these agencies "were not willing to make the efforts needed to secure racial justice. They refused to appoint specialists to keep them posted on Negro problems, and they did not take steps to ensure the distribution of government benefits among Negroes."[27]

Despite such problems, African Americans tended to be positive in their assessment of the New Deal.[28] In the view of the *Pittsburgh Courier*, for example: "Armies of unemployed Negro workers have been kept from the near-starvation level on which they lived under President Hoover. . . . Armies of unemployed Negro workers have found work on the various PWA [Public Works Administration], CWA [Civil Works Administration], WPA, CCC, FERA, and other projects. . . . Critics will point to discrimination against colored sharecroppers, against Negro skilled and unskilled labor. . . . This is all true. It would be useless to deny it even if there were any inclination to do so, which there is not. . . . But what administration within the memory of man has done a better job in that direction considering the very imperfect human material with which it had to work? The answer, of course, is none."[29]

The "very imperfect human material" refers in part to a presumption of racial hierarchy and inequality that persisted even among sympathetic whites. A continuing problem in addressing racial injustice during the New Deal was the tendency among liberals to support improvements in African American lives while stopping short of addressing more fundamental problems that perpetuated racial disparity. John Kirby argues that white ambivalence in the New Deal "came from racial assumptions, shaped by past and present experience, and an intense loyalty to reform liberalism that encouraged them to work for improvements in Black life but not to attack the racial as well as the political patterns of American society which frequently compromised their interracial hopes and their reform goals."[30] Kirby's assessment fairly reflects the cautious concern expressed by the Park Service on race issues. This caution stymied progress in park provision for Black southerners, even as the Park Service and its partner agencies were nothing less than prolific in the construction of parks nationwide.

The prolific development during the New Deal era reflected a shift in Park Service perceptions of what ought to be considered as an appropriate park space. For state parks, the ideal of preserving only the most special landscapes was embraced by many advocates, including Colonel Richard Lieber of the Indiana park service and executive director of the National Conference on State Parks during the 1930s. Much of the New Deal park development, however, was taking place on condemned land near cities or on donated or purchased land of questionable scenic value. In many cases, park development required revegetation and even the creation of scenic features, such as lakes.[31] This shift was part of a broader movement by the Park Service away from an exclusive focus on monumental and sublime scenery toward an expanded emphasis on access and recreation.

As a staunch defender of park ideals, Lieber was among the more vocal critics of this trend.[32] In his keynote address at the 1935 National Conference on State Parks he remarked on the tremendous gains that were brought by this federal effort but also cautioned against degrading the scenic park concept. Speaking at Virginia's Skyland State Park, he expressed concern about "undesirable or sub-standard additions" to the ranks of the state parks, stating that the effort had been "overrun" with questionable proposals that attempted in effect "to make Silk Park Purses out of an over supply of 'sow's' ears." Loath to allow the degree of landscape modification that would come to characterize state parks, such as the construction of artificial ponds, Lieber urged his audience to "keep these things out of the real parks."[33] A decade earlier he had stated a preference for terms such as "recreation area," "wayside park," or other labels indicating an area of diminished landscape value.[34] (Fig. 2.3)

Fig 2.3. The constructed swimming pond at Tennessee's Booker T. Washington State Park in 1950. Courtesy Tennessee State Library and Archives.

Such questions of nomenclature and landscape quality were part of discussions about the construction of the South's so-called Negro state parks. Rather than applying an alternative label to these typically inferior landscapes, both federal and state planners would normally embrace the "state park" label to identify the park spaces reserved for African American use. By calling an area a "state park," state agencies could mask, at least on paper, the significant qualitative differences between park spaces for whites and those for Black visitors and could boast of having provided a facility for African Americans. Lieber did not address that issue, since at the time of his 1935 address, the provision of parks for African Americans was only beginning to be seriously considered. Lieber had warned that "merely to obtain the land, provide a gate, an occasional shelter house, etc., should not entitle the place to the rank of 'State Park.'"[35] But the Park Service quickly learned to ignore such advice, realizing the pragmatic necessity of compromise in securing park facilities for African Americans.

Early Parks in Oklahoma

Oklahoma was among the first of the southern states to make a park facility available to African Americans. By the late 1930s it had constructed two dual-use parks that included separate white and African American sections. One of these facilities was a small, segregated picnic area included at Roman Nose State Park.[36] Located in western Oklahoma north of Watonga, the land for the park had been purchased by the town's

citizens in 1935 through a bond in hopes of benefiting financially from the federal park construction program.[37] A second African American section was added to the state's existing flagship facility, Lake Murray State Park, east of Ardmore near the Texas border. Land for the park was acquired in 1933, and its development began in 1935, although consideration of adding an organized group camp for African Americans did not commence until the following year. After a delay, the camp was opened in time for the 1939 summer season.

Given that New Deal park construction had been under way nationwide since 1933, it was evident that despite the infusion of federal money, the neglect of African American recreation needs in Oklahoma remained a problem at both state and municipal levels. From his prominent position at Oklahoma City's *Black Dispatch*, Roscoe Dunjee expressed outrage at a 1935 report from the city's park board, which revealed that none of the planned parks, paid for by federal tax dollars, were to be accessible to the city's 20,000 Black residents.[38] African Americans had access to none of the 2,200 acres of parks in and around the city, with amenities including a zoo, swimming pools, ball fields, and tennis courts. Dunjee noted in his editorial column that an (unnamed) city councilman had expressed the common belief that Black poverty and lack of transportation made it unlikely that the population would make use of larger parks outside the city. White residents, on the other hand, were apparently entitled to park provision regardless of economic circumstances. In response, Dunjee asked, in the midst of the Great Depression in dust bowl Oklahoma, how many poor whites in the city could find the means for such travel? Editors of other area newspapers supported Dunjee. While affirming segregation as a necessary "safeguard" against racial tension, the *Oklahoma News* pointed out that "Negroes are citizens and taxpayers. As taxpayers they are entitled to a fair share of park facilities." The *Oklahoma City Times* asserted that "Oklahoma City is making a sad mistake when it continues to procrastinate on the Negro park problem. . . . The Negro residents of Oklahoma City are entitled to park facilities."[39]

While much of the local discussion was about municipal playground parks, Dunjee also argued for African American access to the "large diversion parks" around the city, since "there are a lot of kids in town who never saw a hill or a pond bigger than a wading pool who ought be given a chance to know more about geography." As a means of persuading white decision-makers who doubted that such facilities would be used, he offered his assurance that the large diversion parks could host attractions such as pageants, amateur nights, and inspirational programs. Thus, "we assure our white neighbors that our poor, within our group, will find the means to reach these centers of recreation just as do the whites."[40]

Following Frederick Law Olmsted Jr.'s advice in 1929 about state park selection, the initial sites throughout Oklahoma represented its variety of landscapes while also attempting to accommodate the ideal of locating parks within a day's drive of its residents.[41] By 1936 Oklahoma was making progress toward the general goal of access, with state parks located within fifty miles of 60 percent of the state's population.[42] African American access was considered separately, however, and was envisioned with the more limited goal of finding sites near locations with the largest Black populations, which were mainly in the eastern parts of the state and in its cities. Ultimately, though, neither of the two African American state park facilities was located in these higher density areas.[43]

In general, the architecture of Oklahoma's state parks exhibited the rustic style that characterized Park Service design, and architects utilized materials that reflected local natural and cultural histories.[44] The architect Herbert Maier, the Park Service's preeminent expert on structures, directed state park development in the administrative region that included the state of Oklahoma.[45] His influence on design and construction is evident in state parks throughout his region, as in the many CCC-built parks in Texas.[46] Park Service administrators including Wirth and Evison had feared "the threat of standardization" in state park design, but Maier worked to ensure variety that was tailored to location. Maier's influence, as Park Service historian Linda Flint McClelland writes, "allowed for designs that were unique, yet unified by principle."[47] (Fig. 2.4)

The Roman Nose State Park site was selected primarily for its unique physical and scenic features. Located in semiarid western Oklahoma, the site occupied a wooded canyon in Blaine County between the North Canadian and Cimarron Rivers.[48] The park location was known as Big Springs, named for the various

Fig 2.4. CCC-constructed picnic shelter at Oklahoma's Roman Nose State Park. Photo by the author, 2012.

natural springs that flowed from the canyon cliffs at a rate of 500–600 gallons per minute into Bitter Creek, which ran along the length of the park. M. C. Weber's history of the park describes the distinctive landscape that made the site worth preserving: "Flat lands break into a maze of bluffs and canyons that are wrapped in walls of reddish brown shale and capped with massive ledges of silvery white gypsum. The enchanting views seem misplaced for northwest Oklahoma."[49]

The location had once been a winter home for Plains Indians, including the Cheyenne chief Henry Roman Nose. A Cheyenne–Arapahoe reservation in the area had been dismantled by the federal government in 1890 and the land allocated to Indian families.[50] At the start of the twentieth century, a rancher named Will Cronkhite purchased land around the springs and canyon and eventually acquired the canyon itself. In the early 1920s his sons, J. B. and Cab Cronkhite, envisioned the construction of Big Springs Resort at the location and constructed a large lake on the grounds which attracted interest in the project. But in 1926 J. B.'s wife drowned while swimming in the lake, and the plans for the resort were canceled.[51] When federal funds became available park development in 1935, local residents purchased the site with the intention of turning it into a state park.[52]

Roman Nose State Park was designed by Park Service staff, including the architect Gordon Janecek and the landscape architect Harold Phillis, and was constructed with CCC labor.[53] The park, which opened on May 16, 1937, featured some of the New Deal era's most compelling state park architecture, largely constructed from local stone, including a unique bathhouse and pool that drew its water from the springs. The concrete pool was framed with dolomite slabs, one of which served as a diving platform, making it appear as if the entire pool structure was made of natural rock. It could accommodate three hundred swimmers and at the time was "the only concrete swimming pool in the State Parks system." The park also offered "the most picturesque picnic area of any park in the Parks system," as well as group camping facilities and overnight cabins.[54]

Roman Nose State Park included a segregated picnic area for African American visitors, though it remains unclear why the park was selected to allow segregated African American access, since it was not located in a high-density Black section of the state. In 1940, planners commemorated the site's Native American heritage by constructing a twenty-acre segregated camping area for Native Americans in a different area of the park.[55] The feature was unique in the Oklahoma state park system. The section for African Americans was a relatively small day-use facility, referred to as the "Negro Picnic Area" on the park's master plan. The facilities, which occupied a small area of land relative to the rest of the park, included picnic tables, barbeque pits, restrooms, a playground, and a parking lot. The area was located "in the undeveloped, extreme northeast sector of the park," away from areas reserved for whites on the western side of the park that included the swimming pool and other amenities.[56]

This early experiment in segregated state park provision was not a great success as the site reportedly went largely unused. Its limited amenities, day-use status, and significant distance from the more densely populated areas of the state contributed to the lack of visitors, but even local African American residents reported difficulties accessing the site. One local resident "noted that most local blacks did not use the picnic area during the 1940s because they did not have the means to travel to the park. At the time few black families in Blaine County owned an automobile."[57]

The picnic area for African Americans at Roman Nose State Park was closed in 1951. The decision to construct Lake Boecher as a new feature of the park resulted in the inundation of most of the space under its rising waters.[58] A lodge for the accommodation of twenty white guests was subsequently constructed in the vicinity, opening its doors in 1956. In the years following the picnic area's demise, the Oklahoma Planning and Resources Board proposed building a resort-style state park exclusively for African Americans in a new location in eastern Oklahoma. By then, however, most African American leaders in that state and elsewhere were seeking the desegregation of all facilities rather than the provision of separate parks, and the resort was never built.[59]

While Roman Nose State Park was selected for its unique scenic qualities, Lake Murray State Park, located along the shores of a newly created recreational lake, was justified by the land's marginal economic value. Consideration of the site began in 1933, when the state appropriated $90,000 to purchase 16,500 acres from private landowners. An additional 2,700 acres were added through the federal RDA program, and construction got under way in 1935. It would take three CCC camps to complete the project—two of white workers and one of African Americans. The CCC built most of the park structures and infrastructure, although the Lake Murray dam was constructed with WPA labor, as was the park's iconic Tucker Tower and some of the RDA development.[60] The park would remain the largest and by far the most frequently visited in Oklahoma's system.

Park Service architects designed both the RDA and the state park areas at Lake Murray, which were officially merged in 1943. The Lake Murray construction used native stone for structures, oak logs for rafters, and shake shingles for roofs to blend with the environment. The architects paid close attention to details:

Picnic shelters and overnight cabins also demonstrate the diligence used to build non-intrusive structures. The stone for the shelter was excavated from the nearby shoreline of the lake. Great care was taken that the size and color of the lake stone matched the stone in the natural rock ledge on which the building was located. Stone used to construct overnight cabins was also taken from the lake shoreline. The men handled each rock carefully so as not to disturb the mosses and the color of the natural surface.[61]

Discussions about creating an organized group camp for African Americans, originally intended for inclusion in the federal RDA area of Lake Murray, were begun in 1936. The RDA concept was envisioned as a means of finding more suitable uses for condemned, exhausted farmland. The intention was to provide recreation opportunities on federal land for lower-income families near cities while compensating the impoverished families that had struggled to survive on the submarginal land. RDAs came in several varieties, including wayside parks and extensions to national parks, but most important were the "vacation areas" designed to provide accessible outdoor recreation opportunities. The majority of RDAs were turned over to the states during World War II and years following, as their designers intended. While under federal control during the New Deal, however, the Park Service maintained day-to-day supervision over use of the RDAs in accordance with federal rules and policies.[62]

The Lake Murray RDA was one example of the vacation-area concept, and it was among ten in the South where the Park Service planned to include a segregated area for African American use. In planning such facilities, Park Service administrators acknowledged African American recreation needs, although according to policy they also sought assurance that the sites would be used sufficiently to justify the expense. Such assurance was in doubt, however, regarding the Lake Murray project. An assessment of local African American organizations, undertaken in 1936 by a Park Service recreation engineer, indicated that the number of campers from local groups, including the Carter County Community Club, the Boy Scouts, Douglas High School Girl Reserves, and the Douglas High School Hi-Y Club, might be too few to justify the camp.[63] Nonetheless, the Park Service tentatively moved forward with its plan to construct it.

The RDA at Lake Murray was originally designed to include two organized group camps: Camp No. 1 would be reserved for white groups, and Camp No. 2 was intended for African American groups. Located adjacent to each other on a peninsula at the north end of the park, both camps included cabins, mess houses, and other amenities and were slated to open for the 1938 season.[64] Shortly before the grand opening, the *Daily Ardmorite* noted the comparative equality of the facilities: "The two camps, one for white and one for colored, are identical in structure. They consist of 17 separate building units as follows: three unit lodges; three leader's cabins; one combination dining hall and kitchen; three unit latrines; one infirmary; one administration building; headquarters staff quarters; one unit for service staff; complete water system; complete sewer system with 5000 feet of sewer line, and one 5400-gallon tank for the water system."[65] A

newspaper editorial had announced that the African American camp's opening to the public would occur in June and proclaimed that "it will, across the years, be the answer to much for which Negroes in this state have prayed."[66]

But Camp No. 2 would not open in 1938 as a group camp for African Americans. It succumbed to Park Service contradictions regarding race and also to southern white expectations that African American facilities be inferior to their own. The Park Service persisted in its worry about underutilization, while the editorial expressed a concern that some local whites resented the relative equality of the facilities. "Discussion in some quarters," it stated, suggested that the accommodations provided at Camp No. 2 were "far too elaborate for Negroes"; there was a danger that the camp might be appropriated for whites if sufficient African American support was not built.[67]

Two years earlier, Herbert Maier had also expressed concern that the attempt to create an African American group camp would fail because of the inability to ensure adequate usage. While prominent white organizations, including local Kiwanis, Lions, and Rotary Clubs, were enthusiastic about creating a group camp for underprivileged white children, Maier lamented that the camp for African Americans "has not been met with quite the enthusiasm expected," particularly on the part of the local Black community. Maier noted that relatively few African American advocacy groups existed in the area and that the other civic organizations "are not in close contact with the problems of the colored people." Furthermore, Maier pointed out that "the colored people of this region have never before been provided with such opportunities and are, therefore, rather skeptical as to the proposed camp being carried to completion."[68]

In an attempt to bolster local interest in Camp No. 2, the Park Service organized a meeting in April 1938 of the leaders of African American organizations within a hundred-mile radius of Ardmore. According to the minutes of that meeting, there was lack of organizational support for the camp and "very few colored agencies doing organized camp work" within the radius. Local educational leaders, although interested, "have done practically nothing in this field." Officials attributed the limited support partly to the relatively small proportion of African Americans in the area—only 9 percent of the population—and the fact that this small group was reportedly widely scattered and lacked finances. It was also true that the exclusion of African Americans from scenic recreational opportunities meant that such experience and interest had not been cultivated to any significant degree.[69]

Added to the concern about usage was the Park Service's acquiescence to "local custom" regarding Jim Crow (despite the fact that the RDA was federal property). Beyond the expectation of inequality, white residents also expressed extreme rules about avoiding Black and white contact. In his report on the group camp meetings, Milo Christenson, a Park Service supervisor of recreation area planning, related local whites' deep-seated concern about avoiding even indirect physical contact with African Americans: "It will be unfortunate if negro occupancy of No. 2 camp is unsatisfactory as white groups will never use these facilities if they have ever been used by negro groups."[70] Just a month before opening day, having received no applications to use the camp from the African American organizations, the Park Service decided to reserve both Camps No. 1 and 2 for whites only.[71]

The availability of an African American facility at Lake Murray State Park was delayed for another year, when a third camp was constructed before the start of the 1939 summer season. Camp No. 3 was located on state (not federal) park land and was a significant distance from the RDA camps and other developed areas. As part of a newly designated "Negro Recreation Area," the camp was on the opposite side of the lake in the southeast section of the park, distant from the white camps and isolated from the other more extensive amenities of Lake Murray State Park. The camp comprised just 200 acres of the nearly 20,000-acre park.

Completed by May 1939, Camp. No. 3 was modeled on Camps No. 1 and 2, but its facilities were of a lower quality. Cabins and other structures in the white camps were more elaborately designed and included log wall supports and rafters and stone chimneys. In contrast, cabins in Camp No. 3 were of basic wood frame construction. State park officials declared that equality between the camps was not even considered because of the limited time available for construction before the summer season and increasingly constrained program funding.[72] In an attempt to sell the new location as comparable, the Park Service claimed that it was "located near the water on one of the finest sites in the Lake Murray State Park." The completed camp was turned over to the state's director of state parks for operation and maintenance.[73] (Figs. 2.5, 2.6)

Despite the qualitative differences and its new location, Anne Caution, the NYA state supervisor and an African American, urged local groups to make use of the newly constructed Camp No. 3, which, she reported, would have

Fig. 2.5. A cabin in white-only Camp No. 1 at Lake Murray State Park, constructed in 1938 as part of the Lake Murray RDA. Photo by the author, 2012.

Fig. 2.6. A cabin in Camp No. 3 at Lake Murray State Park's "Negro Recreation Area." Photo by the author, 2012.

buildings and facilities similar to those of the other camps. Expressing a sense of urgency for submitting applications, she noted that she had learned "from reliable sources that unless some Negro groups use the camp this year we will lose it for another season."[74] Responding to her call, over two hundred boys and girls used the facility that year, bringing in $172 to the Oklahoma State Parks Division. The biggest individual group included fifty campers, and the groups included Boy Scouts, Girl Reserves, and recreation clubs, among others.[75]

The Oklahoma State Parks Division nonetheless expressed skepticism about the viability of the camp, declaring the revenue in the 1939 season as inadequate given the operating costs. The Southern Oklahoma Boosters Club, a group of prominent African Americans from around Ardmore, responded by producing a booklet that promoted increased attendance in the 1940 season. Circulated across southern Oklahoma and northern Texas, *Beautiful Lake Murray Camp Site No. 3* was aimed at generating awareness and interest in the park's organized group camp for African Americans. According to the booklet, much of the new recreation area's construction still remained incomplete by its January 8, 1940, publication. The planned facilities, however, included a picnic area for day users and cabins and camping facilities with sanitary facilities, drinking water, garbage disposal, firewood, and maintenance staff for overnight and extended use. Beach and swimming facilities would be improved with floating markers for shallow and deeper water, and a floating dock was to be provided, along with fishing and boating activities.[76] The booklet asserted that African American visitors could access the park's Tucker Tower, which was located a few hundred feet west of Camp No. 3 and was visible from its beach. It described the vantage point as "poised like a feudal stronghold on a loft cliff which juts out into the blue waters of the lake."[77] Beyond these facilities for general use, the youth camp was already complete and ready for occupancy. Built by Negro Veteran CCC Camp No. 1825, the camp reportedly contained twenty-two buildings, including a large mess hall/recreation building, an infirmary, and three groups of cabins, each with a separate counselor's cabin and latrine/wash house.[78]

Alongside the enthusiasm generated for the site by the Boosters and park officials, the booklet acknowledged the realities of Jim Crow in Oklahoma in 1940. Its authors reminded readers that a misunderstanding or a wrong turn could bring danger. The directions to the site were headed by a bold "CAUTION," warning visitors: "Please don't come to camp without making definite arrangements beforehand and getting proper directions."[79]

A Nominal State Park in Arkansas

In neighboring Arkansas, the construction of what was to become the South's first separate state park exclusively for African Americans resulted from the persistent efforts of Dr. John Brown Watson, president of Pine Bluff's Agricultural, Mechanical and Normal College (AM&N), a historically Black college.[80] (Fig. 2.7) Originally from Tyler, Texas, Wat-

son earned a degree from Brown University and taught at Morehouse College from 1904 to 1908; the latter institution conferred his Master of Arts and Doctor of Letters degrees. After more than a decade working as secretary of the Colored Men's Department of the International Young Men's Christian Association (YMCA), he was appointed as the first president of AM&N by the state board of education in 1928.[81] Seeking ways to benefit his community, Watson attempted to create an African American recreational space near Pine Bluff in the early years of the New Deal; as with Okla-

Fig 2.7. Dr. John Brown Watson. Courtesy John Brown Watson Collection, John Hay Library, Brown University Library.

homa's Lake Murray State Park, the plan was originally proposed as an RDA.

Among the RDAs proposed in 1935 was a site for an African American park that was referred to administratively as "Arkansas R-4, Pine Bluff Regional Negro Park."[82] Rural park construction in the state had been focused on the Ozark and Ouachita Mountains and the hills in the northeast and included state parks such as Petit Jean, Mount Nebo, Devil's Den, and Crowley's Ridge. The remaining 47 percent of the population, particularly in the southern and eastern areas, had not been provided for, including those living "within the densely negro populated section of the State."[83] The RDA facility in Pine Bluff would be a significant gain in addressing that situation.

The selling points of the Regional Negro Park proposal included its location in an area that was 90 percent African American, its proximity to a highway, the relatively short distance to town, and its support from Dr. Watson and the college. AM&N had even agreed to "assume the responsibility of administration, maintenance and policing of the area."[84] The proposed tract comprised 1,637 acres of submarginal land that qualified for acquisition by FERA's Land Program for RDA development. The site's proximity to 130,000 African American residents had also helped gain the endorsement of the proposed park in both the Park Service and the Land Program.[85] While all RDAs were considered "experimental," this project would be doubly so given its potential status as the first rural reserve intended exclusively for African Americans. And, like the park spaces developed for African Americans

in Oklahoma, this one would encounter serious obstacles.

The proposal for the park near Pine Bluff emerged mainly through Watson's ongoing requests starting in 1933, and the idea was endorsed by the president of the University of Arkansas as well as the state's governor.[86] Federal consideration of the proposal had begun early in 1935, reflecting the emerging concern within the Park Service regarding neglected African American recreation needs.[87] An early memo on the project argued for such provision throughout the South: "Since there are around ten million negroes in the country, largely concentrated in the eleven Southern states, this problem is inescapable and must be dealt with."[88] The memo writer, identified only as "Mr. Stockton," was a Park Service employee who identified himself as a southern man who understood the region's race relations. In his view, the Park Service needed to maintain a policy that recognized segregation as "a fact" of the South, and he predicted white support for the exclusive park project since it abided by the rules of Jim Crow:

As a Southern man myself, I personally look with favor upon the establishment of recreational projects in the South, to be used by negroes exclusively. Conditions of the negroes themselves and the social attitude of the dominant white race would bar them from the use of areas not designated as areas for colored people. White people, however amiable they may be, do not commingle with negroes socially, and certainly not recreationally. I believe the white people would favor the proposal and give it their hearty support.[89]

The Park Service, as well as its partner agencies, was already conforming to this view, but to expect goodwill among southern whites would routinely bring disappointment. Stockton had seemingly misread his southern compatriots—indifference or hostility, rather than "hearty support," was the normal white response during the 1930s.

The proposed RDA facility at Pine Bluff, however, was blocked not by white resistance but by new administrative guidelines; despite widespread support from the state and Park Service, it would never be constructed. Only months after the formal proposal for Pine Bluff, the RA, which took over the Land Program from FERA in April 1935, cited new policies for establishing RDA projects which stemmed from reduced funding for land acquisitions and led to the abandonment or curtailment of some worthy plans.[90] Herbert Maier explained that this change would impact the Pine Bluff RDA for African Americans as well as one planned for whites in Texarkana: "Under these new policies we are permitted to consider only a limited number of areas in certain states of our Region: Arkansas was not allotted any new areas in this new set-up, consequently we have withheld any further action on the Texarkana matter. For this same reason we doubt that the Pine Bluff proposal will be approved."[91]

On learning the likely fate of the park, Watson wrote a letter to L. C. Gray, acting director of the Resettlement Administration's Land Utilization Division, imploring the RA to provide a park for African Americans through the federal RDA program, given that white Arkansans seemed inclined to ignore African American recreation needs. He noted, "We have depended upon our white friends in the South to help us to get a little of this large expenditure, but it seems that this type of development will be over, and we probably will be left out after all."[92] Perhaps with tongue in cheek, Watson commented that the relatively positive relations between whites and African Americans which made such a park even possible were "due to the fact that there has been but one lynching in this state in nearly nine years." Despite that "positive" sign of improved relations, he knew that getting only an unequal share of park space was the best outcome he could hope for. He related to Gray the desire among African Americans in the state to obtain "at least two or three small parks for our people or one state park after the fashion of Petite Jeanne [sic], but not nearly so extensive, of course, and two or more small parks located near some of the areas where Negroes are a large part of the population."[93]

Despite the failure of the Pine Bluff RDA, Watson persisted, building on the already existing support for such a project among federal and state officials. In June 1937 he deeded to the state a hundred-acre parcel of his own land, located eight miles west of Pine Bluff, and a consortium of six government agencies, federal and state, agreed to spend $20,000 for park development. The condition for the deed transfer was that arrangements would be made to improve the property, and initially the Arkansas State Parks Commission, the NYA, and the CCC pledged contributions.[94] The *Atlanta Daily World* hailed the project as "the nation's first all-colored state park."[95] The site contained woods, hills, and valleys, as well as a location where a six- to eight-acre lake could be impounded. Watson envisioned recreation facilities that included tennis courts, a baseball field, and a golf course.[96] He told an Associated Press reporter that "there was a question in the minds of some as to whether the State Park agency would accept the property and assume the responsibility of its development and maintenance."[97] Despite such doubts, he hoped the project would proceed as planned, stating that it "would satisfy a little pride in us all to have Arkansas take this lead." Watson envisioned the park as "a resort for all types of youth groups, such as 4-H clubs, Boy Scouts, YMCA and YWCA, Campfire girls, also for large gatherings of Negro societies and churches."[98] Schoolchildren and teachers helped raise the $5,000 needed to obtain a federal grant of $15,000 for park development. With NYA labor, the construction process was anticipated to take three years, and as the *Pittsburgh Courier* reported, "nearly 100 youths between 18 and 25" began work on the facility in May 1938.[99]

The new facility, Watson State Park, opened that year with one thousand visitors in its first season. But since no CCC camp was allocated for its construction, development of the site lagged. The State Parks Commission report for 1939 described the construction of a caretaker's residence, a large barracks building, and dining hall/kitchen as completed that year.[100] Despite this work, no further improvements were made to the facility. After Dr. Watson died in 1942,

his widow, Hattie M. Watson, sued for the return of the land to the Watson estate, charging that the State Parks Commission had not followed through on its promise of development. The decree issued in Pulaski County Chancery Court in November 1944 expressed agreement, stating that the commission had indeed violated the terms of the original land transfer. Specifically, the court ruled that "there has been an abandonment of said property as a public Negro park" and that the state was not attempting to maintain the facility.[101] With that 1944 ruling, the land was returned to Hattie Watson, and the first state park in the country exclusively for African Americans was officially closed.

The State Parks Commission had counted the site among its units from 1938 until its 1944 demise. With the label "Watson State Park," the agency could claim to have made provision for its African American citizens despite its relative neglect of the site.[102] In contrast with the 18,261.65 acres devoted to state parks for white Arkansans, mainly in the state's most scenic areas, there were just those 100 underdeveloped acres on the outskirts of Pine Bluff allocated to the state's entire African American population.[103] After the court ruling, Arkansas would add no additional state parks for African Americans, and over the course of the coming decades it would remain the lone southern state without any such facility.

Two Relative Successes in North Carolina

The development of two New Deal–era recreational reserves for African Americans in

North Carolina did not appear to encounter the degree of difficulty evident in Oklahoma and Arkansas. Located near Elizabethtown, Jones Lake State Park opened in 1939 as one of the most successful rural parks for African Americans anywhere in the South. Farther north, one of the few successful Park Service attempts to develop an RDA camp for African American youth opened in 1940 near Raleigh at Crabtree Creek RDA.

North Carolina had established Mount Mitchell State Park years earlier as one of the South's first scenic state parks. The state's General Assembly on March 13, 1915, allocated $20,000 for its creation while endorsing the dual values of preservation and use. The establishment of Mount Mitchell State Park was preceded in 1911 by an act of the assembly that retained public ownership "for the use and benefit of all people of the State" of the larger lakes of 500 acres or more in Bladen and Columbus Counties, located on North Carolina's coastal plain.[104] The effort was intended to preserve examples of a unique landscape feature in the region—the concentration of "elliptical, southeast-northwest oriented depressions [that] are found scattered over much of the Coastal Plain of North Carolina and South Carolina." In 1929 protection was extended across the state to publicly owned lakes of fifty acres or more, which were to be used for recreation purposes. A decade later, two of these, Jones Lake and Salters Lake, located north of Elizabethtown, would become the site of North Carolina's first state park reserved for African American use. In 1936 the federal government acquired land for the park in Bladen County under control of the Resettlement Administration. The forested site, which had been used for turpentine production, timber, and cotton farming, was declared submarginal by 1935. These lakes, together with nearby Singleterry Lake, were first administered as a unit called the Bladen Lakes Land Use Area, which was developed through the collaborative partnership of the state and Park Service and contained a CCC camp that engaged in reforestation and road construction. In 1937 additional land was acquired by the state through condemnation, which made possible the construction of a beach area at Jones Lake. Although much of the park land "consisted of bog-bay and swamp forest" and was thus difficult to develop, there were higher areas including a sand-rim around Jones Lake and sand dunes to the east of Salters Lake.[105]

The land around Jones and Salters Lakes became known as the Jones and Salters Lakes Land Use Project, which was transferred to the USDA's Soil Conservation Service in 1938. From the time the land was first acquired by the Resettlement Administration, these federal agencies had envisioned the twin lakes as one of the sites in the South to be allocated to African American recreational use. When the land was transferred by lease to state control the following year, the site for African Americans was named Jones Lake State Park.[106] Neighboring Singleterry Lake was reserved separately as a state park for whites. (Fig. 2.8)

Opened on July 1, 1939, Jones Lake State Park enjoyed immediate popularity. The North Carolina Department of Conservation and Development counted 22,000 visitors in the park's first season, noting that they came from all over

Fig. 2.8. Jones Lake State Park in 1940. Courtesy State Archives of North Carolina.

the state using "private cars, taxis, trucks, and trailers equipped with church pews. Groups of several hundred were common." Success was credited in part to the hiring of African American staff, and attendance at the park grew in the next two years before the war, from 25,000 in 1940 to 38,000 in 1941.[107]

The creation of the park was hailed in the Black press as a sign of progress. Claiming (incorrectly) that the site was the "first State park for Negroes in the South," Norfolk's *Journal and Guide* announced that it had twelve spacious buildings, as well as "picnic booths with rustic tables and seats, a boat house, concession stand, rest rooms for both men and women, bath houses and a board walk leading from the bath house to the pier." Citing its electrification, modern plumbing, ample parking, beautiful beach, and well-stocked lake, the paper proclaimed the site as "superior to any in the State for members of the race." The article concluded with praise for the agencies that made the park available: "The Jones Lake Recreational Area is indeed a demonstration of the fact that North Carolina thinks of the welfare of all of its citizens, physically, as well as intellectually and spiritually."[108] (Fig. 2.9)

Despite the popularity and success of Jones Lake, inequality among the parks remained evident. White-only Singleterry Lake State Park included a hundred-person camping area in its first season, while Jones Lake was restricted to day-use facilities including its beach, bathhouse, bathing pier, picnic shelters, and boats.

Furthermore, by the following year, the North Carolina system encompassed six state parks for whites but only the one park for African Americans. The Park Service would soon add the federally controlled Crabtree Creek RDA, near Raleigh, which included an organized group camp for African Americans in its Reedy Creek section.[109]

The camp in the Crabtree Creek RDA for African Americans was called Camp Whispering Pines and was touted as existing "for the health, recreation, enjoyment, education and

Fig. 2.9. Swimming at Jones Lake State Park, 1940. Courtesy State Archives of North Carolina.

development of Negro boys and girls." Its inaugural season in 1940 appeared to be a great success. Fifteen groups with a total 487 girls, boys, and counselors used the camp in its first season of operation. Four-H Clubs, Boy Scouts and Boys Clubs, Girl Scouts, and Girl Reserves were among the groups drawn from five states: North Carolina, South Carolina, Virginia,

West Virginia, and New York. The camp appraisal report for the first season noted that a number of groups and their leaders had little prior camping experience—as in Oklahoma, likely because of the unavailability of camping areas open to African Americans in the South generally—which meant that the RDA staff often found it necessary to assist in activities.

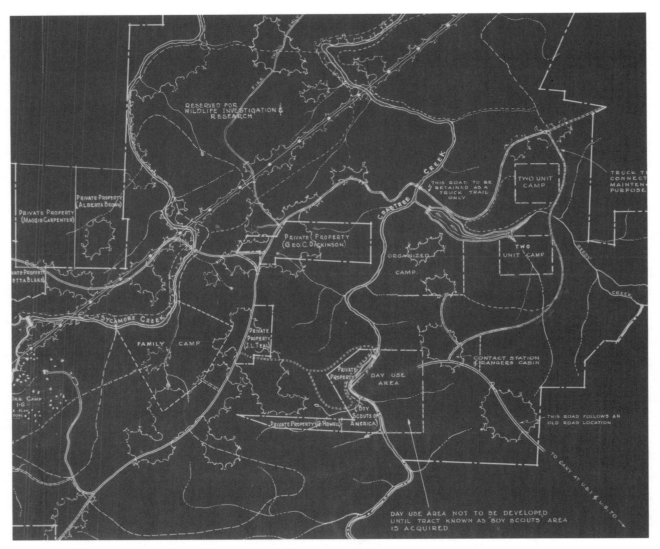

Fig. 2.10. Crabtree Creek RDA Master Plan (detail). Camp Whispering Pines is just south (to the right on the plan) of Crabtree Creek, which divided the white and African American areas. Courtesy State Archives of North Carolina.

Fig 2.11. African American campers at Camp Whispering Pines, 1943. Courtesy State Archives of North Carolina.

Of all the groups using the camp that summer, the Raleigh Girl Scouts received the most glowing review. The last group to use the facility, they were, according to the report, "the best organized, disciplined and trained of any other group of campers, they seemed to have appreciated the camp to the extent that they were willing to do anything for its success."[110] The girls even published a camp newspaper "named the 'Ra-Gi-Sco' meaning, Raleigh Girls Scouts." Having immensely enjoyed the experience, the group adopted the slogan "Back to Whispering Pines in 1941." (Figs. 2.10, 2.11)

Crabtree Creek RDA was transferred to state control in 1943, and in 1950 Crabtree Creek State Park was formally divided into two parks: one larger park for whites (3,135 acres) which bore the original name and a smaller section for African Americans (1,234 acres) named Reedy Creek State Park.[111] Before this the RDA included no facilities for general public use other than temporary picnic areas. New development began in 1950 at both Crabtree Creek and Reedy Creek, including the construction of swimming pools in each (the *Raleigh News & Observer* noted that the pool for whites was

"slightly larger"). New construction also included bathhouses, picnic shelters, and toilet facilities. Remarking on the segregated arrangement, and probably providing reassurance to anxious whites, the *News & Observer* noted the large buffer zone that separated the parks: "The two areas will be better than a mile apart at the Crabtree dividing lines."[112] (Figs. 2.12, 2.13)

Fig 2.12. (left) Girls picnicking in Reedy Creek State Park, 1964. Photo by Charles Clark. Courtesy State Archives of North Carolina.

Fig 2.13. (below) Playing horseshoes at Reedy Creek State Park, n.d. Courtesy North Carolina Collection, Louis Round Wilson Special Collections Library, UNC at Chapel Hill.

In 1952 the *Rocky Mount Sunday Telegram* reflected on North Carolina's creation of the two exclusive state parks for African Americans. During a year of mounting legal challenges to park segregation, the paper declared that their existence was evidence "of the State's progressiveness by the vast majority of North Carolinians."[113] By that time, however, the true progressive stance, adopted by African Americans and supporters nationwide, was to reject the idea of segregated facilities, demanding instead the desegregation of all institutions.

Parks in Tennessee

Tennessee's state park planning got under way in 1935 with the creation of its State Planning Commission, and reorganization in 1937 resulted in the Division of State Parks, housed in the Department of Conservation. The division would develop the sites planned by the planning commission, which during the New Deal worked with a range of federal agencies including the Park Service, CCC, WPA, USDA, and TVA.[114] Remarkably, two of Tennessee's first four state parks—T. O. Fuller in Memphis and Booker T. Washington near Chattanooga—were reserved for African American use. After the auspicious start, however, the state was unable to develop any additional state parks for African Americans despite a search for sites that continued through the 1950s. This failure was largely attributed to the opposition voiced by local white residents to proposed sites. As one observer noted, "fear of white reaction seemed to be prominent in all considerations for Negro parks."[115] Even the two existing African American parks were burdened by delays.

Booker T. Washington appears to have been a state park in name only until most of its facilities were completed in 1950. Twelve years earlier, it was sited on TVA land along Chickamauga Lake and development was expected to commence in the spring of 1939.[116] The Chattanooga area had a relatively large African American population, which used existing municipal parks frequently but for whom few such sites were available.[117] County planners envisioned cabin camping outside the city for African Americans, who lacked "a really open space, away from the city in healthful surroundings."[118] These officials also sought such accommodation to benefit "Negro tourists [who] often slept in their cars because there were no hotels or courts in Chattanooga to accommodate them."[119]

The park master plan displays a broad array of proposed facilities on the largely wooded site, including a recreation lodge, picnic facilities, swimming and boating, ball fields, and tennis courts. A group camp was also recommended with a lodge for dining and recreation, shower facilities, and cabins, all of which would be accessed by a road network that curved its way around the park.[120] Despite the elaborate plans, a variety of aesthetic and functional problems made the park less desirable among Chattanooga-area African Americans than planners had hoped. As Nancy L. Grant notes, "The initial complaint regarding Booker T. Washington Park involved its proximity to an industrial site, which diminished its esthetic value and hampered the park's development.

The park proved to be an even greater disappointment in the 1940s, when it was not properly maintained: for example, the swimming pool remained closed for lack of pumping equipment. In addition, there were no lavatories in the park."[121] (Fig. 2.14)

The park remained in disrepair until after 1948, when a superintendent was appointed and more concerted development work began. Speaking to a reporter in the late 1960s, the long-time park superintendent William C. Bell recollected, "We spent the first two years out here just cleaning the place up. . . . This was a real wilderness."[122] The new postwar construction

included picnic grounds and playing fields, concessions, boats, water and sanitation, and would be staffed by "a Negro as a full-time park ranger with the authority to patrol the park and make arrests inside the reservation." While acknowledging the long-standing need for such a facility, B. R. Allison, director of the Division of State Parks, explained that the reason for earlier inaction was a lack of funding for improvements.[123]

Across the state, the other African American facility took shape more quickly. T. O. Fuller State Park, a thousand-acre site nine miles south of downtown Memphis, was situated on a bluff at the edge of an oxbow lake

Fig. 2.14. Master Plan of Booker T. Washington State Park, 1940. Courtesy Tennessee State Library and Archives.

Fig 2.15. Aerial view of T. O. Fuller State Park, 1938. Courtesy Tennessee State Library and Archives.

adjacent to the Mississippi River. The Division of State Parks selected the site largely because of its proximity to the city, with its large African American population, and also because it was the best site that could be purchased at a reasonable price. The property was deemed worthless for agriculture and therefore its rehabilitation for recreation "would follow the present trend of land utilization" as seen among the RDAs.[124] Rehabilitation of the park grounds required managing the extensive erosion of the site's loess soils and reforesting its overcultivated ridge tops. (Fig. 2.15)

Efforts within the African American community to persuade the state to provide park space began with a proposal by the NAACP to the Park Service in 1937. On the northern side of the city, development had already begun at Shelby Forest RDA, a 13,000-acre park that would serve white residents and, like most

RDAs, eventually become a state park. The Memphis chapter of the NAACP sent a resolution to the Park Service expressing dismay over the exclusion of African Americans from Shelby Forest, which had been under construction by the CCC and WPA since 1935. The resolution noted that 39 percent of the Memphis-area population lacked facilities for outdoor recreation. Owing to "official custom or administrative practice," African Americans were "excluded from the benefits of the many large, well-equipped city parks, play grounds, etc., and confined to three small, ill-equipped, inadequate, unsanitary spaces wholly impractical for their needs." As another means of persuasion, the NAACP argued that the park was needed to help combat juvenile delinquency, explaining that youth in their formative years would, in the absence of productive alternatives, roam the streets and reinforce "the deplorable record of our city for high mortality, morbidity and criminality, causing it to be known as the homicide capital of the world." On these premises, the Memphis NAACP resolved to request that the Park Service provide a facility for the city's African Americans that had the qualities of the Shelby Forest park (not simply a city park). The proposal was endorsed by eighteen civic groups in addition to the NAACP.[125]

The Park Service deferred to the state on the ultimate decision of whether to create specific facilities for African Americans. In a letter to the NAACP Special Counsel in New York, Conrad Wirth emphasized the agency's cooperative role in relation to the state regarding the possible Memphis park: "The State Department of Conservation will administer and maintain the Area when the work of development on which we are now engaged is completed. Therefore, any plans for the development of facilities specifically for Negro use would have to be approved by that Department."[126]

The state ultimately agreed to create the park partly because of NAACP pressure and support from the Shelby County Commission, but also because the issue had the attention of top levels of the federal government. The county commission enlisted the support of First Lady Eleanor Roosevelt, during her visit to Memphis in November 1937, and Mrs. Roosevelt's secretary contacted Interior Secretary Harold Ickes directly to inquire about the chances of the park coming to fruition.[127] Ickes responded to Mrs. Roosevelt in early December, stating that no definite assurance could be given to the county commission since funding to the CCC had been curtailed.[128] After learning of this response, E. W. Hale, chairman of the commission, noted that a "colored" CCC camp had been working on the Shelby Forest RDA for the past two or more years and suggested moving this camp to the new park site.[129] Park Service director Arno Cammerer agreed to Hale's plan, and later that year the CCC camp was transferred to the location to construct the new Shelby County park for African Americans.[130]

In April 1939 the *Atlanta Daily World* described the CCC's progress at the park in erosion control, bank sloping, sodding, and surveying, along with construction work. Envisioning eventual completion, the paper noted that the space would "show the works of CCC labor and nature in beautiful trees, shrubbery, rolling prairies, drives, flowers and scenic places."[131] Included in the original vision were plans to develop day-use recreation facilities including a baseball field with grandstand, a swimming pool, and an amphitheater. Additional vacation facilities would be created according to "need and proposed use."[132] The article described the amenities the park would offer: "Splendid lodges will be constructed. These lodges in other camps have been great show places for convenience and beauty as well as rustic art. Plans show that parking areas will be placed at a number of vantage points. Drives, trails, and guard rails will be found in places where needed. Barbeque pits and picnic areas should be of interest to summer campers, and other structures are included in the plans for the colored citizens, the like of which cannot be found in the South."[133]

The lack of a swimming pool inhibited attendance in the early years of the park. Although a pool was included in the original design, its construction was interrupted in 1940 when CCC workers discovered the remnants of an Indian village dating to as early as 1000 CE.[134] The 188-acre site, called Chucalissa Archeological Park, was fenced off but remained officially part of T. O. Fuller State Park and was reportedly open to both African Americans and whites.[135]

Visitors had been entering the park ever since the summer season of 1941 amid construction.[136] At first called Shelby County State Park, Shelby Negro State Park,[137] and then Shelby Bluffs State Park, the site was finally named for the Reverend Thomas O. Fuller,

who presided over the park's dedication on June 14, 1942, just a week before his death.[138] The local press reported that 3,000 people attended the dedication ceremony.[139] Later that year, Tennessee Conservation Commissioner J. Charles Poe wrote to Conrad Wirth to explain the park's name. Poe described T. O. Fuller as a prolific writer and minister with a theology degree from Shaw University who had served as a senator in the North Carolina legislature. Fuller had moved to Memphis in 1900 to preach and established the First Colored Baptist Church. Poe noted that Fuller spent his last few weeks "in cooperation with the County and State officials in perfecting plans for the dedication and presentation of a State Park for Negroes."[140] Development of some amenities at T. O. Fuller State Park was slow, apparently because of widespread park system budget constraints; basic camping facilities were unavailable until 1950, and its swimming pool was finally constructed in 1954.[141] An 18-hole golf course was added to the park in 1957.[142]

Park Development in South Carolina

In addition to the limited New Deal–era park development taking place in Oklahoma, Arkansas, North Carolina, and Tennessee, South Carolina constructed three state parks that accommodated African Americans. Greenwood and Hunting Island, opened in 1940 and 1941 respectively, were dual-use parks that included a smaller segregated African American facility within the larger park grounds. The third, Mill Creek, opened in 1941 as a nominally separate facility for African American use, although it was administered from nearby Poinsett State Park for whites. In total, sixteen state parks were constructed in South Carolina during the New Deal, and its three racially segregated facilities represented a larger number available to African Americans than was provided in any southern state up to that point.[143] Hostility among the state's white population, however, obstructed most plans to expand that number after World War II.

Given the minimal progress in establishing state parks for African Americans in the states discussed here, the New Deal did little to rectify the tremendous inequality in recreational access. Only nine of the many state parks constructed in the South and four of its fifteen RDAs were accessible on a segregated basis to African Americans. The state of Texas alone had constructed about three dozen state parks but had made no provision for African American use. Although all southern states expressed a need for such projects—evident in their Park, Parkway, and Recreational-Area studies produced in the late 1930s and early 1940s—most had made no state parks available to African Americans by the onset of World War II.

THREE

PARK SERVICE PLANNING
MEETS RESISTANCE

The National Park Service was the dominant force in state park development from the time director Stephen Mather initiated the National Conference on State Parks in 1921 until the end of the New Deal in the early 1940s. During that era, when most states were only beginning to establish parks and park systems, the Park Service saw its mission broadly as leading a nationwide effort to encourage park development and visitation. The expansion of state parks was a central element of that work, evident in the close collaboration between the Park Service and the National Conference on State Parks.[1] Membership in the conference included dozens more Park Service professional staff than state park directors, while high-level Park Service administrators served on its board, including Mather, Herbert Evison, and Conrad Wirth, who was later appointed as a "life" member.[2] Horace Albright, Park Service director from

1929 to 1933, had even commented that "state parks are, in many ways, more important than the national parks."[3]

The pace of development accelerated tremendously starting in 1933 as the Park Service took charge of New Deal park and recreation planning and used the opportunity to emphasize state park construction. During each year in the life of the CCC, the number of camps allocated to state park development under Park Service guidance exceeded the number in the national parks. In 1935, the zenith of CCC activity, the state parks garnered 435 camps nationwide in contrast with 115 camps in the national parks.[4] (Fig. 3.1)

The Park Service also directed the Recreational Demonstration Area program, which came to fruition during the second half of the decade and supplemented its state park work. In his memoir Conrad Wirth recalled the RDA

Fig. 3.1. Segregated bath and latrine building at a CCC camp in Florida's O'Leno State Park, under construction in 1935. Signs indicate facilities for "white" (left) and "colored" (right). Courtesy State Archives of Florida.

program "as one of the really fine accomplishments of the New Deal."[5] Under Wirth's direction, the RDAs were modeled on state park design and were usually between two thousand and ten thousand acres in size and located within fifty miles of major population centers.[6] They typically included separate day use and overnight areas for the general public as well as organized group camps, which were designated "for use and management by private and semi-private social, educational, and welfare organizations, such as the Campfire Girls or a local board of education."[7] The intention from the start was that the Park Service would hand over most of the RDAs to be administered as

state parks, although the authorization for such transfer had to await congressional approval, on June 6, 1942. Once turned over to the states, these areas contributed "almost three hundred thousand acres of new state park land."[8]

Wirth's commitment to the state park idea and emphasis on cooperating with local and state interests was vital to his success in both state park and RDA construction. Given the relative newness of state parks in much of the country and especially in the South, Park Service involvement in the development process was "major" and in some cases even "total."[9] The Park Service not only controlled the allocation of CCC camps, which greatly influenced site selection, but also planned the parks, supervised their construction, and made recommendations on all park projects.[10] Despite its dominance, however, the agency took pains to maintain effective relationships with state and local entities, opening field offices so that staff could remain closer to action on the ground.[11] Ney Landrum describes the Park Service during this time as "a truly sympathetic and helpful 'big brother' to the state park systems" that emerged.[12] (Fig. 3.2)

But the Park Service efforts to expand African American access to parks through the RDA program also opened up tensions over the issue of race in the South. With its goal of providing recreational opportunities within easy access of the urban poor, the program was poised to provide at least a partial solution to the nearly total exclusion of African Americans from scenic parks in the region. In that context, "recreational demonstration" took on extra meaning, demonstrating to state officials that African American facilities were needed and could be successful. The program's potential in that regard, however, was largely overwhelmed by the contradictions generated by Park Service pol-

Fig 3.2. A float representing an African American CCC camp called Camp Booker T. Washington in a Labor Day parade in Chattanooga, Tennessee, n.d. Courtesy National Archives, College Park.

icy of acquiescence to Jim Crow in its desire to maintain good relations between the agency and local and state interests. The result was that the RDA program's potential to significantly expand African American park access went largely unrealized.

In August 1937, as plans for RDAs were being implemented across the United States, W. J. Faulkner, president of Nashville's Inter-Denominational Ministerial Alliance, an organization of African American clergy, wrote to Tennessee's Department of Conservation, wanting to know whether the new Montgomery Bell RDA would be accessible to "members of our racial group," who were "citizens and taxpayers" of the state.[13] Faulker knew full well that in Tennessee, as elsewhere in the South, any access would be racially segregated. There was, however, no lack of space for a separate facility in the large reserve. Montgomery Bell RDA encompassed 3,996 wooded acres in the rolling hills west of Nashville, which after transfer to the state in 1943 would become one of Tennessee's premier state parks.[14] Faulkner explained that a lack of facilities had hampered the provision of summer camps for Nashville's African American youth and hoped to receive assurance that the "vast appropriations which the Federal Government has made for parks and playgrounds" would be available "for the use and enjoyment of all of the people of Tennessee."[15]

Faulkner mailed a copy of the letter to National Park Service director Arno Cammerer, adding a cover note that displayed an understanding of both the possibilities and the constraints of federal involvement in these matters: "While we realize that your office must necessarily work through local committees in carrying out programs for local communities, we are also aware that the Federal Government can do much toward seeing that the local policies are fair and just to Negroes who have not always been fairly treated by white committees in Southern communities."[16] The official Park Service response to Faulkner revealed its ambivalent stance: "We are aware of the great need that exists for adequate recreational areas and facilities for the use of the Negro people," but the problem of state and local white assent was another matter. The agency provided their usual explanation: "The State has agreed to eventually take over and administer this area so that plans for its use must necessarily be worked out in cooperation with State authorities."[17] Faulkner was assured that the Park Service would discuss the concern with the state commissioner, but it was ultimately up to the Tennessee Department of Conservation to decide.

In responding to all such inquiries, the Park Service expressed a persistent interest in expanding access to African Americans. Its pursuit of the matter reflected a growing effort within the Roosevelt administration to address the nation's so-called Negro problem in a variety of arenas. In January 1937 the administration had convened the National Conference on the Problems of the Negro and Negro Youth, which included officials from various federal agencies and more than one hundred prominent African Americans. The three-day meeting was chaired by Mary McCloud Bethune and featured her good friend First Lady Eleanor Roosevelt as a keynote speaker.[18]

The need to improve African American recreational access for both youth and adults was one theme of a conference that also addressed employment, housing, and education, among other topics. Of the recommendations offered, one suggestion was that federal officials should stipulate that any recreational facility created or maintained with federal assistance be "made available to Negroes without discrimination on account of race or color."[19] Implementing such a policy would be especially difficult in the South since it would pose a direct challenge to a Jim Crow system that touted "separate but equal" but, in fact, was designed to make racial inequality and discrimination plainly visible. Park Service leadership was sympathetic to the taxpayer-access argument, but weighing such sympathy with the realities of southern white recalcitrance and the need to maintain regional support for New Deal programs, the Park Service declined to adopt the conference recommendation. Rather than use its significant power to equalize park opportunities, the agency chose to defer to state and local wishes.

Some Park Service staff were frustrated with the results of this accommodation. Fred T. Johnston, working under Conrad Wirth, wrote in fall 1937 that even some RDAs originally designed to include African American facilities were ultimately reserved for white-only use. Observing the situation around the South, he identified a familiar combination of prejudice and indifference: "Prejudice makes it practically impossible to provide for Negroes on areas also intended for white use, and has so far prevented us from developing even the few portions of some of the Recreational Demonstration areas originally planned for Negro use." After four years of park planning and construction, on this issue Johnston could point to only "slight progress" in some of the southern states. He noted more specifically that "no developments of this kind have been actually carried out by this service," which suggested that "progress" was limited merely to promoting of the idea of access. Johnston saw a solution to the problem but also recognized the dilemma it posed: "It might be possible to develop parts of some of the large Recreational Demonstration areas for Negro use and make it a condition in turning the areas over to the states that these be maintained. However, the states have so little interest in the problem that we might be faced with a task of maintaining these areas for sometime [sic] to come if we insisted that this be done. It seems that the best we can do now is to consider each area an individual problem to be worked out with the State Park Authorities in the way most satisfactory to them and to us."[20]

With the decision regarding access in state hands, Tennessee's Department of Conservation answered that it would not allow African American access to the Montgomery Bell RDA. Faulkner's inquiry would be the first step in a failed quest by him and then others, unfolding over the next twenty-five years, to construct a state park in the Nashville vicinity that allowed African American use. Failure persisted mainly because local white interests rejected all suggested sites.[21]

Curtailed Plans for African American Recreation

The Park Service intensified its push for African American recreational access in early 1937. The Resettlement Administration was disbanded in spring, which left the Park Service in control of the RDA program and other park projects on submarginal lands. As part of their development work, Park Service planners assessed the state of current recreational efforts being considered for African American use on these sites. One list of projects included the nationwide proposals for all RDA vacation areas, waysides, and extensions to national parks.[22] A significant number of these were to be located in the South, and most of the fifteen vacation areas planned for the region were envisioned to allow some form of segregated African American access. The agency also reviewed a list of nineteen RA Land Utilization Projects in twelve southern states.[23] These were not RDAs but were located on submarginal lands and were intended specifically to provide African American recreational access. The proposals ranged from small picnic areas to relatively large rural parks.

Having reviewed the success rate of projects on this second list, Evison stated that the "sum total of actual results obtained in this phase of general recreation planning is not particularly encouraging." He attributed the lack of success to "the unwillingness of local communities to permit desirable areas to be made available for negro use."[24] That conclusion was based on inquiries by R. C. Robinson, a Park Service recreation planner in Region I.[25] Robinson reported that none of the Region I states of the South—not Alabama, Florida, Georgia, Kentucky, Louisiana, Maryland, Mississippi, North Carolina, South Carolina, Tennessee, Virginia, or West Virginia—had yet created any facilities for African American use, although significant opportunities existed. The responses he received described a mixed pattern of construction under way in some cases, and in others plans that had not moved forward or had been abandoned. Robinson's overall outlook was pessimistic, and his explanation echoed Johnston's perception of the situation faced by the Park Service: "In a number of instances areas and facilities which at one time were apparently intended for Negro use have later been allocated to the use of white people. This re-allocation has no doubt been due to the desire of the white people to have access to such facilities and to a lack of sympathy and interest for the Negro's need among a large portion of State and local leaders."[26]

By the time of Robinson's review only about one-third of the nineteen proposals had seen any significant movement toward development.[27] In his opinion, any solution to the problem of supplying quality facilities to African Americans would be found by developing alliances with white supporters. As he put it, "It is unquestionably going to be necessary to stimulate and crystallize the interest of the more liberal and far-sighted white people in this problem." Even sympathetic southern whites tended to be unreliable supporters of Black causes, however, as Robinson pointed out regarding white support for African American education:

In spite of the efforts of political, social, and civic leaders and organizations on behalf of Negro education over a period of seventy years or more, we still have illiteracy figures running from 10% to 25%. The contrast between the figures on illiteracy for the white and Negro races indicates the lack of interest on the part of the white race in the general welfare of the Negro. When we learn, for example, that 25.4% of the Negroes living in Greenville, Mississippi, are illiterates, we are justified in concluding that a community which will permit such a condition to exist cannot be expected to cooperate in the provision of a recreational area for its Negroes.[28]

In addition to casting doubt on the southern will to provide recreational facilities for African Americans, Robinson suggested that the proposed sites on the RA list were poorly selected in relation to potential demand. Instead of the "state park every 100 miles" slogan that influenced Park Service discussions of state systems generally, Robinson advised a focus on "principal Negro urban centers" as indicating places with the "greatest need." He suggested that the RA list of land use projects was problematic since it included sites for African Americans that in his view were too far from "the more heavily congested centers of the Ne-

gro population." To ensure adequate demand, he suggested that the African American facilities should be closer to such centers, within a "radius of thirty miles" as the "maximum distance" given perceived travel constraints associated with African American poverty. His suggestion was intended to overcome the Park Service's requirement that demand be proved in advance, although proposals still faced the hurdle of local white acceptance.[29]

Several months earlier, Robinson had addressed the lack of progress in a different report that provided a general inventory of state-supported "Recreational Areas for Negroes" throughout Region I. He noted that in the region's northern states some communities still expected segregation of facilities, albeit unofficially, but his focus was on the South, where "the Negro is not permitted to use parks developed for the use of the white race." While pointing to "a few outstanding proposals" in the South, he indicated the lack of current facilities of any type and suggested the need for greater federal pressure. He wrote that "without substantial Federal encouragement, it is seriously doubted whether any of these proposals will materialize in concrete developments."[30] The RA had already acquired significant tracts of submarginal land, including some in areas with high African American population density. Robinson envisioned that this land could provide the basis for the federal effort to extend park access for African Americans, and over the next few years the RDA program would become a focal point of this encouragement of state action.

The nationwide list of forty-six RDA sites

included fifteen vacation area projects located in nine southeastern states. Ten of the sites were originally envisioned to allow segregated African American access and five were proposed for exclusively white use. The white-only sites included Georgia's Alex H. Stephens and Pine Mountain RDAs, Tennessee's Fall Creek Falls and Montgomery Bell RDAs, and South Carolina's Cheraw RDA. One of the sites—Hard Labor Creek RDA, located east of Atlanta—was initially intended for exclusively African American use. The remaining nine sites were envisioned to include separate white and African American facilities. Facing local pressure, however, Hard Labor Creek and most of these dual-use sites were soon added to the white-only list, and the number of RDAs that might allow African American access quickly shrank. By the time construction commenced, more than half of the proposed segregated sites were reallocated to exclusively white use.

Overseeing this growing number of white-only federal parks, it was evident that the Park Service needed an answer to the charge that its de facto discriminatory policy conflicted with its official nondiscrimination stance. To extract itself from the contradiction, the agency explained that it would remain officially race-neutral in administering the RDAs, applying no racial designation to any of the facilities nationwide. The essence of the conflicted policy was expressed by Park Service employee Kenneth B. Simmons: "There has been no color line drawn in the selection or the development of the . . . recreation areas. It has, therefore, been deemed advisable to leave the matter with the individual states or the local advisory groups."[31]

This largely semantic distinction would help smooth the cooperative relationships between federal, state, and local interests, albeit at the expense of progress toward resolving the problem of African American recreational access.

The prerequisite of ensured African American demand also loomed large over these projects. Concerned that constructed camps would go underused, Director Arno Cammerer applied this policy not only to the RDAs but also to the national parks located in the South: "In the Shenandoah and Great Smoky Mountains National Parks," he stated, "I have always said that we have a location for colored camps in each park, but that these will not be built unless there is a proven demand therefor."[32] Associate Director Arthur Demaray's response reflected his concern that the policy ran counter to Park Service claims of nondiscrimination. With Cammerer's policy in place, whites could expect parks as an entitlement, while African Americans would need to prove in advance that they would use them. Regarding camping in the national parks, Demaray cautioned that although few African Americans might demand camping facilities at first, "if one comes to the Park he cannot be denied such facilities and he will either have to be placed in a camp ground where white persons are camping or there must be available a separate camping area for negroes with facilities equally as good as for white persons. I do not see how this can be avoided."[33]

Demaray also pointed out the double standard regarding the RDAs. He cautioned that no such demonstration of preexisting demand had been required of underprivileged whites. "In neither case," he explained regarding African Americans and poor whites, "has there been a *demand* for such facilities in advance of the facilities being made available." Suggesting that "there is just as much need for camps for negroes as for whites," Demaray asserted that Interior Secretary Harold Ickes was aware of the issue and soon would "insist that some Provision be made for the negroes, if funds can be obtained for that purpose and maintaining and operating agents can be found."[34] Despite Ickes's strong support for the program, however, the funding caveat included by Demaray would govern the program in practice. Intended to promote the careful use of available funds, the policy of demand proven beforehand remained in place.

Since the RDA proposals had been drawn up without the Park Service's direct knowledge of local white opinion or of potential African American demand, the futures of the ten RDA sites remained uncertain. In addition to Hard Labor Creek RDA, proposed for exclusively African American use, those envisioned with dual-use facilities included Alabama's Oak Mountain RDA, located near Birmingham, the largest center of African American population in the state, and Maryland's Catoctin RDA, part of which was retained by the federal government to house the Camp David presidential retreat.[35] Much of Virginia's Chopawamsic RDA would also retain federal status as a National Park Service unit renamed Prince William Forest Park. Other sites with proposed dual access in the region were Swift Creek RDA, located near Richmond; Otter

Fig. 3.3. Entrance to Crabtree Creek RDA, 1943. Courtesy State Archives of North Carolina.

Creek RDA, west of Louisville, Kentucky; Shelby Forest RDA, near Memphis, Tennessee; King's Mountain RDA at the northern border of South Carolina; North Carolina's Crabtree Creek RDA; and Oklahoma's Lake Murray RDA. (Fig. 3.3)

Despite initial intentions for segregated access, however, the policy of accommodation and requirement of predetermined demand would remove such consideration from six of these parks. Wirth, in a reply to a camping inquiry from the Boy Scouts of America, had written, "Local custom and sentiment will probably make it impossible for us to provide camping facilities for Negroes on the Fall Creek and Kings Mountain Recreational Demonstration Areas at any time in the near future."[36] Alabama's Oak Mountain RDA was removed from dual-use consideration "because of lack of organization and interest among Negroes for this type of recreational program."[37] Such plans at Oklahoma's Lake Murray RDA were canceled for the same reason.

Only four of the ten RDAs planned for African American access successfully included the segregated group camps, with the first of these opening in summer 1938 at Chopawamsic RDA, just south of Washington, D.C. The others were located at Crabtree Creek, Otter Creek, and Swift Creek RDAs. The remaining six, including Hard Labor Creek RDA, were reallocated to white-only access. Despite its non-discrimination policy and its expressed interest in addressing the problem of African American recreation, the Park Service found itself administering eleven white-only RDAs in the South in addition to the four segregated facilities.

Secretary Ickes's Negro Affairs Advisor, William J. Trent Jr., sought to assess the progress made in providing African American camps in the RDAs.[38] Having conducted inquires since his appointment to the post early in 1938, he wrote a memo in June 1939 to the secretary summarizing his findings. Trent placed most blame for the lack of progress on the curtailment of New Deal funds. Noting that "a great deal of attention had been paid to the problem" by Park Service officials, and that "very effective work is being done in this connection," the tendency by decade's end was that dwindling funds meant that often "the Negro areas were left out." He recounted that plans for the camp in Catoctin RDA were dropped for this reason as were plans at Hard Labor Creek in Georgia, despite its proximity to Atlanta's large African American population. Trent lamented that "this camp was developed for use of white people and no camp is available for Negroes."[39] He noted that the Otter Creek RDA had still planned for such facilities, although development thus far had been limited to the construction of two camps for whites. Perhaps because of pressure brought by Trent's inquiries, that facility would successfully include a tent camp for African American groups in time for the 1939 season.[40]

Given that the limited available funds tended to go to white facilities, Trent recommended that specific funding be earmarked for the development of African American projects. Ickes responded that he would consider requesting funds for such purposes from the Public Works Administration, as Trent suggested, given curtailment of CCC and other funds. "The National Park Service assures me," he wrote, "that any funds it may have available will be utilized to the best advantage in meeting current recreational needs, both for Negro and white use."[41]

Just two weeks after this assurance, however, Ickes learned from Demaray, by then Park Service acting director, that while a portion of the funding had been restored, the allocated amount was 60 percent less than requested.[42] The result, according to Demaray, was that no new RDA group camps could be constructed but that work would continue in camps already under construction, including "some contemplated for Negro use."[43] The funding problems that beset New Deal programs in their later years would only deteriorate as the war drew near.

Recreational Studies in a Reluctant South

Park Service hopes for the future were boosted by the emphasis on long-term recreational planning envisioned in the Park, Parkway and Recreational-Area Studies that were carried out as the New Deal waned. The studies were congressionally mandated by the Park, Parkway and Recreational-Area Study Act of 1936, which had followed a preliminary study by the newly created federal Natural Resources Board in 1934.[44] Conducted by state planning commissions beginning in 1937, with close assistance from the Park Service, these studies were designed to assess existing park and recreation facilities (municipal, county, state, and federal) and recommend systematic improvements. The results of the individual studies were intended to inform recreational policy and planning at the national scale. The outcomes of individual state studies were synthesized by the Park Service in its 1941 report, *A Study of the Park and Recreation Problem in the United States*.[45] The federal interest in improving rural park access for African Americans ensured that this goal appeared prominently in the state studies. The body of the final report, however, emphasized its national scope and focused on the general need for parks and recreation. Consideration of African Americans in the South was confined to the appendix, albeit with significant coverage. In that section, information for each state included a map of its recreational facilities, demographic data, a tabular list of federal, state, and local parks, and a written summary of recommendations.

Each southern state's written summary emphasized the importance of providing for African American needs, but these were shaped in part by federal supervision of the individual studies. Tentative reports from the state planning committees underwent a review process that included Park Service planners and administrators. With this feedback informing the assessments and recommendations, the state planners were urged to be candid in assessing the problem faced regarding access for African Americans. Remarking on South Carolina's tentative report, for instance, Park Service planners suggested that it "should include a mention of the meagre facilities now provided for Negro camping and should deal with the glaring needs of this race for more camping opportunities."[46]

The recommendations, however, did not propose equality between white and African American facilities, in either number or size. North Carolina's report specifically recommended, for example, that six state parks for whites and three for African Americans be added to its current offerings.[47] Additionally, assessments and recommendations were often grounded in the stereotype that African Americans were disinclined toward using "natural" areas like state parks, suggesting instead that efforts focus on providing playfields and playgrounds in cities. A contributor to Louisiana's Park, Parkway, and Recreational-Area Study, for example, framed the state's African American recreational needs in relation to the "nature and talents of the Negro." The author writes, "By nature, the Negro is gregarious. His chief pleasures come from those things which enable him to participate in activities, and to share in the joy or sorrow with others of a group."[48] Louisiana's survey suggested the systematic provision of recreational areas for its African American population, 37 percent of the whole, although mainly on smaller sites of between forty and one hundred acres, providing facilities catering to physical and social activity. While a few large reservations were viewed as needed for group camping, the report emphasized smaller parks and playgrounds that were within a short distance of population centers and available at low cost.[49]

Florida's report also applied stereotypes to determine the characteristics of its recommended African American facilities. On the positive side, the commission acknowledged a significant need for such recreation areas in this state with a 30 percent African American population. The report of a meeting to discuss the survey conveyed broad consent: "It is agreed that the State Forest and Park Service should assume an aggressive role in the development of Negro areas."[50] The report recommended, however, that such areas be designated as community or county parks, and not as state parks. The justification was that African American poverty and travel constraints would keep such users close to population centers.[51] A consultant for the Park Service suggested that the proposal was a "reversal of general policy and practice." Noting the double standard in the report's logic, he explained, "If the same reasoning were applied with respect to provision of parks for white people it is probable that more than half of them would not be able to use the State areas."[52] The Park Service's regional planning office was even more direct in its critique of what the staff saw as Florida's evasion of responsibility:

It appears to us that the State is intentionally dodging its responsibility for the provision of non-urban park opportunities for Negroes. To date, it has not acquired a single area of State park character for the Negro race, nor does the report recommend areas for State ownership to serve this race. The State Park Director states in his side comment that areas for Negroes should be community or county rather than State parks. In our opinion, the State of Florida has a definite obligation to provide its Negro with equal per capita opportunities.[53]

Perhaps not surprisingly, Florida was among the many southern states that provided no large rural parks to African Americans during the New Deal years. Its first was opened in 1951 at Little Talbot Island State Park, near Jacksonville.

The Case of Mississippi

Mississippi's study and the effort to implement some of its plans illustrate the difficulties encountered in achieving success. Its 1938 Park, Parkway, and Recreational-Area Study envisioned a significant distribution of parks accessible to its 50 percent African American population, and the report was persistent in discussing this provision. The relative poverty of both its residents and state government, however, constrained recreational plans. Most of the recreational facilities existing in Mississippi were provided by private groups including churches, schools, 4-H clubs, and lodges.

Given the state's poverty, there were insufficient public facilities even for the white population, and the state relied almost entirely on federal funds to provide the limited spaces available. The study highlighted such limitations, indicating, for example, that the white population was deemed large enough to require 215 public swimming areas, though only 67 were available. For African Americans, the report described an even more dramatic lack: "The Negro population is sufficient to use 214 swimming pools. There are none."[54]

While acknowledging the state's significant recreational potential, the study suggested that a lack of resources would preclude elaborate plans for state park expansion beyond those already constructed or under construction with federal assistance. To meet Mississippi's recreation needs for the future, the report recommended instead a primary focus on day-use recreational facilities constructed separately for both Black and white residents. Sites between forty and one hundred acres and located adjacent to schools were recommended since the state already controlled such land. The report suggested that most but not all of the state's counties include at least one site for each race. The number for each was not proposed to be entirely equal. Mississippi's whites would ostensibly receive eighty-six locations while seventy-nine were proposed for African Americans.[55]

The report generally recommended against providing larger reservations of five hundred to one thousand acres or more, for both whites and African Americans, citing the travel constraints of 75 percent of the state's population. There were already nine state parks in Mississippi, although none of them permitted African American access and the report entertained no idea of expanding these parks to include segregated facilities. This lack of consideration was likely informed by the results of a survey of recreational habits and interests among Black and white Mississippians which reinforced familiar stereotypes. Survey responses from both whites and African Americans emphasized a desire for swimming pools, athletic fields, tennis courts, golf courses, and other such "active" recreational pursuits; only the white respondents were credited with a desire for hiking and auto trails, gardens, hunting and fishing grounds, and reading rooms.[56]

In any case, none of the existing larger reservations were accessible to African Americans. Along with the state parks and forest lands, even the larger federal areas in Mississippi, which included areas along Natchez Trace Parkway, two WPA lake areas, and national forests, were restricted to white use. The larger sites were deemed unnecessary for African Americans, but providing even the smaller areas would prove to be difficult. The report acknowledged that existing facilities would address at least some of the recreational needs among whites throughout the state, but "in nearly all cases for the Negro, there were no facilities provided whatsoever."[57] It noted that four federal projects for African Americans were under consideration, including two RA sites at Okolona and Starkville and a site in Clinton. Most of these proposals were not situated in close proximity to the highest concentrations of Black population, and thus, according to the report, they hardly altered the statewide need for additional African American recreational facilities.

Providing recreational areas around schools was viewed as the best hope for serving Mississippi's African Americans, but the report offered several additional proposals. One was to convince plantation owners in the Delta region, where African American numbers were highest, to lease or donate land for recreational use. According to the suggestion, the state park agency would administer the properties and user fees would be collected from African Americans living both on and off the plantations, to provide a maintenance fund. A willing plantation manager was even identified, one Oscar Johnson, who might serve as an example for other plantations in the Delta. Johnson agreed to supply land for "numerous small Negro recreation areas," which his British-owned plantation would maintain and operate but which the state would develop and supervise.[58] Another suggestion for the Delta region was to use CCC labor already in the area working on malaria control projects to construct recreational facilities through the use of "side camps." Neither suggestion was accepted—the plantation arrangement in particular faced administrative questions regarding state control of essentially private park lands.[59]

The report presented one significant recommendation, that two coastal areas along the Gulf of Mexico be acquired for the creation of two new state parks—one for whites and one for African Americans. None of the existing state parks were located in the coastal region, despite the perception that the Gulf Coast was "Mississippi's greatest recreational asset."[60] The report suggested a coastal park for white use, envisioned as "Magnolia State Park," to be located somewhere in the vicinity of Biloxi and Gulfport. The state's planning commission suggested that the revenue generated from this potentially popular site could help underwrite the entire financially challenged state park system. The other location was envisioned as "Gulfside State Park," to be reserved for African Americans and located near Waveland. The prospects for success with the latter effort were buoyed by the existence of state-owned coastal land in proximity to an African American resort called the Gulfside Assembly that had been successfully operating for over a decade. The site was unique in its potential to become the only "State owned colored Gulf-coast area in the South," and the commission pointed out that it was an opportunity the state ought not pass by. It warned, "This may be the only possibility of providing for the Negro in this State."[61]

In a letter to Herbert Evison, the Park Service recreation planner R. C. Robinson described the unique and potentially profit-generating opportunity that "Gulfside State Park" would provide. Situated about midway between New Orleans and Mobile, the site was controlled by the Gulfside Association, which owned some of this land and had leased the rest from the state. The site comprised 1,240 acres of gently rolling coastal landscape that was covered with mixed pine, oak, elm, gum, and beech, along with broom sage and Johnson grasses. Most important, the site included one and a quarter miles of Gulf beach frontage, protected by a sea wall.[62] The location was already widely used and well known to the region's—indeed the nation's—African American population.

The Black-owned Gulfside resort was created and run by Robert E. Jones, a Methodist bishop from Greensboro, North Carolina. He had purchased the property, which included a mansion once owned by President Andrew Jackson along with 300 acres of overgrown and swampy land, in 1923. The property was adjacent to 320 state-owned acres that Jones also acquired that year under a lease.[63] The resort was developed to promote adult education as part of the Chautauqua movement and emerged as a popular destination for African Americans who traveled to the site from great distances. The *New York Amsterdam News* in 1926 hailed the resort as "the only project of its kind that has ever been launched in America."[64] The resort hosted conferences, summer school activities for teachers, music performances, home economics training, religious education for pastors, and camping excursions for the Boy Scouts and Girl Reserves, among other events.[65]

In 1934 the *Pittsburgh Courier* called the Gulfside resort "one of the finest in America" and "the best known and most widely used center of constructive recreation for the Negroes in America."[66] But despite the positive image the resort enjoyed, the Great Depression had taken a significant toll on the financial health of the Gulfside Association. Small donations (as well as visitation) had declined dramatically during the 1930s, while major philanthropic support, such as that from the Rosenwald Fund, had

been reduced or withdrawn. Meanwhile, local banks were demanding loan repayments and the property tax burden had increased.[67] It was during this difficult time that the state planning commission contemplated converting the resort into Gulfside State Park. The request to consider the conversion had reportedly come from Bishop Jones himself.[68] With its existing facilities and nationwide fame, the beachfront location had evident potential for success as a state park. Robinson understood the site's great potential, suggesting that it could "become the focal point of Negro recreation for the entire Southeast."[69]

The state officials in charge of administering the Mississippi park system, including State Forester Fred Merrill and State Park Director J. H. Fortenberry, were much more wary of the proposal. They were, as Robinson explained, "dubious of their agency's assuming the responsibility for maintenance and operation." They also questioned the location, which, despite the potential to serve what Robinson pointed out were five million African Americans living within a four-hundred-mile radius, was not near a major center of Mississippi's Black population. Robinson remained hopeful, however, noting that the state officials were suspending their judgment pending assurance that civic and recreational organizations serving African Americans in the area would provide sufficient support.[70]

In the end, Gulfside State Park was not realized, more than likely because the state declined to pursue the project.[71] The state did, however, approve the creation of Magnolia State Park, for whites, which was constructed soon after with CCC labor in Ocean Springs, just east of Biloxi. That park was later incorporated into Gulf Islands National Seashore in 1971.[72] After the failure of the Gulfside proposal in 1938, Mississippi would remain without any state park access for African Americans until 1954, when Carver Point State Park, constructed in conjunction with Hugh White State Park for whites, was opened on the north shore of Grenada Lake, a two-hour drive north of Jackson.

Pushing Back on Jim Crow

The Park Service did occasionally press harder to allow African American park access and so invited controversy.[73] In his May 1937 inventory of recreation projects for African Americans, R. C. Robinson noted that local opposition to the segregated camp at Swift Creek RDA, near Richmond, Virginia, put plans at that site in jeopardy. Herbert Evison, however, assured his superiors that the concern was overstated, asserting that only "one or two people" were opposed and he felt "very confident that this attitude can be changed."[74] Discussion at a December 23 meeting with the local Camp Advisory Board, however, showed that Robinson was not exaggerating the issue. Eight of the nine board members attended the meeting, which was organized by Stanley M. Hawkins of the Park Service regional office in Richmond. At the meeting, Hawkins demonstrated the measures being taken by the Park Service to ensure the adequate segregation of races in the park, describing the physical features of the spatial arrangement on a map that

showed how the African American camp in question would be separated from the white areas of the park. The landscape features that would serve to buffer white and Black areas included "the Court House Road, the size of the Area and the natural cover."[75] The map also showed "that it was possible to have an entirely separate entrance road to the proposed Negro area," and, to emphasize the completeness of this physical separation, Hawkins pointed out that the "Negro camp" was located in a different watershed from the white areas.[76] To further placate the board, he had proposed that, if desired, the Park Service would even provide a separate name for the African American group camp.[77]

Despite the carefully segregated design and the concessions offered, after Hawkins's presentation all but one of the local board members voted to exclude the African American camp from the RDA. The lone supporter of the Park Service plan was a Mr. Guild, director of the Richmond Community Fund. Among those voting against the proposal was Fannie Crenshaw, director of physical education at Westhampton College and member of the YWCA camp committee. Hawkins related that Crenshaw's objection "seemed to sound the key note of the discussion." Citing her experience with the college and with young women's institutions, Crenshaw "felt it would be very difficult to continue the operation of any girls' camp on the Swift Creek Area, due to the reaction of the parents, if a Negro camp were allowed in the same general vicinity." With Crenshaw raising the specter of Black males mixing socially with white females, Hawkins wrote that "she was quite pointed in her remarks that the hiking and nature study radius of each Race would be limited and would be very difficult to control the intermingling of the campers during the camping season."[78]

In rejecting the proposal, the Camp Advisory Board passed a resolution stating, in part, that "the present camp site in Swift Creek Area be retained as a camp for white persons." Two additional clauses expressed a desire to develop existing parts of the RDA and to form a subcommittee to consider a location for an African American organized camp "in some other area."[79] Upon receiving this news, Herbert Evison sent a memo to Conrad Wirth that hardly disguised his annoyance with the board's decision: "It is the profound conviction of this office that neither logic nor Southern sentiment with regard to Negroes can justify the stand taken by this committee. Furthermore, there is immediate need for group camping facilities for Negroes in this area. We are then brought face to face with what appears to us to be a major matter of policy."[80]

Evison proposed three alternatives to resolve the issue to the Park Service's satisfaction. The first was to defy the resolution and weather the ensuing "storm," given that local officials had no jurisdiction over the federal RDA land. A second suggestion was to declare the proposed "Negro camp" a completely distinct RDA, thereby removing the area as a matter of concern for the Swift Creek Camp Advisory Board. Evison's third suggestion was to accept the committee's resolution and search for an alternative parcel for development of the camp.[81] None of these options was pursued in the end. Conrad Wirth was also disappointed with the advisory board's resolution, although he maintained that cooperation and negotiation, rather than confrontation, would yield the best result. Wirth explained to the Region I director that inclusion of such a camp near Richmond had "been our intention from the start," and that "we desire that every effort be made to carry out our plans in this regard."[82] Wirth managed to negotiate a resolution, and in the end the "Negro camp" at the RDA was ultimately constructed, although its site was moved significantly farther from the white areas than originally planned. It was open for the 1939 camping season.

In 1940 the Park Service took a similarly determined stance in allowing a mixed-race group to camp at Oklahoma's Lake Murray RDA, adjacent to Oklahoma's Lake Murray State Park. As discussed in chapter 2, the Park Service had constructed two organized group camps, one intended for whites, one for African Americans, in the RDA to be available for the 1938 summer season. In response to local dissension, however, both camps were allocated for exclusively white use, and the following year a separate camp for African Americans, Camp No. 3, was created outside the RDA on state-owned land.

There was no circumstance under which a mixed-race group would have been allowed in Camp No. 3 or either of the RDA camps, if the decision were left to the local Camp Advisory Committee. But in the fall of 1939, RDA manager Dean Bell authorized use of white organized group camps by a mixed-race group, and he did so again in October 1940, generating

Fig 3.4. Girls at Camp No. 3, Lake Murray State Park, 1939. Courtesy National Archives, College Park.

outrage among committee members. The circumstance involved requests from YMCA and YWCA groups from twelve colleges around the state, which included Oklahoma's Langston University, an African American institution. The groups were sponsored by the Southwest Council of Student Christian Associations, which had been holding its conferences for the past fifteen years at various locations, usually on college campuses. With the Lake Murray park facilities available, they wanted instead to hold the meetings there regularly. Bell granted the organization permission to use the RDA's (white-only) Camp No. 2 for its 1939 meeting. When the group's representative asked if a second visit in October 1940 would create any difficulty, Bell responded that "the Federal Government did not discriminate against any of its citizens."[83] But Bell had granted the permission without consulting the advisory committee, which without question would have demanded denial of the request.[84] An affiliated mixed-race student organization from Southern Methodist University had made a similar request to use the park in April 1940, and the advisory committee, angered by the past approval, had refused permission.[85] (Figs. 3.4, 3.5)

Hearing of this denial, and having intended to bring the YMCA and YWCA groups back to Lake Murray in the fall, Fern Babcock, the regional secretary of the YWCA, wrote directly to Interior Secretary Ickes to ask him to use his influence to convince the advisory committee to change its policy on disallowing mixed-race groups. The response to Babcock's request came from Arthur Demaray, the acting director of the Park Service. In his letter to Babcock, Demaray reiterated the Park Service nondiscrimination policy and, referring to the RDA camps, assured her that the agency "does not forbid their use for meetings of this type nor does it discriminate against groups on grounds of race, color, or creed." Regarding the role of the advisory boards and committees, Demaray explained, "their functions, as their title indicates, are purely advisory in nature."[86] He blamed the denial of permission to the Southern Methodist University group on "a misunderstanding" of this role and said that a board recommendation of denial was not an absolute bar to acceptance

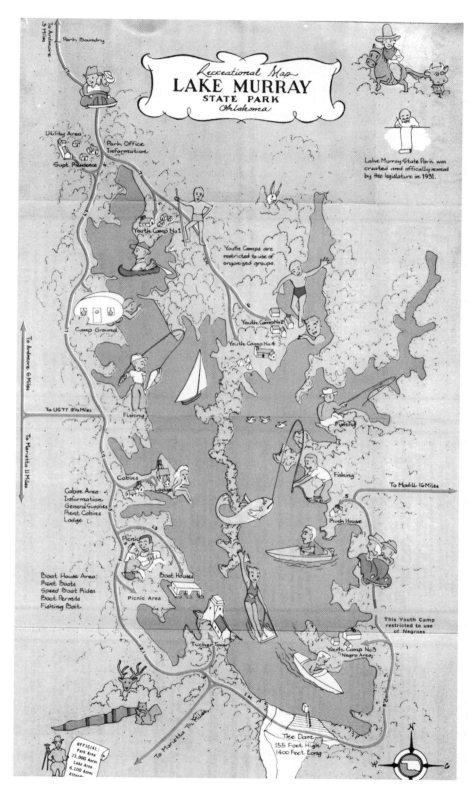

Fig. 3.5. A 1941 map of Lake Murray State Park showing the "Negro Area" on an isolated peninsula along the lake's southeastern shore. Courtesy Oklahoma Historical Society Research Division.

of an application to use the camps. He pointed Babcock to the appropriate personnel within Park Service's Region III to direct her application. Since the request was for short-term use of the camp, the application was directed to the RDA manager, Dean Bell, who had approved the previous year's request.[87]

Bell granted approval for the mixed-race group to use the white-only Camp No. 1, and the conference sponsored by the Southwest Council of Student Christian Associations took place as planned from October 11 to 13, 1940. The unusually bold Park Service stand generated a predictable and vocal backlash from the advisory committee. A meeting held on November 5, 1940, just weeks after the mixed-race conference included Park Service regional director Minor R. Tillotson, Dean Bell, several members of the Camp Advisory Committee, a representative of the Ardmore Chamber of Commerce, and the state supervisor of parks. The attendees admonished the federal employees for what they perceived as a transgression, asserting "that this section of Oklahoma would not tolerate Negro use or inter-racial use of the organized camps within the Recreational Demonstration Area." The advisory committee's chair, Reverend George Quarterman, its secretary, and another member threatened to resign unless the Park Service prohibited the interracial use of the Lake Murray RDA. The group was "most emphatic in denouncing" the nondiscrimination policy that was used to justify the permit and would "bring every pressure to bear against the [Interior] Secretary and the Service" through their congressional delegation.[88]

Committee letters to the delegation in turn prompted inquiries from Senator Josh Lee and Congressman Wilburn Cartwright to Ickes and Demaray. Reverend Quarterman's letter to the senator detailed his version of events leading to the 1940 conference taking place at the park. Quarterman said he had personally told the student group's representative "that following the traditions and customs of this area and the position of the whole Advisory Committee permission for such use could not be granted." He said he had been assured by Bell a week later "that the conference would not be conducted" only to learn of its ultimate approval during the second day of the meeting. According to Quarterman, the manager was taking his orders from higher up: "In telephone conversation on that day with Mr. Bell he told me that he was given explicit orders by his superiors of the National Park Service to permit this council of student associations to conduct this conference as they had planned." Quarterman asked the senator to convince Park Service officials to see the issue from the viewpoint of the local white community: "It is apparent that the National Park Service refuses to acknowledge existing race relationships in this area. It is our considered opinion that if they persist in this position they will not only cause serious difficulties in those relationships where no difficulties now exist, but will also decidedly limit the use of these camps by white groups."[89]

Demaray drafted a response for Ickes that was mailed to Congressman Cartwright under Ickes's signature with only minor modifications. In the letter, Ickes said that his position regarding the case was unwavering, declaring,

"In similar future circumstances, I would be disposed to follow the same procedure." The letter justified the decision to issue the approval, explaining the circumstances as an expression of the official race-neutral policy, which allowed the organizations to utilize the camps according to local racial standards. Ickes explained that the camp permit approval was based on the premise that this interracial group did, in fact, represent local values. The request came from a "predominantly white religious organization, which this Service believed represented the local viewpoint."[90]

The Park Service had assumed that whatever accommodation or separation of races occurred at the conference was "satisfactory to the white persons and to the Negroes concerned." Ickes assured the congressman that had the group comprised exclusively African American attendees, they would have been directed to the area of the park provided for their use in Camp No. 3. As for the declaration from the advisory committee that whites would not use the camps if they were also used by Negroes, even occasionally, Ickes was most adamant: "I believe that the Department should not accede to what appears to be a narrow point of view in order to be assured that white organizations would continue to use those camps."[91]

Without Ickes's direct intervention, Park Service staff might have acquiesced to the advisory committee's wishes. By 1940, however, momentum was building toward a more concerted push for civil rights among the nation's African American population. Ickes was clearly happy to support that fight. Staff in Region III, however, appeared weary from battling over the race issue for two consecutive camping seasons. Regional director Tillotson was "frank to admit" that he saw no way of reconciling the Park Service's nondiscrimination policy with "the racial feeling that exists in the Lake Murray area in common with other southern communities." He commented that the Park Service would be relieved of the issue only when the RDA was transferred to the state, still several years into the future, although he understood that the outcome would be to the detriment of interracial groups such as those enlightened Oklahoma students representing the YMCA and YWCA.[92]

Toward a New Era

There was never any doubt that Harold Ickes was very interested in promoting an agenda of racial justice. Soon after his appointment in 1933, Ickes desegregated Washington, D.C.'s National Capital Parks as those units were folded into Park Service administration. In 1937 he ordered the department-wide capitalization of the word "Negro," which had been promoted generally by African American leaders as a sign of greater respect, in official communications. In 1939 he ordered the removal of racial designations on park maps and creation of a nonsegregated demonstration area in Shenandoah National Park. In 1941 he extended the policy to other national park units, and in the following year Ickes ordered the desegregation of the system's southern parks.

The implementation of that directive, however, met predictable southern white resistance. A memo in May 1942 sent by Interior's first assistant secretary, E. K. Burlew, to Park Service director Newton B. Drury adds an important qualification to the order. Burlew requested an update regarding "lifting the segregation of Negroes, as far as possible, in the southern national parks and monuments."[93] The caveat, "as far as possible," suggested that for pragmatic reasons the segregation ban was not necessarily total. For instance, the continuing "unofficial" segregated use of the organized group camp areas at Virginia's Prince William Forest Park (formerly Chopawamsic RDA), a unit in the National Park system, would last for more than a decade after the end of World War II.[94]

The war years would prove pivotal to both federal recreation efforts and race relations in the United States. New Deal programs were disbanded, including the CCC and WPA, bringing to a close the tremendous expansion of state parks and RDAs, with most of the latter transferred to state control during the 1940s. The 1941 *Study of the Recreation Problem in the United States* had been intended as the starting point of an era of national recreation planning. Because of the war, the recreation report would ultimately have little impact.[95] A supplemental foreword by Harold Ickes, included with the report on its release in early 1942, downplayed the study's importance at that moment, emphasizing instead that "our present war effort must take precedence over all other activities."[96] After World War II, the Park Service never did reestablish the intimate link to state park development that it had in the 1930s. And, as one source states,

there "was a general feeling among Park Service officials that it was time to pull back, to consolidate gains and to become . . . a land administration bureau, whose focus was on the national parks."[97]

The war years were also a pivotal time in U.S. race relations, marked by intensified efforts to challenge racial discrimination. The shift toward demands for desegregation reflected a watershed transformation in African American activism that occurred during this time. The emboldened stance was influenced in part by the experiences of African American soldiers serving overseas, which offered them a glimpse of life beyond discrimination. More generally, the fight against fascism in Europe forced larger numbers of Americans to question the accommodation of white supremacy in the South. Harold Ickes himself decried the contradiction, expressing his views at a dinner in honor of Albert Einstein on June 6, 1944. Ickes exclaimed that "in the United States we cannot ignore the stark cold fact that we have a racial problem of significant proportions," warning his audience that "we make certain our own eventual defeat so long as we tolerate intolerance."[98]

Meanwhile, with Charles Hamilton Houston and then Thurgood Marshall heading its legal efforts, the NAACP had been increasingly successful in challenging Jim Crow in the federal court system.[99] In 1948 its Legal Defense Fund initiated a strategy that demanded the desegregation of institutions rather than their equalization, and it soon included cases aimed at southern state park systems. Facing courtroom pressure and seeking to protect Jim Crow, southern states reacted in the postwar years with belated plans to expand segregated park access for African Americans. These efforts signaled a significant turn from the relative indifference to the issue expressed by the region's park agencies in the 1930s. The postwar result was an increase in African American state park access that significantly exceeded the limited provision by the National Park Service during the New Deal. These state efforts, however, would soon prove to be too little and too late to rescue the "separate but equal" doctrine that had justified racial segregation and discrimination for more than half a century.

FOUR

PURSUING "SEPARATE BUT EQUAL" AFTER WORLD WAR II

Having been prodded by the New Deal–era efforts of the National Park Service to provide park access to African Americans, state agencies in the South had slowly accepted the necessity of this idea. But the financial and labor support from the federal government had ended with the war, which meant that subsequent design, planning, and construction had to be undertaken by the agencies themselves with financial support from their legislatures. Nonetheless the expansion of access continued without federal funding. By 1955, when the U.S. Supreme Court ruled that public park segregation was unconstitutional, the number of accessible state parks had increased from the nine built before the war to thirty, and by the early 1960s state agencies had constructed ten additional facilities for African Americans. Still, the number paled in comparison to the many state facilities that were constructed exclusively for white visitors.

The irony of this effort to expand access was that African Americans largely were no longer seeking to increase segregated spaces. There remained a significant number of "racial diplomats" among African American leaders in the South, who were willing to negotiate and compromise with whites to smooth the path to eventual desegregation.[1] But after the war, the direction among African Americans throughout the country was toward insistence on the equality that was promised to all Americans. Consequently, the main motivating force behind the modest postwar expansion came not from the goodwill of whites but largely from the pressure brought to bear by African Americans.[2] Legal action and threats of legal action spurred state park agencies to improve park access, and this chapter highlights some of these expansion efforts along with the difficulties they encountered.

In the postwar era, advocacy groups such as the NAACP were consistently calling to desegregate institutions, including state parks. The federal court system provided a major venue for applying this pressure, adjudicating lawsuits filed mostly by lawyers affiliated with the NAACP and its Legal Defense Fund. The state park cases it pursued were typically initiated by testing the ability of African Americans to enter the gates of parks designated for whites only.[3] Alarmed by the prospect of integrated state parks, agencies moved quickly to establish segregated facilities for African Americans. Agency officials accepted and even embraced and defended racial segregation as foundational to their regional traditions and perceived way of life. With a showdown looming over the *Plessy* doctrine, they hoped to demonstrate to the courts that a "separate but equal" standard was at least in the process of being met. Florida's parks director articulated the equalization strategy at the 1954 meeting of the Association of Southeastern State Park Directors: "It is hoped that, if equal facilities are available, the Negroes will use their own areas and leave the white areas alone."[4] Mississippi's Board of Park Supervisors was even blunter in its expression: "Our hope for maintaining segregation within our State Parks depends to a large extent on our furnishing equal facilities for both races."[5]

One important indicator of the shift in African American views and tactics was inscribed in the 1944 volume *What the Negro Wants*, which included essays by Black intellectuals from across the political spectrum. From social critic W. E. B. Du Bois to the conservative George S. Schuyler, all contributors agreed that the time had come to demand racial equality and desegregation. The NAACP's Roy Wilkins explained in his contribution that, in fact, African Americans had always sought equality, though until recently political circumstances had rendered pursuit of that goal impractical. Pointing to World War II as pivotal, Wilkins noted that there had been more discussion of the so-called Negro problem since Pearl Harbor than at any time, which led to the desegregation demands that characterized the postwar era. Wilkins recounted, "The war stimulated the discussion. The war stimulated the Negroes."[6]

The experiences of African American soldiers traveling both nationwide and abroad had heightened expectations and emboldened demands for change. Although the military enforced Jim Crow within its ranks for nearly the entire war, the writer Jerrold Packard notes that "these blacks nonetheless interacted with whites on a basis other than servile."[7] Military personnel overseas found relative freedom from the race restrictions they faced back at home. Additionally, the changing wartime economy in the South had increased pressure for change. The struggle among African Americans for entry into new industrial jobs, such as building planes or making ammunition, were added to struggles over discrimination in education, voting, and other areas of life.[8] The result of the momentum building through the war years was that, as the historian George Tindall states, for the first time since even before *Plessy*, "segregation itself became, at last, an open question."[9] Remarking on reactions of southern white leaders against this trend, Wilkins commented that in seeking full equality, "Negroes are demanding nothing new or startling. They are asking nothing they had not asked before Hitler came to power. . . . They are asking nothing inconsistent with the declared war aims of the United Nations. They are asking nothing inconsistent with the Constitution and the Bill of Rights."[10]

Disparities among States in Expanding Access

Between 1949 and 1956 nearly all southern states operated at least one state park facility for African Americans. Arkansas, which had closed Watson State Park in 1944, was the lone exception. Louisiana was the last to provide any facilities, opening a segregated area at Lake Bistineau State Park in 1956 and building similar additions at Chicot State Park and Fontainebleau State Park by 1961.[11] Georgia, Florida, and South Carolina were the most prolific, constructing twenty-three of these segregated parks by the early 1960s. The three states alone accounted for nearly 60 percent of all the state park facilities made available to African Americans over the course of the Jim Crow era. The most productive years in all of the states' efforts were between 1950 and 1955, coinciding with the most intensive period of postwar legal challenges to Jim Crow.

In 1950 Georgia's Division of State Parks, Historic Sites and Monuments began constructing George Washington Carver State Park, named for the famed botanist and inventor and designated for exclusive African American use.[12] The park was located on the shore of the new Lake Allatoona in the mountains north of Atlanta near Red Top Mountain State Park for whites. The Flood Control Act of 1944 authorized the recreational use of reservoirs controlled by federal agencies including the Army Corps of Engineers (COE), which leased land to states for a number of new state parks.[13] John Atkinson, a Tuskegee airman during World War II who sought to create a recreational area for Atlanta-area African Americans, is credited with the successful construction of the park. Atkinson was appointed as park superintendent, and during his tenure from 1950 to 1958 he oversaw the construction of the park's "clubhouse, concession stand, playground, boat ramp, beach and residence."[14] According to Georgia's park agency, the site proved to be popular, attracting visitors from nearby Atlanta and the surrounding region. A Girl Scout camp created on a leased section of the park in 1962 provided the only such space for use by north Georgia's African American Girl Scouts.[15]

In addition to Carver, the park agency added Keg Creek State Park in 1952, another exclusively African American facility, on the western shore of the Clarks Hill Lake north of Augusta. Two smaller, urban parks were added by mid-decade; fifty-two-acre Lincoln State Park was developed within Millen city limits in 1955, and the five-acre Yam Grandy State Park opened in Swainsboro in 1956.[16] Despite their deviation from the state park ideal, these small, unremarkable parcels could be rationalized as providing easy access, as they were within walking distance for the many African American residents in these cities. Fairchild State Park was Georgia's final exclusively African American facility, also constructed in 1956. It was a more traditional park in size and scenic quality, though limited to day use. Distant from major population centers, the relatively isolated park occupied the extreme southwest corner of the state on COE land along Lake Seminole.

Georgia's park agency included two dual-use facilities among its seven units providing African American access.[17] In 1952 the agency added a segregated camping area for African Americans at Georgia Veterans Memorial State Park, west of Cordele. A 150-acre space on the eastern edge of a larger park that was constructed in 1946, the site was separated from the white area by both distance and a railroad track that crossed in front of the camp's

Fig. 4.1. Georgia's Fort Yargo State Park in the 1960s; the segregated section for African Americans is located in the upper right corner. Courtesy Georgia Archives, Vanishing Georgia Collection, spc13-051.

gate. The press referred to the site as "Colored Georgia Veterans Memorial Park," which included a separate entrance, a recreation building, playground, ball fields, and boat docks that were "similar to the ones now on the white side of the park."[18] The other dual-use park in the Georgia system was Fort Yargo State Park near Winder. The park was acquired in 1954 and named for the restored eighteenth-century frontier fort located on its grounds. A separate entrance led to what is now called Section B, which was the smaller African American area located in the park's southwest corner. The African American sections of both Georgia Veterans and Fort Yargo State Parks did not include the best amenities the parks had to offer, such as the historic Fort Yargo structure or the modernist recreation center at Georgia Veterans State Park.[19] (Fig. 4.1)

Florida opened its first park for African Americans in 1951 at the south end of Little Talbot Island State Park.[20] A dual-use park containing separate Black and white sections, the coastal facility was situated on a barrier island with a wide beach, located northeast of Jacksonville. By 1955 the Florida Board of Parks and Historic Memorials had opened additional African American sections in St. Andrews State Park near Panama City, Florida Caverns near Marianna, Fort Pickens near Pensacola Beach, Tomoka at Ormond Beach, and Myakka River State Park near Sarasota. By the early 1960s park facilities for African Americans were extended to include John C. Beasley, Frank B. Butler, Jim Woodruff, and Magnolia Lake

State Parks—two beachfront and two lakefront parks respectively.[21] Three of these late additions were set aside for exclusive African American use (Woodruff, a dual-use facility, was the exception) and were the only state park facilities in Florida of this type. By the early 1960s Florida was responsible for more than 25 percent of all facilities in the South that were accessible to African Americans. Its relatively prolific output did not, however, signal equality. All of the park spaces were small and limited to day-use activities, while the rest of Florida's nearly fifty state parks were reserved for white use.[22] (Fig. 4.2)

Little Talbot Island State Park was the most notable addition because of the conscious attempt by the park agency to demonstrate full equality between white and Black sections. Plans had been formulated for the dual-use park arrangement since 1949, and the land was deeded to the Florida Board of Parks and Historic Memorials for development as a recreation area in 1951, just prior to the park's opening.[23] Despite the plan, the issue of creating a beach area for African Americans was predictably contentious. Park board member Elizabeth Towers told the agency's director, Lewis Scoggin, "You are perfectly right—the Little Talbot question with the Negro Beach Problem is going to be a Hot Potato."[24] Besides the possibility of local white resistance, it was evident that the African American section had lagged in both funding and agency commitment. A letter from Park Board vice chairwoman Eileen Butts to a fellow board member expressed her concern that the African American beach development at the site was not

Fig. 4.2. A group photo at the bathhouse on Butler Beach in the 1950s, prior to the site's development as a state park. Courtesy State Archives of Florida.

being pursued vigorously: "We felt, with due reason, that the negro project was in the Tally [Tallahassee] office discard. However, promise was extracted to rush work. Please keep the heat under them so that this promise is fulfilled by Labor Day. . . . With a good will, such simple construction can be finished by the above date."[25] In addition to board members, local advocates also pressed for the park's completion. Several months before the park opened, Martin Williams, president of Jacksonville Beach Chamber of Commerce, wrote to the Board of Parks: "The increasing number of requests we are now receiving from the colored personnel of the Armed Forces in training in the Southeast add additional pressure to the long felt need."[26]

The agency made a concerted effort in the design and construction process to demonstrate that the facilities for Black and white were virtually identical. Of the park's 1,651.12 acres, the white recreation facilities occupied an area of 5.74 acres while those in the African American section included 4.59 acres.[27] Planners noted that the recreation facilities provided were the same in both areas, while the local media highlighted this emphasis on equal though separate facilities. (Fig. 4.3) On September 1, 1951, just before opening day, the *Florida Times-Union* published a photograph of the park with a caption explaining that "the picture shows structures at the white section—at the northern end of the island. Those for the negro area on the southern end of the island are identical with those

shown." The paper reported that in each area, "the park board has drilled a 535-foot well at each center, providing a good artesian flow; covered the sand with pine tree bark, placed three wooden walks toward the beach, with shower heads at the end of each, and erected what will for [the] time being answer the purpose of dressing rooms, picnic areas with tables, benches and fireplaces, concession stands and toilet facilities. . . . An additional facility planned is a play area for each center, to include swings, seesaws, etc., for use of children."[28] After a year of operation, Florida Park Service acting director Walter Coldwell reported that the "use of the two beaches, one

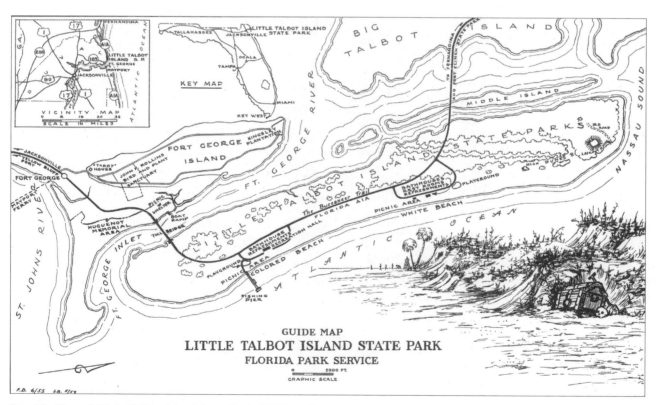

Fig. 4.3. Map of Little Talbot Island State Park (1959), indicating separate white and "colored" beaches. Courtesy Jacksonville Historical Society.

Fig. 4.4. A trail in the north section of Little Talbot Island State Park, 1959. Although separate beach facilities were reportedly similar in size and quality, this photo indicates that the white section had access to more varied ecological communities than the south end, which included only the beach and sand dunes. Photo by Charles H. Schaeffer. Courtesy State Archives of Florida.

for colored and the other for white, has exceeded all estimates."[29] (Fig. 4.4)

In West Virginia, a state that produced the slogan "wild and wonderful" to honor its scenic beauty, the lone facility for African Americans—Booker T. Washington State Park—was striking for its small size and limited amenities. West Virginia created no state parks for African Americans until after the war, when this park was opened in 1949 on the edge of the largely African American town of Institute.

Like many states, West Virginia had laid the groundwork for its park system in the 1920s. Its State Forest, Park, and Conservation Commission, established in 1925, identified a number of scenic and historic locations as potential state park sites. The first of these were developed after 1933 under the New Deal and included spectacular scenic settings such as Babcock, Cacapon, Hawk's Nest, and Watoga State Parks.[30] About 30,000 acres were acquired and developed for state parks by the mid-1930s, but African American access was restricted to a 4-H camp, constructed by the WPA on a 583-acre site adjacent to 3,227 acre Babcock State Park. Initiated in 1937 and dedicated in 1942, the 4-H site was operated by the extension services of historically Black West Virginia State College and was named Camp Washington-Carver. Providing recreational and outdoor opportunities for African American youth, the site contained unique and impressive features, such as The Great Chestnut Lodge, built of local chestnut wood, which was the largest log building in the state.[31]

But Camp Washington-Carver was not a unit in West Virginia's state park system, which restricted access to white visitors. When the NAACP asked in 1940 about African American access, West Virginia's Division of State Parks responded that "our Negro citizens would feel ill at ease" in sharing the parks with whites.[32] The agency added that it was considering constructing a state park for African Americans but had not yet made a decision. Before the end of the decade, the Division of State Parks had decided to undertake such construction, although the addition of Booker T. Washington State Park was hardly notable.

In his agency's annual report for 1951–52, Division of State Parks chief Kermit McKeever had invoked the words of Col. Richard Lieber. An icon of the state park movement and a defender of park ideals, Lieber had stated that the purpose of state parks generally "is not to merely satisfy but to uplift" and that "our parks are not merely picnicking places. They are rich store-houses of memories and reveries. They are guides and counsels to the weary and faltering in spirit."[33] Those words would have applied to other units in West Virginia's system, but surely not to the day-use state park for African Americans, which comprised just 7.43 acres. Occupying land donated by private citizens, Booker T. Washington State Park opened in 1949 with a well, ten picnic tables, fireplaces, toilets, and a parking area.[34] The site did not include trails and scenic views, nor did it provide camping, swimming, or any other recreation.[35] It was merely a picnic place. Booker T. Washington did not keep track of visitation, unlike all other parks in the state, and was apparently so insignificant that historical accounts of West Virginia state parks, including one written by McKeever himself, a long-time head of the park system, do not even mention it.[36]

In Kentucky, state planners had intended to assess the financial feasibility of expanding state park access to African Americans. To do this, the state's Park, Parkway, and Recreational-Area Study of 1938 suggested converting the Blue and Gray State Park in Todd County from white-only status to exclusively African American use. The idea was that with adequate visitation, more such sites would later be added.[37] Circumstances changed with the war, however, and the plan was never implemented.[38]

By 1945 the idea for a state park designed exclusively for African Americans was reportedly renewed by Kentucky governor Simeon Willis. State parks director Russell Dyche predicted that "Chickasaw State Park" would open within two years, pending an appropriation of funds from Kentucky's General Assembly. Ultimately $150,000 was allocated to its construction.[39] The space that came to be called Cherokee State Park was taken from land adjacent to Kentucky Lake (now Kenlake) State Park on the western shore of the TVA lake near the town of Aurora. Constructed by the TVA, Cherokee State Park occupied the northern end of the tract, and following familiar patterns of inequality, comprised 360 acres in contrast with Kentucky Lake, which was 1,414 acres.[40] The two parks were physically separated by forest and by state Route 80, which linked the western shore of Kentucky Lake to the Land Between the Lakes. (Fig. 4.5)

Cherokee State Park was formally dedicated in 1953, once all facilities had been com-

Fig. 4.5. A portion of Kentucky Lake State Park under construction in 1947. Cherokee State Park opened four years later along the lakeshore north of the bridge. Photo by G. K. Gunderson. Courtesy National Archives, Morrow, Georgia.

Fig. 4.6. Children posing at the Cherokee State Park entrance sign, 1953. Courtesy Kentucky Department of Parks.

pleted, although it had been open for day use since May 31, 1951.[41] *In Kentucky*, a state public relations magazine, included a description of Cherokee State Park on its grand opening that summer. (Fig. 4.6) Enthusiastic in tone, the article declared that the park was "in one of the most scenic spots on the entire lake."[42] Managed by L. G. Mimms, himself African American, who oversaw a staff of thirteen, the park was by then well developed with ten vacation cottages and a restaurant. Rustic in design, the restaurant was situated on a bluff overlooking the lake and the park's swimming area. (Fig. 4.7) The cottages were equipped with electric appliances and kitchenware as well as bedding and linens. Two of the ten structures were efficiency units, six had one bedroom, and two were two-bed-

room family cottages. (Fig. 4.8) All included a screened porch that faced the lake.[43]

The significance of Cherokee State Park was expressed by *Louisville Courier Journal* staff writer Joe Creason, who pointed out that given the previous near-total deprivation, it would "amaze many folks" that such a facility could exist in Kentucky. He described the park as "a giant step forward" and noted that "before Cherokee, except for a picnic area near Kentucky Dam, the state had done nothing in the recreational line for its Negro citizens and travelers." He added, "It would be difficult to convince most skeptics that such a park has been built and set aside for Negro Kentuckians."[44] Perhaps most unexpected was the quality of the facilities, which he judged "equal" to those of

Fig. 4.7. The Cherokee State Park restaurant, 1953. Courtesy Kentucky Department of Parks.

Fig. 4.8. A family enters a cabin at Cherokee State Park, 1953. Courtesy Kentucky Department of Parks.

neighboring Kentucky Lake State Park or any other such park in the state. Cherokee State Park did offer unusually fine accommodations, but Creason's assertion of equality was overstated. The neighboring Kentucky Lake State Park for whites was four times its size and featured beautiful lake views with more vantage points as well as the 58-room Kenlake Lodge.[45] Nonetheless, Cherokee State Park was remarkable and attracted African American visitors not only from Kentucky but also from Chicago, St. Louis, and other major population centers in the region.

By the early 1950s, segregated state park facilities were controversial, among both whites and African Americans. While most African Americans were pursuing a path to desegregation, many also desired park access in the meantime. Kentucky's conservation commissioner Henry Ward remarked on this tension at Cherokee State Park's unofficial 1951 opening

ceremony. Speaking to the substantial crowd of two thousand African American park visitors, he stated: "The question of whether parks of this type should be built is one that is subject to continuing debate in the nation. . . . Those of us charged with the responsibility of developing a park program for Kentucky do not claim that we have the final answer. But," he continued, "there is one thing that is clear and that is that while the debate over segregation rages, the colored people of Kentucky are entitled to a park they can enjoy without confusion, conflicts, or race riots."[46]

Ward's address presented what in the postwar decade was a commonly expressed goodwill toward Black citizens, tied to a pervasive white perception in the South that segregation was a mutually agreed upon arrangement aimed at the best interests of both whites and African Americans. He also included, however, an acknowledgment of the uncertainty of

Jim Crow's survival. Predicting that some day the struggle over segregation would be settled, Ward said that in the meantime it was the state's obligation "to provide equal recreation facilities for all of its people." Of course, the fact that there were ten state parks in the Kentucky system restricted to white use only compared with this single facility for African Americans, highlights the relativity in his use of the term "equal." At the same time, however, Ward attributed the construction of this park to an expressed African American request: "Colored leaders of this area have indicated by their interest that they prefer a park of their own that their people can enjoy now than to wait until the segregation problem has been settled."[47]

Cherokee State Park proved popular, although its existence as a separate African American state park was relatively short-lived. Kentucky's park system would be desegregated in 1955, soon after the U.S. Supreme Court declared public park segregation unconstitutional. Cherokee continued to operate until it was eventually closed and its property absorbed into neighboring Kentucky Lake State Park in 1964.

Mississippi was yet another southern state that managed to construct only a single park for its African American residents, who comprised nearly half of the state's total population—higher than in any other state. After the Gulfside State Park project in Waveland fell through in the late 1930s, the state waited another fifteen years to address African American park access. The Mississippi's State Board of Park

Supervisors suggested in its 1953–55 biennial report that the legislature should provide funds to create three African American parks.[48] But the only one constructed was Carver Point State Park, which opened in 1954. The exclusively African American park was situated on the north shore of Grenada Lake, not far from the city of Grenada, in the north-central area of the state. Its construction was paired with the simultaneous development of Hugh White State Park, restricted to white use, which was located on the lake's opposite shore.

A comparison of the parks suggests that the design of Carver Point State Park was aimed at achieving relative equality with its neighbor. Located on land leased from the COE, the two parcels, at just over seven hundred acres each, were nearly identical in size, and both included a large, hotel-like lodge to house guests. As construction commenced, the State Board proclaimed that the lodge at Carver Point would be "exactly the same as the one to be built for the Hugh White State Park."[49] The park for whites had a few extra amenities not found at Carver Point State Park, including its ten duplex vacation cabins, but Carver Point did have three group camp buildings, and there was even a plan to add a golf course, though that plan never materialized.

Despite its attractive features, Carver Point State Park persistently struggled to attract visitors. After the first two years of operation, the newly created Mississippi Park Commission reported, "The attendance at the Hugh White State Park has been very outstanding. Attendance at Carver Point State Park has been rather disappointing."[50] The main problem was not facilities, but location. The state park for whites was conveniently located just a few miles east of Grenada, while Carver Point was much less accessible, requiring a relatively long trip around the lake to reach its north shore. The roads leading to the remote park were poorly maintained (the entry road was unpaved) and formed a confusing network that made navigation difficult. As a result, attendance at Carver Point continued to lag. Mississippi's state parks were desegregated in the mid-1960s, and neither of the additional facilities envisioned for the state's African Americans was constructed.

White Resistance to Segregated Parks

In Tennessee, the postwar period began with badly needed improvements to the Chattanooga-area Booker T. Washington State Park and to T. O. Fuller State Park in Memphis. The refurbished Washington park was reopened on May 1, 1950, after two years of clearing vegetation and construction led by its African American manager, William Bell.[51] New facilities at the park included a swimming pool and concrete wading pool, bathhouse, picnic shelter, tent camping, concessions building, and caretaker's residence, as well as improved roads and parking.[52] (Figs. 4.9, 4.10) In 1950 T. O. Fuller received a new dining hall, tent facilities, a new water pump and filtration system, new picnic shelters, and bleachers at the park's baseball field.[53] Attendance swelled when a swimming pool and bathhouse were finally built in 1954. Twenty-one cabins were added to the park's

group camp in 1956, and the following year a golf course was constructed on land leased to the city.[54] (Fig. 4.11)

Beyond improvements to existing facilities, however, Tennessee's Department of Conservation was unsuccessful in expanding African American state park access, despite repeated attempts. In his history of Tennessee state parks Bevley Coleman explains that plans failed for a variety of reasons. For instance, the attempted lease of a TVA site in Humphries County for the envisioned Trace Creek State Park was scuttled when the federal agency withdrew the offer in favor of building the New Johnsonville steam plant.[55] Planners downplayed the need for a state park near Knoxville, citing the presence of a county park for African Americans built in the late 1940s on TVA land west of the city. A proposal in the early 1950s to set aside part of Chickasaw State Forest in Davidson County was never acted on. Additional proposals near Kentucky Lake, at Stones River, and at Old Hickory reservoir were also "not followed by action."[56]

While limited funding was an obstacle, local white prejudice was often an insurmountable factor in the effort to establish state parks for African Americans. As Coleman explains, "The Division of State Parks recognized in 1943 that there would probably be objection to establishing a Negro park near any center of white population or on any site within the state. The State Planning Commission restated the same handicap in 1952."[57] Even existing African American parks were affected by such resistance; the gates at Booker T. Washington

Figs. 4.9, 4.10. Picnicking (top) and the Picnic Pavilion at Booker T. Washington State Park, 1950. Courtesy Tennessee State Library and Archives.

Fig. 4.11. Ball field and picnic area at T. O. Fuller State Park, 1950. Courtesy Preservation and Special Collections Department, University Libraries, University of Memphis.

State Park were chopped down twice between July and October 1948 by suspected white vandals.[58]

The Conservation Department's expansion plans were also complicated by the increasing demand for desegregation by African Americans. Coleman quotes a 1953 letter from an official who was surprised by the skepticism expressed by two African American lawyers and a minister who visited a proposed site

outside Nashville: "To the astonishment of all concerned, these three negroes reported back they did not think much of the deal and that they preferred to hold up matters." The expressed reason was the momentum that had been building across the South toward park desegregation: "they felt that action would soon be taken to place them with the whites in Montgomery Bell Park." Noting the potential for conflict in this integrationist stance, a department employee wrote: "Thus, we observe at a glance the dynamite that is in this thing."[59]

At the same time, organizations such as the Girl Scouts and Boy Scouts had argued for a new park for African Americans in the Nashville area or at least somewhere in middle Tennessee. The Department of Conservation and the National Park Service had been fielding requests in the area both before and after the war.[60] Tennessee's 1956 ten-year state park plan, called "Operation '66," reasserted the pressing need around Nashville. The plan acknowledged the relative inaccessibility of the existing two African American parks by pointing out that a "Negro citizen in Nashville at present has to travel approximately 140 miles to Booker T. Washington State Park or approximately 225 miles to T. O. Fuller State Park."[61] By 1960 the department believed that it was finally close to a land deal to create a Nashville-area park. The parcel in question was located on the shore of Old Hickory Lake to the northeast of the city, a reservoir created by the Corps of Engineers.[62] Conservation commissioner J. Brents McBride told Tennessee governor Buford Ellington that the 140-acre parcel was "the last available piece of property suitable for this type of Park." Believing that a land deal was in hand but concerned about white resistance to the plan, McBride told the governor that three other proposed locations had "been blocked." Expecting resistance at this new site, McBride warned, "We are reasonably sure that there will be some objections to this and that some folk will be to see you."[63]

Ten days later, in a meeting with a local judge, a mayor, and the landowner in question, McBride acknowledged that local white resistance would persist. As he told Ellington, "We realized that we were placing our friends in Sumner County on the spot and that the feeling there was such that it would be impossible for them to go along with us."[64] Speaking to a reporter, Sumner County judge Stokley Dismukes, who was present at the meeting, explained the situation with frankness: "People out in that section of the county don't want it."[65] McBride declared, "We all agreed that it would be best to drop the matter. This brings us back right to where we were. Where we go from here we cannot see."[66] No further attempt was made to add a state park for African Americans in Tennessee prior to the desegregation of its park system by executive order of Governor Ellington in 1962.[67]

In Alabama, the situation was the same. James L. Segrest, chief of the Division of State Parks, wrote in 1945 to his superiors in the Department of Conservation that he "personally would like to see something done in the not too distant future toward establishing a few recreational areas in the State for the use of the Negro race."[68] The state's 1938 Park, Parkway and Recreational-Area Study had recommended the addition of five African American state parks, but by the date of Segrest's letter, the proposed number had been scaled back to three—one on the coast, another in central Alabama, and a third in the north.[69]

The coastal park for exclusive African American use had been on the state's agenda since it was first recommended in the study.

In 1946 the idea was endorsed locally by C. A. Gaston, an alderman from the town of Fairhope, who noted, "Not so many years ago our bay front was so sparsely populated that there was ample opportunity for segregation. Both races used the water front and neither attempted intrusion on the other." Alderman Gaston endorsed the creation of a "Negro state park" as a pragmatic means of protecting what he called "wholesome segregation" standards in the face of ever-larger beach crowds on Alabama's Gulf Coast. He recognized, however, that "it will prove very difficult to secure a suitable location" on the waterfront.[70] Probably because of local opposition, a beachfront state park for African Americans was never built.

In the middle section of Alabama, the most promising site for a state park was within a federally controlled tract located two miles east of the Tuskegee Institute. Work there toward establishing a rural recreation area for African Americans had been initiated in the mid-1930s after the Resettlement Administration acquired a 10,000-acre tract of submarginal agricultural land. Starting in 1937, two federal recreation areas controlled by USDA's Soil Conservation Service were developed within the project to provide much-needed recreation opportunities for Tuskegee residents.[71] These areas included one 35-acre parcel for African Americans with day-use picnic facilities, a campground, and a baseball field. A similar 25-acre park for whites was also constructed as part of the project.[72]

In March 1940, while construction of the federally controlled African American recreational site was under way, Alabama's Department of Conservation director Walter B. Jones requested development of a 442-acre section at the southwest end of the tract as a state park for African Americans. The plan was to direct the CCC to construct a site by 1941 that included an impounded lake for swimming, boating, and fishing, along with a group camp.[73] An agreement to pursue the project was reached by the involved parties, including the Tuskegee Institute, which agreed that the park would be an asset to its educational mission. Plans were shelved in 1940, however, as the allocation of a CCC camp was deemed unlikely with the approach of World War II. Attempts to develop the parcel as an African American state park subsequently fell through, and the land was given back to the USDA.[74]

After the war ended, Segrest recommended that the state reacquire the parcel and renew the attempt to construct the park. To create a more suitable state park site, he suggested the acquisition of additional land to create a 552-acre unit with an enlarged lake, family cabins and campsites for organized groups, and other facilities. The site was already partially developed, including an 8-acre lake and facilities that were being used for summer camps for (presumably white) Boy Scouts, Girls Scouts, and 4-H clubs. In Segrest's opinion, the expanded project would be an excellent first step in providing for the state's African American population. He stated, "This area has possibilities of being developed into a very fine recreational area for the use of Negroes. . . . I have every reason to believe that this could be developed into a worthwhile State Park that could be enjoyed by all of our colored friends."[75]

Alabama's interest in this project was

heightened by intensifying legal activities organized by the NAACP by that year, which included encouraging African Americans to test their ability to enter white-only state parks. The *Chicago Defender* reported that Alabama officials had been "scurrying about" in search of a state park site for African Americans, and that the effort was being renewed because of these legal threats. The paper reported that when seeking funding in spring 1951, Department of Conservation director Earl McGowin warned a legislative committee that "difficulties will arise in some of the other State parks" if the state did not secure a site soon, adding, "This is a condition that cannot last."[76]

The testing was a clear concern among the southern park agencies generally. The National Park Service, which continued to monitor and consult on state park development, noted these challenges. Reporting to the regional director on the situation in Alabama, Park Service planner Allen Edmunds noted that "Mr. Segrest is somewhat concerned over the use being made of Monte Sano State Park by Negroes," and that there were "other areas also that are being 'tested' by the Negroes." On a broader scale, Edmunds pointed out that around the South, the states "are recognizing this situation as one of considerable import."[77] Despite his concern, however, the Tuskegee project was ultimately abandoned, and the land remained in federal hands as part of the larger USDA tract, which in 1959 was designated as the Tuskegee National Forest.

Having scrapped plans at the Gulf Coast and in central Alabama, the Department of Conservation had one remaining option, in the north. The initial plan was to construct a separate area for African Americans in Monte Sano State Park near Huntsville, but despite efforts to garner support from local political leaders,[78] in October 1951 Segrest announced that the "project there has been abandoned due to intense opposition to such a development by local citizens."[79] After the failure at Monte Sano, the best alternative was to locate the segregated facility at Joe Wheeler State Park.

A former TVA park, Joe Wheeler, named for a Confederate general who had lived in the area, originally came under state control in the fall of 1949. The state leased 2,200 acres of TVA land on both sides of Wheeler Lake that included the TVA's Wheeler Village on the south side of the dam. The inclusion of Wheeler Village provided a ready-made, resort-like environment for visitors, which helped produce the expectation that Joe Wheeler State Park would become "one of the outstanding recreational areas in the state."[80] The former Wheeler Village section of the park contained thirty-five buildings, including a manager's residence, ranger's quarters, guest house, administration building, and community house. There were also thirteen buildings for overnight/vacation rental, including several lakeside brick houses, two-bedroom wood-frame cabins, and seventeen other structures that were at the time being rented as residences.[81] Recreational amenities included boating, fishing, swimming, hiking, and horseback riding, and there were also several picnic shelters, tennis courts, a bait shop, and a café. (Figs. 4.12, 4.13)

The proposed recreational area for African Americans paled in comparison.[82] Not only

Fig 4.12. Road leading into the African American section of Joe Wheeler State Park, 1953. Photo by C. E. McCord. Courtesy National Archives, Morrow, Georgia.

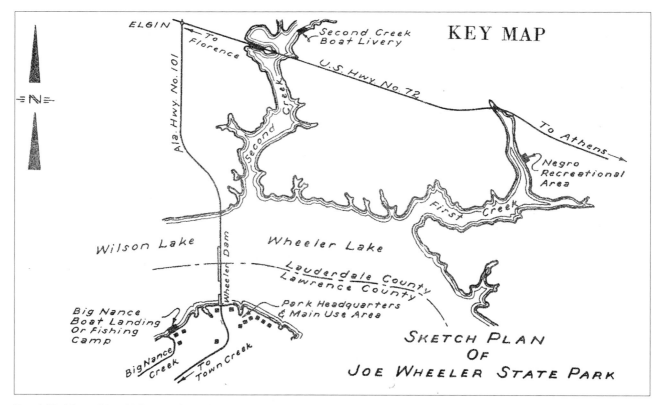

Fig. 4.13. Map of Joe Wheeler State Park showing the "Negro Recreational Area" separated from the white facilities by Wheeler Lake. Joe Wheeler State Park brochure, n.d., Alabama Archives.

was the area to be separated from the rest of the park by the vast expanse of Wheeler Lake, but it was also limited to day-use facilities for swimming, fishing, and picnicking. An earlier effort to convert a nearby Boy Scout camp for African Americans into a state park area did not work out, but the general plan to construct the segregated facility was moving forward by July 1952.[83] The location of the specific site remained in flux, however, requiring negotiations that summer with local landowners and county and state political representatives. The site ultimately selected was on the east bank of the First Creek embayment of Wheeler Lake. As one member of the Conservation Advisory Board put it, "This area will produce as little irritation as any spot we could find for such a development."[84] The deal was settled after Rex Robinson, a white landowner with property adjoining the site who had initially objected, agreed to the plan. After the end of a long discussion on the matter, Segrest reported that "He [Rex] and Mrs. Robinson both stated that they felt the need of such a development for the negroes in that part of the State."[85]

Having finally accomplished the goal of creating a state park accessible to African Americans, James Segrest praised the local white residents around the First Creek location, saying that "the people there should be commended for their attitude in regard to such a project."[86] The 1952–53 annual report of Alabama's Department of Conservation announced that the establishment of the facility at Joe Wheeler State Park "is considered to be the beginning stage in recreation developments for negroes."[87] In reality, it was the final stage;

no additional state park facilities for African Americans were proposed in Alabama.

For South Carolina as well, the largest problem many projects faced, even beyond funding constraints, was routine opposition to site proposals by white residents. The state's limited success did not reflect a lack of effort. Having constructed nineteen state parks for whites by 1948, South Carolina's Forestry Commission was also remarkably active in attempting to expand state park access for African Americans. By then it had created African American facilities in four state parks—Campbell Lake, Greenwood, Mill Creek, and Hunting Island State Parks. The possibility was explored in numerous additional locations including Clarks Hill Reservoir, Edingsville Beach, Santee State Park, Paris Mountain State Park, Sesquicentennial State Park, Croft State Park, Kings Mountain State Park, and Aiken State Park.[88] The state also made several ultimately futile attempts to identify suitable sites near Columbia and Charleston.[89]

Responding to the Southern Regional Council (SRC), which was attempting to tally the numbers of parks accessible to African Americans across the region, South Carolina's State Park director C. West Jacocks was clearly proud of his agency's efforts to accommodate African American recreational needs. In his response, Jacocks detailed various achievements and plans, including its four facilities completed by 1952 and a fifth under way near Greenville, the future Pleasant Ridge State Park. In an attempt to impress a sense of equality among facilities, Jacocks listed the construction of picnic shelters, outdoor cooking facilities, playgrounds, bathhouses, and "fine" group camps and bathing beaches.[90] Adele Minihan, who worked for the South Carolina Citizen's Committee on Children and Youth and assisted with the SRC's survey, offered her support: "I feel that our State Forestry Commission is making an honest effort to 'equalize' the park facilities and much progress has been made."[91]

Regardless of such "progress," the Forestry Commission's search for additional sites revealed the lengths to which planners were willing to go to accommodate racial stereotypes, fears, and taboos. For instance, one criterion was to locate sites in areas "predominantly inhabited by colored people," which was viewed as the most likely means of attaining success.[92] A second criterion was more insidious, catering to the racist white association of Black bodies with pollution (which was also the basis for separate drinking fountains and swimming pools). Regarding a site near Columbia, assistant state forester C. H. Schaeffer stated that "the park should be located on a body of water which is not upstream from another body of water which is used by white people. This means that generally the waters should be near the mouths of the streams."[93] This criterion was reiterated by state forester Charles Flory regarding the possibility of adding an African American section to Sesquicentennial State Park. The addition was requested by state senator James H. Hammond, described as a staunch segregationist who wanted to establish a Columbia-area park for African Americans as a means of avoiding integration.[94] "I do not

believe it is desirable," Flory responded, but asked, "Is there any space below the present lake where another lake could be put in for colored?"[95]

By fall 1949 the Forestry Commission was considering an eighty-acre parcel in Richland County near Pontiac, northeast of Sesquicentennial State Park. According to Jacocks, one advantage of the site, located on Speers Creek, was that the stream "does not drain through white developments."[96] The parcel had other advantages, including the presence of structures that could be used immediately. It also provided easy road access, and Jacocks predicted "no criticism from neighbors" regarding the presence of an African American park. The Forestry Commission decided not to acquire the site, however, noting its disadvantages in terms of size, distance from the city, and relatively small African American population in the vicinity.[97] No other Columbia-area sites were considered.

The heightened concerns about white reaction in the Columbia area were likely prompted by an uproar near Greenville over a search there that began in 1947. From the viewpoint of the Forestry Commission, the most desirable location for an African American park in that area was in a section of the already-existing Paris Mountain State Park. The park superintendent, G. G. Blackmon, identified a three-hundred-acre parcel in its northwestern area on the mountain slope facing the city of Traveler's Rest.[98] Located on the opposite side of the mountain from the main area of the park, the site was not only isolated from white visitors but also suited to lake impoundment and the provision of additional park amenities. Word of the plan got out quickly, however, and opposition from surrounding property owners mounted.[99] A petition with the signatures of nearly one hundred local residents was delivered to the State Forester's office in mid-November 1947. Opening with the statement, "We the undersigners being of the white race," the petitioners asked that the commission consider their opposition and requested that any action take their opinions into account.[100] In response, Flory asked Senator Ray Williams of Greenville, who had delivered the petition, to get word to the petitioners that the proposal for the African American park had been abandoned.[101]

Reporting on a May 1948 meeting with the Greenville City Council, P. R. Plumer, a Parks Division employee, recounted that sites at places called Woods Lake, Stones Lake, and Dreamland were rejected owing to their close proximity to white residential areas. The only site deemed feasible was at Lakeside, located five miles south of Greenville and described as "attractive," with seven hundred acres and "a beautiful 40 acre lake winding among steep hillsides." It too, however, was thwarted by white reaction. In particular, the owner of most of the property, Mrs. C. C. Good, declined to sell. Plumer explained her decision: "Because of moral obligations to her relatives and close friends living nearby it would be impossible for her to sell for the purpose intended."[102]

Plumer suggested that consideration be shifted back to Paris Mountain State Park, where a former CCC site called Camp Buckhorn could be converted into an African American park area. Unlike the previous proposal for the northwest slope of the mountain, this one would locate the park in the eastern portion. There was some hope that it could surmount local resistance since the majority of the land was under public ownership.[103] Camp Buckhorn was also attractive because its existing facilities could be converted and upgraded at relatively small expense.[104]

An editorial in a Greenville newspaper had attempted to bolster the commission's case for the African American park, emphasizing its importance in the effort to preserve segregation. In that light, the paper presented the establishment of the Camp Buckhorn site as a relatively urgent matter. The editors pointed to a lawsuit in Virginia demanding Black access to a white park—the suit that led to the construction of Prince Edward State Park—and although no such legal action had yet been taken in South Carolina, the editors noted reports that lawsuits were coming. Commending the construction of African American parks as laudable in itself, the paper opined that approval of the Camp Buckhorn project would avert legal trouble that would be "distasteful to both white and negro." There would be no other areas that did not also adjoin white sections, the editors noted, and reminded readers that the proposed project would be of low cost to taxpayers and "will maintain segregation of the races required by law."[105]

But white residents placed their local concerns about direct proximity to African Americans above the larger issue of protecting the institution of Jim Crow. The objections were laid out most vividly in a letter from Mrs. G.

M. Hubbard of Greenville, directly responding to the newspaper's editorial with an extended recitation of the prevailing racist views. "How can *anyone* even think of mixing negroes & whites in the same park, even if they do swim in a different lake?" She imagined wild and possibly drunk driving by Black men on the "beautiful curving . . . State Park roads." She believed that park rules would not curb this behavior, stating, "who is going to control the negroes drinking & molesting white girls or women on the park roads? It can't be done!" She recognized that whites drink at the park, too, but asserted that Black people "go crazier than whites when they drink." Hubbard also wrote that the presence of "negroes" diminished the beauty of the park landscape. Doubting that African Americans would stay within their segregated area, she exclaimed, "They'll be all over those beautiful roads at the park and no one will be able to stop them as they'll say they're walking up to Buckhorn." Confident that she could speak on behalf of the area's white residents, Hubbard implored the park agency to avoid diminishing the park's aesthetic values: "I and many many others hope the Commission *will not* spoil our beautiful park by opening any part of it to negroes."[106]

Hubbard's perspective illustrated a central problem faced by the South Carolina Forestry Commission and by agencies throughout the South. "Of course" she understood and accepted the need for parks for African Americans, "but not in Paris Mt. Park where *only* the whites belong."[107] Around the region, such abstract agreement with the principle of Black access would continually and frequently evaporate in the face of actual plans in actual places.

Nevertheless, by June 1948 the Forestry Commission had the assent of the Greenville City Council for the Buckhorn plan and planned to consult further with the legislative delegation from the county. Until the details of the agreements were settled, Flory suggested that the planning "should be kept as confidential as possible."[108] But word had gotten out, and the commission held a public meeting at Paris Mountain High School on July 30. Not surprisingly, the twenty-five white community members attending objected to the plan. The minutes recorded their concerns about concentrating large numbers of African Americans in an area where current numbers were relatively low, increased traffic and declining property values, that the site was inadequate for the expected volume of use by African Americans (and whether it ought to be reserved for whites). One objection was to the possibility of "water contamination."[109]

At the meeting, the commission already seemed to be backing away from the Buckhorn plan. Residents were assured that the camp at Paris Mountain would be considered for African American use only if a suitable site were not found elsewhere in the county. They were also reminded, however, that there was a pressing need for an African American park because of "the pressure being made for colored facilities in the present white park."[110] Nevertheless, despite the idea of keeping Camp Buckhorn as a backup plan, by August 4 it was apparent that the site would be completely removed from consideration. In contrast with the positive assessments of the site's qualities in previous communications, C. H. Schaeffer now had nothing good to say about the former CCC camp. Declaring the project to be "a waste of money," he explained, "I believe that any competent park authority, not swayed by local influence for or against this project, would rule out Camp Buckhorn for use either as a white or colored state park inasmuch as the area is entirely too small for use either by white or colored citizens as a complete park."[111]

After the rejection of Camp Buckhorn, a pair of additional Greenville sites were considered and rejected. Local residents had requested converting a playground facility called the Happy Hearts Park in the New Washington Heights section of Greenville, but their plan was rejected by the Forestry Commission because of size and location concerns. Another prospect was a African American–owned tract of 215 acres located seven miles south of the city. Partly wooded, with rolling hills and a stream, the site was considered to have "very good possibilities," although the planner noted the need for a "close check in regard to the flow of water in the creek."[112] After abandoning consideration of that site, the Forestry Commission finally found one that would work.

The selected site, recommended in October 1949, was 325 acres located twenty-two miles north of Greenville. The parcel, owned by the Enoree River Colored Baptist Association, was considered to have, "without question, the best features of any visited up to now for a Negro Park."[113] It took nearly a year for the Forestry Commission to obtain the $6,000, provided by Greenville County, needed for its purchase.[114]

The location of the site "was a closely held secret until the 1950 summer season ended."[115] By releasing the information after Labor Day, the commission hoped there would be less local attention paid to the issue.[116]

Acquired in 1950, Pleasant Ridge State Park was not officially opened until 1955, with the intervening years bringing delays and even tragedy. Ambitious plans to construct features ranging from picnic to restaurant facilities met with unreliable and inadequate funding from the state. As the historian Stephen Cox notes, "The white state legislature was reluctant to fund permanent improvements on established white state parks, much less a new Negro state park." Funding had stalled by 1952, although pressure from the Greenville press and other park advocates spurred the release of more development money by September 1953.[117] Then three Black youths drowned in the park's unsupervised lake in July 1954, sparking outcry over the continued delays. Pleasant Ridge finally opened in time for the 1955 summer season as the only state park designated exclusively for African American use in South Carolina. Although it occupied wooded land of significant scenic and recreational quality, the park was nonetheless dwarfed by the nearest state parks for whites—Paris Mountain was five times larger, while Table Rock was ten times its size.

It would be another seven years before South Carolina opened its sixth and final state park space for African Americans. Huntington Beach State Park, located a half-hour drive south of Myrtle Beach, was acquired in 1960 and opened in 1962. The park included the sprawling 1930s-era building, Atalaya, the former winter home of New York philanthropist Archer Huntington and his wife, Anna, a sculptor, who had owned the land before it was leased to the state. The segregated area for African Americans at the north end of the park had been the first section constructed after acquisition, although it would exist for only one year as a segregated area.[118] In 1963, the entire South Carolina state park system was closed by an act of the legislature in resistance to court-ordered desegregation of its state parks.

The eventual demise of Jim Crow and its "separate but equal" doctrine had appeared on the horizon more than a decade earlier, brought into view by activism during and after the war and by NAACP lawyers who challenged its constitutionality in federal courts. From the early 1950s it became increasingly clear that equalization strategies, designed to keep state parks segregated, were doomed to failure. The U.S. Supreme Court rendered its verdict on state parks in 1955, repudiating equalization and adding fuel to the intense reaction among white southerners that had followed its *Brown* decision the year before. As the civil rights movement grew in the years that followed, the region's state parks would be mired in the turmoil that characterized the South.

FIVE

GOING TO COURT

By the late 1940s and early 1950s most African Americans were done waiting for change. The leadership of organizations like the NAACP charted a course that demanded more rapid transformation, and beginning in 1940, the creation of the NAACP Legal Defense Fund gave focus to a goal of making "the cost of *Plessy* so great that it would threaten the economic viability of the Southern states."[1] By 1948 the group had resolved to pursue only cases seeking the desegregation of public facilities, abandoning any aim at equalization. At midcentury it had already achieved an impressive record in the federal court system, winning over 90 percent of cases heard by the U.S. Supreme Court.[2]

Parks and recreation facilities were among the targets of legal action. The Atlanta-based Southern Regional Council (SRC), which endorsed desegregation in 1951, described the parks issue as a "less conspicuous legal battle" than school segregation but declared that public parks were Jim Crow's "Achilles heel."[3] Unlike the lip service paid to schools, the SRC noted, it was only recently that southern states had "given serious thought to an equitable dual system of parks and playgrounds."[4] Before the *Brown v. Board of Education* decision in 1954 and a decision the following year extending *Brown* to recreation and parks, there were several legal actions against southern parks that resulted in compromise, and for a time such compromise was an acceptable outcome for African American plaintiffs. But these concessions became less common as the pathway to desegregation emerged.

Early Legal Actions

In 1948 Maceo Conrad Martin, a bank official in Danville, Virginia, was denied entry to Staunton River State Park, and he and his attorneys filed suit in federal court. Asserting that the lack of state park access for African Americans in Virginia violated the U.S. Constitution's Fourteenth Amendment, they asked the court to rule that its state parks be made available to all citizens regardless of race. The complaint noted that the seven state parks available to whites represented a variety of the state's landscapes—"in the mountains, on the plains and at the various seashores." Access to all of them was denied to African Americans.[5]

At the time, the only state-owned facilities open to African Americans in Virginia were a small recreation area in Prince Edward-Gallion State Forest near Farmville and a group camp in a segregated section of Pocahontas State Park near Richmond. The latter was a remnant of the Swift Creek RDA that was built by the National Park Service and CCC and turned over for operation as a state park in 1946. The Virginia Department of Conservation and Development leased the space to a local community organization to run camps but did not provide facilities to accommodate family picnics, camping, or other activities for casual park users. Perhaps for that reason, the department had not claimed the group camp to be a "Negro state park" even as it faced legal action over its system's lack of park access for African Americans.[6] The site was poorly maintained and had no electricity, and a local African American leader who complained about conditions after his son attended camp there called it a "leech-infested" and "forsaken place."[7]

Although Martin's lawsuit alleged a consti-

tutional violation, his attorneys settled for the construction of a new state park for African Americans rather than pressing the case for access to all parks. According to the compromise, the Department of Conservation and Development would expand the Prince Edward-Gallion recreation facility into a fully developed state park.[8] Prince Edward State Park, opened in 1950, was a twenty-eight-acre site on Prince Edward Lake that included lakeside family cabins, a bathhouse and swimming area, and picnic facilities.

In 1948 local NAACP leaders were engaged with South Carolina's Forestry Commission in a search for a state park facility for African Americans in the Charleston area. Marian Wynn Perry, NAACP assistant special counsel, wrote to the local chapter president and secretary praising their "excellent campaign" and reminding them that all requests be phrased to reflect the goal of desegregation rather than equalization. She wrote, "As you know, from the litigation which is being carried to the United States Supreme Court from various parts of the South, it is the position of the N.A.A.C.P. that segregation is illegal under the Fourteenth Amendment since the segregated facilities can never be equivalent to full participation in the facilities offered generally to the public."[9] Perry expressed her understanding that attaining segregated facilities in the South was a step forward, and maybe was as much as could be expected at the moment. But she emphasized the importance of both northern and southern NAACP chapters' sending the same message of desegregation, and offered legal support if accommodations were not made for African American access. The Charleston-area search ultimately failed to produce an acceptable site, and the NAACP there later rejected compromise, suing the Forestry Commission to desegregate the nearby white-only Edisto State Park.

The rejection of compromise was also evident in Oklahoma in the early 1950s as legal trends more clearly signaled eventual desegregation. During the New Deal, Oklahoma had been among the first states to provide facilities for African American use. That early success was largely the result of persistent pressure on state officials by Roscoe Dunjee, editor of the *Black Dispatch,* and other African American leaders in the state. Their concern over funding allocations for exclusively white parks was instrumental in establishing "Negro areas" in both Roman Nose and Lake Murray State Parks, but by the 1940s they were no longer willing to accept separate facilities. In 1952 Dunjee and others adamantly opposed plans by the state to construct an elaborate state park lodge and other facilities for African Americans near Muskogee.

After the segregated day-use area at Roman Nose State Park was eliminated in 1951 by the creation of Lake Boecher, state officials proposed constructing a lodge, cabins, and other facilities for African Americans in the new Sequoyah State Park. Proposing the name Carver Memorial Recreation Area, the Oklahoma Planning and Conservation Board announced in 1952 that it would spend $500,000 on its development.[10] The new park was to be located on the western shore of Fort Gibson Reservoir, segregated from the white facilities by the expansive lake. The board and the press described the project as a "luxurious resort lodge for Negroes" that would include lodge space for 116 guests as well as cabins, a swimming pool, boat dock, and other amenities.[11] The board's magazine, *Resourceful Oklahoma,* provided an illustration of the proposed lodge and swimming pool and described it as "the first state-sponsored project of its kind in the nation."[12]

Before the war, the elaborate Carver Memorial plan might have been viewed in the Black press as a significant step forward in recognizing the recreational needs of African Americans. By 1952, however, the state's plan was behind the times. Responding to the announcement, a delegation that included Dunjee, who was a member of the NAACP national board of directors, filed a protest with the planning board on January 16, 1953.[13] Although the board subsequently dropped the effort, the plan resurfaced in May 1954, when its funding was ultimately approved. Reasserting its opposition and arguing that the recent *Brown v. Board of Education* ruling applied to all state facilities and not just to schools, the NAACP declared that the plan for the lodge was now illegal and threatened to take the board to court to block construction.[14] The board canceled the plan and used the funds elsewhere.[15] Oklahoma's state parks were desegregated just a few years later.

A lawsuit in Texas illustrates the motivating impact of the NAACP legal strategy on southern state park agencies. The extensive Texas system, by far the largest in the South, was constructed mostly during the New Deal with the close assistance of the National Park Service, the CCC, and other federal agencies. By 1949 the number of units had grown from 35 to 44, with a combined area of well over fifty thousand acres, and featured unique scenery ranging "from gorgeous canyons in the plains country of the Panhandle to islands and beaches on the Gulf, and from mountains in the West to the cypress bayous and pines in the East."[16] The state's New Deal–era Park, Parkway, and Recreational-Area Study had considered adding separate park facilities for African Americans, but no plan proceeded following the war. Although Texas prohibited discrimination against its large Mexican American population during the war, African Americans were officially unwelcome in all of its state parks.[17]

Steps toward legal action began in April 1949 when T. R. Register of the Tyler Negro Chamber of Commerce wrote to the Parks Board requesting admission to Tyler State Park. He argued that African Americans had been excluded despite their contributions of tax dollars for park construction and maintenance.[18] His request was denied. The board's executive secretary Gordon K. Shearer stated that African American admission "would be impossible" and pointed to public health problems that would arise from the lack of segregated toilets, as well as a lack of security to monitor mixed use.[19] He rationalized that "there is always the possibility of a clash occurring between park patrons if the park is used by members of the white and negro races." He suggested that Register contact the federal government to request recreational facilities on land controlled by the Army Corps of Engineers at two new reservoir locations.[20]

On behalf of Register, U. Simpson Tate, the NAACP regional special counsel, responded to Shearer the following month. Urging the board to make available to African Americans not only Tyler State Park but all others in the system, Tate reminded Shearer that if the state "insists upon the luxury of segregation, it must assume the burden of providing, at any cost, equal accommodations for the persons or group segregated."[21] Advising Tate on strategy, the NAACP special counsel Thurgood Marshall suggested that Texas park officials be constantly reminded "that their stupidity and selfishness is cutting the ground out from under the separate but equal doctrine." Rather than compromise, he advised Tate to "insist that Negroes be admitted to the existing facilities and keep that clear before the officials of Texas."[22]

By year's end, the governor's office was regretting the decision to deny access to the Tyler-area park, in essence agreeing with Marshall's charges of "stupidity." William L. McGill, secretary to Governor Allan Shivers, said that the Parks Board had had "a way out about eight months ago but they wouldn't take it," despite advice to do so from the attorney general's office. "The Negroes in East Texas said they would be still if the State would let them have the end of a lake in a park in Tyler for picnicking and fishing," McGill wrote to the governor. "Said end of lake was not being used by anyone else, but Parks Board said NO."[23] The board's refusal to make any concession over Tyler State Park prompted a lawsuit, *Register v. Sandefer*, filed on December 29, 1949. Its scope went beyond Tyler, asking the court to open all state parks in Texas to African Americans.[24] The day after the filing, McGill wrote again to the governor, sending the message that African Americans had expanded their demands and were now seeking full access to state parks in Texas.[25]

Hoping to satisfy demands for access, the Parks Board suggested that with adequate funding it was committed to providing "substantially equal" facilities.[26] But an editorial in the *Dallas Morning News* pointed out that the legal action was not about equalization: "They are asking that the facilities that have been built for whites be thrown open to their own people." It observed more generally that "most of the present Negro effort in this direction is opposed to 'equal facilities for Negroes' if they are to be separated from the white facilities." Declaring park segregation to be "a sound and logical policy," the editorial reprimanded past legislatures and administrations throughout the South for not acting earlier to equalize facilities of all types, which in its view would have settled the "separate but equal" issue to the satisfaction of both Black and white. The current inequality, by contrast, "has given to the more radical element among the Negroes the opening they wanted."[27]

Board members went to the legislature in January 1950 to seek funding for an effort to construct African American facilities. They argued that rather than spend money to maintain existing facilities, the construction of

"park facilities for Negroes . . . seem[s] imperative because of the national situation and litigation."[28] Their ideal plan was to spend $800,000, but to avoid outright rejection the board presented a version to the Senate finance subcommittee that sought only $100,000. The so-called equalization plan was quite limited in scope, including some new construction but mostly conversion of existing facilities. The plan for Caddo Lake State Park was simply to change it from being a white-only to an African American park, and would cost virtually nothing. Similarly, the board proposed transferring Lockhart State Park to African American use, with the exception of its golf course. The park included a swimming pool, which the board considered important since it would, as Parks Board chair J. D. Sandefer stated in his Senate testimony, "give us a place to send the Negroes from Samuel Huston and Tillotson Colleges who are now trying to get into Bastrop [State Park]."[29] A section of Possum Kingdom State Park was also to become a separate African American area. It would, according to the board, include cabins, fishing, picnicking and "other facilities equal to those available to white park patrons."[30] At Stephen F. Austin State Park the board suggested either using the existing picnic area and restrooms or constructing a new facility altogether. Finally, two new parks on Corps of Engineers land were envisioned on Lavon Reservoir near Copeville and on a five-hundred-acre site at Whitney Reservoir between Hillsboro and Clifton. The ultimate "equalization" goal was to create "a park for Negroes within 50 miles of Houston, Dallas, Fort Worth, and San Antonio, with future parks to be established in the Beaumont area."[31]

Meanwhile, in a special session, the Texas Legislature passed a law giving the Parks Board the power to maintain segregation in the parks while mandating the need to provide equal facilities. The law also gave the board the power to close the parks or lease them to private operators. Tyler State Park, which was at the center of the lawsuit, was the highest priority. On September 5, 1950, the state used its powers under the new law to close the park entirely pending the development of what the plan called a "separate park" on the site. The county was to construct a separate entrance, which, combined with the construction of facilities including picnic area and shelter, latrines, and ball fields, would cost an estimated $30,000.[32] The park was closed for one year and then reopened on July 4, 1951, with a new bathhouse and concession stand for African Americans.[33]

The Parks Board had been concerned that the Supreme Court might rule to end park segregation before the state could develop and act on their equalization plan. Their concerns were allayed, at least for the short term, on September 11, 1950, when a panel of three federal judges ruled that the *Register* case be sent to state court pending review of the new state law pertaining to the case. The case remained on the federal docket throughout the decade and was eventually dismissed in January 1960. By then, the main plaintiff in the suit, T. R. Register, had died.[34]

The federal decision to send the case to the Texas courts provided the time the Parks Board had hoped for to implement its plans,

although the allocation of funds remained uncertain. A Senate committee had approved the plan on February 8, 1950, but the prospects for passage in the full legislature remained poor. In subsequent months, board member Frank Quinn implored legislators to understand the high stakes involved. The board was asking for a mere $100,000, but failure to adequately pursue equalization might result in the state's closing or selling its state parks, putting the entire $30 million system at risk. To those who saw the equalization plan as a lost cause, Quinn argued that failing to act would "be the same as failing to give adequate hospital and medical care to a patient that you felt reasonably sure might pass on three or four years from now."[35] Since the legislature had "gone all out" to protect segregation in the schools, the "emergency" in the state parks, he argued, warranted a similar "immediate assistance."[36] Ultimately, the Parks Board could not convince the legislature, which declined to appropriate the funds, and the modest equalization plan was never pursued. Tyler State Park remained the only unit in the system that included an officially designated area for segregated African American use.

Raising the Stakes: Sandy Point, Seashore, and Edisto State Parks

In the early 1950s important high court rulings on education indicated that the *Plessy* doctrine might soon be overturned. By then, the legal scholar Walter Murphy writes, "every careful student of constitutional law knew that, given the climate of judicial—as well as national—

opinion, the 'separate but equal' formula was doomed."[37] In 1951 four African Americans—Lavinia G. Tate, Samuel R. Robinson, Leon A. Woodhouse, and Otis B. Watts—sought entry to Seashore State Park on Cape Henry in Virginia and were turned away.[38] A lawsuit, *Tate v. Department of Conservation and Development*, was filed in the federal district court in Norfolk by NAACP attorneys. Governor John S. Battle refused to meet with the NAACP on the issue and declared that if the federal courts ordered integration, then "Virginia would, in my judgment, abandon her park system."[39] The Department of Conservation and Development hoped to resolve the case quickly by expressing its willingness to construct an African American facility in the vicinity that was comparable to those available to whites, but the plaintiffs rejected the offer and the agency took no action to provide such a facility.[40] The case was continued by Judge Walter E. Hoffman for several years. (Fig. 5.1)

Fig. 5.1. This photo of a cabin at Seashore State Park was displayed in the Virginia Room exhibit at the New York World's Fair in 1939. Courtesy Library of Virginia.

Meanwhile, *Lonesome v. Maxwell*, which aimed to integrate Sandy Point State Park in Maryland, was filed in the summer of 1952, not long after the park's grand opening.[41] The facility, also on the Chesapeake near Annapolis, was Maryland's first and only attempt to provide state park access for African Americans. It included separate facilities for Black and white visitors on the same grounds, including segregated beaches and bathhouses. According to the *Atlanta Daily World*, eight plaintiffs, represented by NAACP Legal Defense, claimed that "they had been refused admission to well-equipped South Beach [for whites] . . . and directed to nearby East Beach, a virtually unusable area reserved exclusively for the use of Negroes."[42] The attempt strategically took place on July 4th and included an African American World War II veteran and his children.[43] Judge Calvin Chestnut initially agreed with the plaintiffs, ruling in June 1953 that the segregated facilities were unequal, but he vacated the order the following month after the state improved the East Beach facilities in an attempt to demonstrate equality.[44] The NAACP appealed.

With the *Lonesome* appeal pending before the Fourth Circuit Court of Appeals, the U.S. Supreme Court on May 17, 1954, issued its monumental ruling on *Brown v. Board of Education*. Although the decision was focused on school segregation, its broader implications regarding parks and recreation would soon be evident. *Brown* drew an enormous backlash from the white South. In a lengthy speech, Senator James Eastland of Mississippi declared that "the South will not give an inch," arguing that the ruling violated not only the Constitu-

tion, but also "the laws of nature, and the law of God."[45] He insisted that "racial instincts are normal, natural, human instincts. It is natural that persons of every race, hybrids only excepted, desire to associate with their own kind, and to maintain the purity of their own race."[46] Southern newspapers also attacked the decision. The *Jackson Daily News* decried the "radicals and rabble-rousers and race agitators" who expressed "glee," warning that their victory might lead to "tragic consequences."[47] The *Richmond News-Leader* wrote, "Let us pledge ourselves to litigate this thing for 50 years."[48] The NAACP was targeted with accusations that it was communist, or a fourth branch of government of "outside agitators" determined to destroy the southern way of life. By 1956, several states including Texas, Louisiana, South Carolina, Alabama, and Florida passed laws restricting operation of the NAACP and banning membership by public employees.[49]

In the midst of the ensuing uproar, the *Brown* decision prompted discussion at the 1954 annual meeting of the Association of Southeastern State Park Directors under the heading "Effect of Supreme Court Ruling on State Park Use." Striking a defiant tone, the South Carolina director said that the state "has always resented others who tried to tell them how to run their internal affairs" and that they expected to continue the current program of providing state parks for both races.[50] Georgia's director claimed that "there is no trouble between races in Georgia, except that which is dictated and stirred up by outside influences. The Negro is not a free man since he lets outside organizations do his thinking for him and tell him what he wants." Speaking of his own park service, the representative from West Virginia took a more resigned stance, simply declaring, "They will obey the law of the land."[51]

After several years of continuance, a hearing date for the Seashore State Park case (*Tate*) was set by Judge Walter Hoffman for April 26, 1955. By then, Virginia officials anticipated an adverse ruling and the governor had already decided in late February that the Department of Conservation and Development would lease the park to a private operator to avoid a possible desegregation order.[52] The General Assembly had passed a law in 1952 that allowed the governor to take such actions when deemed "in the public interest."[53] Other legislatures passed similar laws aimed at avoiding court-ordered integration, including those in Texas, South Carolina, Florida, Georgia, and Louisiana. Preempting the tactic, Judge Hoffman issued a temporary injunction on March 12 that barred any such leases until after the April court hearing.[54]

Meanwhile, on March 14, the Fourth Circuit appeals court had reversed two of Judge Chestnut's rulings on park segregation, declaring unconstitutional the operation of segregated public parks in both the *Lonesome* case regarding Sandy Point State Park and in a municipal park case regarding Baltimore's Fort Smallwood Park. Guided by *Brown*, the appeals court ruling was groundbreaking within the Fourth Circuit and beyond. It confirmed that *Brown* applied beyond schools and served as further evidence of a steady trend toward the desegregation of southern institutions. The reversal held immediate implications for the Seashore State Park case, heard within the Fourth Circuit, signaling that the park would soon be forced to desegregate. The court declared, "It is now obvious that segregation cannot be justified as a means to preserve the public peace merely because the tangible facilities furnished to one race are equal to those furnished to the other." It argued that since segregation is no longer allowed in schools, which require compulsory attendance, then "it cannot be sustained with respect to public beach and bathhouse facilities, the use of which is entirely optional."[55]

The Seashore State Park case moved forward under this new reality. At the April 26 hearing, Virginia's attorney general did not contest the state's new obligation to allow African American access to the park, but focused instead on arguing the legality of leasing parks to private operators to maintain segregated operation.[56] Judge Hoffman ordered a subsequent hearing to allow NAACP attorneys to prepare their counterargument that the court had the power to require nondiscriminatory leases. Unable to lease the park owing to the injunction, the governor and the Department of Conservation and Development closed Seashore entirely for the 1955 season rather than open it on a desegregated basis.

Judge Hoffman ultimately prohibited the state from leasing the park, ruling in July in favor of the NAACP plaintiffs. The *Chicago Defender* reported his declaration "that if the state of Virginia leases Seashore State Park to a private operator as is contemplated, the lease must not discriminate against any race."[57] As the *Wilmington Journal* put it, "The State could not do indirectly what it had no right to do directly."[58] Hoffman's ruling also had implications for plans to resist implementing *Brown*, stating that the prohibition on park leases for discriminatory purposes also applied to the lease of public schools for the same purpose. Still contending that a federal judge had no authority to intervene in a lease to a private individual, the attorney general appealed the case. With the lease denied and the case now moving to appeal, Seashore State Park remained closed. Defying the ruling that ordered public parks open to all, Governor Stanley ordered that the rest of Virginia's state parks operate as usual, on a segregated basis. His defiance was greeted enthusiastically by white Virginians. Lewis Roop of Blacksburg exclaimed, "I am proud to have such a wonderful and fearless governor as you."[59]

In August 1955, as Virginia took its stand, NAACP lawyers filed another high-profile lawsuit in South Carolina. Three years earlier Charleston-area African American leaders had discussed going to court to gain access to state-owned beach areas in South Carolina. Focusing on Edisto Island and Myrtle Beach, they were reacting to a report declaring that the Forestry Commission had achieved the goal of a state park within fifty miles of every white resident, but that African Americans needed to travel farther to reach a park. The only beach park accessible was at Hunting Island, opened at the end of the New Deal and located ninety miles

south of Charleston and nearly two hundred miles from Myrtle Beach.[60]

In May 1955, Edisto State Park superintendent Donald Cooler responded with a letter of denial to a series of mailed requests from African Americans asking to use the park.[61] Pointing to the existence of the Negro area at Hunting Island State Park, he stated that he was "not empowered with the authority" to permit such visitors in a park established "for the exclusive use of white persons, and based on custom and precedence we will have to deny your request."[62] With this reply, a group of African Americans backed by the NAACP sued South Carolina's Forestry Commission on August 6, 1955, to open Edisto State Park to all users regardless of race.[63] In response, South Carolina governor George Bell Timmerman Jr. stated that he would prefer to see the park system closed rather than integrated and that he would not support legislative funding for a desegregated park system.[64] With 46,000 acres in the system and more than three million visitors annually, abandoning the parks would be a major step and a significant loss. The risk was particularly acute since donated park lands were typically governed by reversionary clauses that would return parcels to their original owners if the land was no longer used by the state as a park.[65] An editorial in Columbia's newspaper, *The State*, opined that the NAACP action put the entire park system at risk for no good reason. Presuming that the parks would close rather than desegregate, and pointing out that South Carolina at the time led the South in the number of state parks available to African Americans, the newspaper declared, "If the suit is pressed and won it will be a victory of destruction and an empty piece of pointless and baseless vindictiveness, robbing all the people of the state of outstanding privileges—for nothing."[66]

District court judge Ashton H. Williams met with the parties in late August, advising them that an expected U.S. Supreme Court ruling in the Maryland case of Sandy Point State Park would ultimately guide his decision. In the interim, Judge Williams sent the case to the state court for review. In the course of presenting that decision, he also revealed the extent to which he essentially agreed with the editor of *The State* and others who harbored hostility toward what they perceived as the overly aggressive tactics of the NAACP. Advocating a gradual path to racial change, Williams agreed that change must come, but admonished the NAACP for what he viewed as its tendency to push too hard. He criticized the attorneys for declining the state's offer to appropriate $50,000 to create a beach resort for African Americans. The judge asked, "Would you rather see this beach at Edisto closed altogether and the state surrender it back to its former owners?"[67] Predicting a disastrous and even violent outcome if the park was integrated, he claimed that the activities of the Ku Klux Klan and the NAACP were equally dangerous. In his view, both were "secret organizations" that used illegal force to get their way. He accused the latter of using "undue influence, threats, or force . . . to seek personal rights given them under the Supreme Court decision."[68] Williams even admitted that he would have dissented in *Brown* if he were a Supreme Court justice, and asked the NAACP lawyers to heed the caution-

ary advice presented by Dr. Frank P. Graham, president of the University of North Carolina, in a recent law review article. The judge called Graham, an influential white southern liberal, "the most enthusiastic supporter that you have in the United States." Paraphrasing Graham's gradualist stance, Williams warned, "Don't try to press your victory too far."[69]

Supreme Court Decision and Southern Reactions

The hearing on the Edisto State Park case took place a few months prior to the release of the most significant federal ruling to date on the subject of public parks. As an aftershock of *Brown*, on November 14, 1955, the U.S. Supreme Court weighed in directly on the constitutionality of park segregation. It upheld the Fourth Circuit rulings in the cases regarding Maryland's Sandy Point State Park (*Lonesome*) and the City of Baltimore's Fort Smallwood Park. The decision also included a Georgia case from the Fifth Circuit regarding African American exclusion from a public golf course in Atlanta. Affirming that public park segregation was unconstitutional, the high court's decision touched off a renewed wave of reaction among white leaders in the South.

Under the headline "Dixie Fumes Over New Supreme Court Ruling," the *Chicago Defender* quoted the reactions of state officials from around the region.[70] South Carolina governor Timmerman promised, "There will be no mixing of races in our state parks." Georgia's former governor Herman Talmadge decried the threat to public recreation and called for the lease of park facilities to private interests. The *New York Times* reported that Georgia's governor, Marvin Griffin, declared "that Georgia would abandon all state parks before race mixing would be allowed." He stated, "Co-mingling of the races in Georgia state parks and recreation areas will not be permitted or tolerated. While I cannot speak for city officials, I can make the clear declaration that the state will get out of the park business before allowing a breakdown in segregation in the intimacy of the playground."[71] The following year, Georgia's state park agency leased twelve of its parks to private operators to avoid desegregation.[72] In Alabama, Birmingham mayor James W. Morgan struck a chord that best characterized the mood of post-*Brown* resistance, "We must either bow in meek obedience to this decision or we must take steps to prevent the cramming of this policy—so alien to our way of life in the South—down our throats." Georgia's attorney general Eugene Cook declared that the decision was yet another step by the NAACP "to further its program to force inter-marriage."[73]

Earlier in 1955, the Supreme Court had issued its guidance for implementing *Brown* in a ruling known as "*Brown II*," which allowed school desegregation take place "with all deliberate speed" (i.e., not immediately but at some undetermined point in the future). This allowance for delay was seized on in most southern states as permission also to delay state park desegregation. As Florida governor Leroy Collins declared, "We can calmly and soundly proceed as we have in respect to our schools." Delay was justified, according to officials, to prevent the violent encounters they expected should race

mixing be allowed in the parks. South Carolina's attorney general declared that desegregation would "inevitably lead to bloodshed and public turmoil."[74]

In this general atmosphere of post-*Brown* defiance, and with the momentum of a "massive resistance" campaign building, only a few states attempted to implement the Supreme Court's ruling. Maryland governor Theodore McKeldin said, "Officials of the State of Maryland have never to my knowledge questioned the supremacy of the law of the U.S. Constitution or the interpretators [*sic*] of that document by the Supreme Court of the U.S. I see no reason to do so now."[75] Within two weeks of the *Brown* decision, West Virginia's conservation director Carl J. Johnson announced that the state's Booker T. Washington State Park would now be open to "the general public."[76] In Kentucky, the state court of appeals ruled on an earlier case, declaring that segregation in all of the state's public recreation facilities was unconstitutional. The combination of federal and state rulings prompted a swift end to segregation in Kentucky's state parks, ordered by Governor A. B. "Happy" Chandler in 1955.[77] Two years later, Oklahoma desegregated its state parks when faced with a threatened discrimination suit from the NAACP.[78]

In Texas, discussion of state park desegregation had subsided after the Tyler State Park facility was opened in 1951 and the *Register* case was sent to state court, but the issue quickly reemerged after the 1955 Supreme Court ruling. With public park segregation now declared unconstitutional, the fate of the segregated Texas system seemed in doubt. Municipal golf courses in Dallas, Houston, and Beaumont had already been desegregated either voluntarily or by court order, and with some school desegregation taking place in west Texas, the general trend toward integration was clear.[79] The Texas State Parks Board had presumed that the ruling would apply to its system but awaited input from the Texas attorney general. Texas newspapers expected an immediate impact; the *Sweetwater News,* for instance, ran an Associated Press story under the headline "Texas Park and Recreation Facilities Soon Open to All."[80]

By early 1956 an African American delegation that included NAACP members asked Texas officials to open all state parks and remove any statutes mandating segregation and discrimination. The Texas attorney general promised to "look into it," but by then Governor Shivers was considering joining with other southern governors in the massive resistance campaign and declaring "interposition," a claim that states had the right to nullify federal laws to avoid compliance with the courts.[81] The Parks Board decided to await resolution of the Tyler State Park case, which remained dormant on the federal docket, before making any decision regarding park segregation.[82] Arguing that court-ordered park desegregation suggested no set time scale, Attorney General John Ben Sheppard stated, "No court has ever held there must be forced integration."[83] The Texas State Parks Board maintained its policy of segregation for another seven years.

In Virginia, the conservation director and attorney general responded to the 1955 ruling by declaring "that the 'only course' left to the state is to lease state parks and other recreational facilities to private operators."[84] While the Supreme Court upheld the ban on separate public parks, the legality of leasing them to evade desegregation remained an open question. Seashore State Park was closed for a second season in 1956, pending the outcome of the appeal of Judge Hoffman's ruling that such leases were illegal. With the announcement that the judge's ruling was upheld in the Fourth Circuit court on April 9, 1956, it became clear that the NAACP had won another major victory. In October 1956 the U.S. Supreme Court declined to hear that case, allowing the appeals ruling to stand. With no option to lease the park, and with desegregation a looming reality, Governor Stanley decided to keep Seashore State Park closed indefinitely. He and Attorney General Almond had floated the possibility of selling the park system entirely, but the public balked at such a drastic move. Virginia remained defiant, continuing to operate its state park system on a segregated basis while Seashore State Park stood closed for eight years.

In South Carolina, Judge Williams had sent the Edisto case to state court for review but retained federal jurisdiction pending resolution of the public park segregation issue. The case was heard on February 6, 1956, and, understanding that the judge would be compelled to rule against the state, South Carolina's attorney general advised the Forestry Commission to close Edisto State Park indefinitely in hopes that the judge would subsequently dismiss the case.[85] The Forestry Commission ordered the park closed on the evening of February 7, 1956, and the General Assembly followed the next day with a bill formalizing the closure, which was signed by the governor in March.[86] With the park now closed to both whites and African Americans, Judge Williams dismissed the federal case in April, declaring, "No one contends that this Court has the power to operate any park."[87] The Fourth Circuit appeals court upheld the ruling that fall, agreeing that the federal courts could not force the state to keep the park open.[88] Edisto State Park remained closed from 1956 until the 1964 summer season. The rest of the South Carolina state park system continued to operate on its normal, segregated, basis.

Around the time of the 1955 Supreme Court ruling, the different stances on park desegregation in Kentucky and Virginia—compliance versus massive resistance—had the potential to derail the creation of the new Breaks Interstate Park in the Cumberland Mountains, planned as a racially integrated facility. (Fig. 5.2) The park was situated on the border between the two states and was scheduled to open that year. The site was referred to as "The Grand Canyon of the South," a five-mile-long gorge over 1,600 feet deep. The Clinchfield Coal Company had donated one thousand acres, and requests for a park at the site had been ongoing for a decade. During the summer before its opening, however, residents of the area grew concerned that the intense discussion over segregation would block the planned park. Virginia's conservation director explained that segregation would not be an issue since the Commonwealth of Virginia would technically not be operating the

park. Catering to white fears on both sides of the border about race-mixing, the special commission appointed by the states to plan and construct the park had decided to include neither cabins nor swimming facilities.[89] The *Richmond News-Leader* reported that at Breaks Interstate Park the "master works of nature" should be open to all visitors, but that an "overwhelming majority" of people from both races would be unwilling "to accept the prospect of mixed bathing and close social mingling."[90] Despite Virginia's committed park segregation policy, Breaks Interstate Park was opened to all on Labor Day 1955.

After the 1955 Supreme Court ruling declared that public parks must be open to all, state park officials around the South braced for whatever trouble might come. Anticipating reaction in South Carolina, state park assistant director T. D. Ravenel wrote to his boss, "You . . . and I know that this state, certainly in our lifetime, will never accept integrated parks."[91] The state's Forestry Commission was expecting attempts by African Americans to enter its state parks in the 1956 season. A memo from State Forester Charles Flory to all park superintendents warned of such attempts, noting that already "some Negro groups have found their way into State Parks designated for white use." While these situations had been resolved "in a satisfactory manner and without any trouble," Flory urged park staff to be diplomatic in addressing the "highly delicate subject" should any such circumstance arise. In the event that diplomacy broke down, the attorney general

Fig. 5.2. Visitors at a scenic overlook in 1951 at the site of Breaks Interstate Park on the Virignia–Kentucky border, officially opened in 1955. Courtesy Library of Virginia.

recommended that superintendents establish a plan with their local sheriff to assist as a last resort in resolving any such incidents.[92] The potential for violence persisted as a concern among park staff in the South. In one example in 1960, the manager of Georgia's Unicoi State Park refused to allow entry by an official from the Pakistan Embassy in Washington, D.C., who was in the area on a trade mission sponsored by the U.S. Department of Commerce.

The manager was worried that local whites might mistake Mr. Wasir Ali for a Negro, which in turn might "cause trouble."[93]

In fact, there was little evidence of any trouble, let alone violence and bloodshed, in the South's state parks after the Supreme Court's 1955 ruling. Expecting such problems in Tennessee, for instance, officials late that year reported "no instances where Negroes had sought to use facilities in state parks oper-

Fig. 5.3. A float celebrates Mississippi's state parks during a parade in downtown Jackson, 1950s. Courtesy Mississippi Department of Archives and History.

ated for whites."[94] With concerns about trouble in the parks largely unfounded, the end of the 1950s was characterized by relative calm and maintenance of the segregated status quo. The two parks that were specifically ordered desegregated by the courts—Seashore State Park and Edisto State Park—remained closed in defiance. But beyond the border states, little else had changed in the operation of the park systems. The remaining states presumed that they could proceed with desegregation at their own pace, which for most meant indefinite postponement. The federal courts, meanwhile, provided no clarification. For the next eight years after the *Brown* rulings, the Supreme Court backed away from taking on racial segregation cases, leaving room for the states to pursue race matters as they wished.[95] (Fig. 5.3)

A Stronger Push for Desegregation

The situation changed with the start of a new decade, when a new phase in civil rights action began that included the rise of more confrontational organizations and greater national visibility. Intensifying in February 1960 with sit-in protests at a Woolworth's lunch counter in Greensboro, North Carolina, acts of civil disobedience came to characterize the movement and quickly expanded to include church "kneel ins" and beach "wade ins."[96] Through the visibility generated by their direct-action tactics, the Student Nonviolent Coordinating Committee (SNCC) became the preferred organization of younger activists, and the Southern Christian Leadership Conference (SCLC), led by the Reverend Martin Luther King Jr., soon superseded the NAACP in national attention.[97]

While the NAACP was vilified by southern whites, it was also criticized from within the civil rights movement. Its reliance on funding from white liberal foundations and its privileged relationship with the Roosevelt administration during the New Deal had cemented an image of moderation. Its preference for slow-moving legal tactics and its focus on racial segregation rather than economic injustice generated complaints from younger and more militant members.[98] The NAACP nonetheless maintained its relevance and even provided legal support for jailed protesters from other organizations. The association also added its substantial network and influence to the direct-action campaign. As the summer of 1960 approached, NAACP executive secretary Roy Wilkins sent a message to southern chapters calling on members to engage in acts of civil disobedience on the South's segregated beaches and in its state parks. Such demonstrations, he said, "proclaim . . . our determination not to forego any of our constitutional rights."[99]

That summer there was a notable spike in news reports of civil disobedience at parks in the South. In Mississippi, the Harrison County sheriff averted a potential racial clash on July 4, 1960, in a park area in Desoto National Forest. Sheriff Curtis Dedeaux had expected that an Independence Day desegregation attempt would be made at Gulfport's beaches, but a group of about eighty African American family groups showed up instead at the National Forest park to picnic and play ball. Dedeaux told the reporter, "It appeared to be a well-planned effort to integrate the park," which despite its federal status had been historically used only by whites. Tension mounted when the African American players declined to yield to whites who showed up wanting to use the baseball field. Before that moment, the sheriff stated, Black and white visitors had been using the same toilets and drinking facilities without trouble. In the midst of the tension, one white man was reported saying, "If those Negroes don't get out of the park, let's go get our guns and clean them out." Officers expelled both Black and white visitors, threatening resisters with arrest, although the sheriff stated that he tried to give the picnicking families time to finish their lunches before making them leave.[100]

Also on July 4, 1960, the Associated Press reported an incident near Chattanooga, Tennessee, involving two dozen African American youths. They were attending an Independence Day event at Booker T. Washington State Park and left its grounds to swim at a nearby white-only swimming beach on Chickamauga Lake. The youths reportedly threw rocks at cars in the parking lot and "taunted white swimmers with threats to disrobe" before fleeing back into Booker T. Washington park, blending with the crowds.[101]

Florida's State Park Board decided to close Tomoka State Park after two attempts to desegregate it in July 1960.[102] Located near Ormond Beach on the east coast of the state, the park included a small picnic area for African Americans located outside the main park grounds. On two separate occasions, busloads of an estimated one hundred African American children and supervising adults held a picnic in an area restricted to white visitors, prompting the park's closure.[103] The board had claimed that facilities in the white and African American areas were of equal quality, but Rev. E. C. Tillman of Daytona Beach stated, "The Negro picnic area is definitely inferior," explaining, "That's why we went into the white section."[104]

Over the next half decade, the direct-action campaign raised the national profile of the civil rights movement. Efforts to desegregate public and private accommodations, expand voting rights, and achieve other goals through protest and acts of civil disobedience were met with an intensified and often violent white backlash. Some of the most infamous acts of white violence against the movement occurred in this period, including the murder of the Mississippi civil rights activist Medgar Evers in June 1963, and a few months later the bombing of the 16th Street Baptist Church in Birmingham, Alabama, which killed four African American girls.[105] During Freedom Summer the following year, three voting rights activists were found murdered in Philadelphia, Mississippi.[106] In the midst of this regional turmoil, a number of southern states outside the Deep South began quietly rethinking their park segregation policies.

Virginia took its first step toward desegregation with the partial reopening of Seashore State Park in spring 1961, when the park's "wilderness area," a small portion of the site, was opened on an experimental basis to all visitors for hiking, scientific exploration, and education. All other facilities, including picnicking, remained closed.[107] With that experiment deemed a success, the Department of Conservation and Development opened the park's campsites on an integrated basis in September 1962, although its twenty-five cabins and swimming area remained off-limits to all visitors.[108] Applauding the news that Seashore State Park might reopen on a desegregated basis in 1962, Harrisonburg resident Robert L. Hueston sent a letter of support to the governor: "It is not the emotional issue that it was several years ago and its facilities will certainly provide the citizens with another wonderful seashore area to enjoy." He emphasized his desire to make Virginia more attractive to industry, which required shedding "a reputation of still living in the 19th century."[109]

Of course, not all white Virginians shared Hueston's enthusiasm. Margaret Hales of Norfolk expressed to the governor her concern that it was "the White race" that is being discriminated against. Deploring the possibility of integrating Seashore State Park, she declared that Negroes were "about to take over" in Norfolk and Richmond and decried the few white "extreme intergrationists [sic]" who together with Negroes were "trying to ruin the way of life for the white people." Regarding both parks and schools, Hales exclaimed, "Everything is done for the negro, and while I am not against them, I do not want to mix with them and be thrown with them."[110]

Most letters simply expressed appreciation that camping was available at the park once again. Its Chesapeake Bay beachfront area, as well as the cabins and picnic areas remained closed, but the success of the limited reopening prompted the Department of Conservation and Development to quietly open the entire state park system to integrated access in 1963.[111] That year at Seashore State Park, close to nineteen thousand overnight campers visited from April through September even though the park was no longer listed in camping guides because of its long period of inactivity.[112]

Resistance in South Carolina and Georgia

As Virginia waded cautiously into state park desegregation, the official stance in South Carolina remained adamantly defiant. On July 8, 1961, nine African American plaintiffs, all members of the NAACP, sued the South Carolina Forestry Commission in federal court for access to all of its state parks. The process had begun on August 30, 1960, with a failed attempt by three of the plaintiffs to enter Myrtle Beach State Park. The suit was filed after a second failed attempt nearly a year later at Sesquicentennial State Park near Columbia.[113]

In his ruling, filed two years later on July 10, 1963, Judge J. Robert Martin noted, "There can be no doubt that the plaintiffs were denied admission to the State Parks because they were Negroes."[114] Ruling in favor of the plaintiffs, the judge was guided by the recent U.S. Supreme Court decision on May 27, 1963, in *Watson v. Memphis*, which clarified a timetable for public park desegregation. In *Watson*, city officials in Memphis had admitted continuing to oper-

ate segregated parks and agreed that they must end the unconstitutional practice. Their contention was that to maintain peace and avoid violence, the process of park desegregation had to be gradual; both the district court and appeals court had accepted their argument. But the Supreme Court, in a unanimous decision, reversed the ruling. Writing the opinion, Justice Arthur Goldberg stated that to continue racial discrimination, which violated "now long-declared and well-established rights," the city "must sustain an extremely heavy burden of proof" to demonstrate the claim that a delay in establishing these rights was necessary. "This burden," he declared, "has not been sustained." Justice Goldberg's opinion cast aside any attempt to maintain separate parks, as was being done by statute in South Carolina. He declared that it did not matter if facilities for white and Black were equal, as "it reflects an impermissible obeisance to the now thoroughly discredited doctrine of 'separate but equal.' The sufficiency of Negro facilities is beside the point; it is the segregation by race that is unconstitutional."[115]

Judge Martin ruled that South Carolina's law requiring separate parks violated the 14th Amendment. In ordering the desegregation of the state park system, he allowed the Forestry Commission a sixty-day transition period to carry it out. The state was not ready, however, to accept race mixing in its parks. In the most dramatic development occurring in any southern state, the South Carolina Forestry Commission followed the recommendation of Attorney General Daniel R. McLeod, who advised that the entire state park system be closed to the public on September 8, 1963, the day the court order was to take effect.[116] The state had already announced the intention in April, when attorneys told Judge Martin that in the event of an adverse ruling it would have "no alternative" but to close its parks rather than desegregate them.[117]

The decision to close the parks in September was officially announced in a press release on August 20, 1963.[118] White opinion was clearly mixed on the prospect of giving up the parks. One former Forestry Commission member expressed doubt that racial conflict would result from integration, stating that "we should not close our parks and thus abandon a wonderful resource because of fears which may never materialize."[119] The general public support for this opinion was soon made evident to state leaders. Prior to the July court ruling, the state House of Representatives had assembled a five-member committee, chaired by Rep. J. Clator Arrants of Kershaw County, to study state park issues generally. With the district court desegregation order and the state's decision to close the parks, the Arrants Committee quickly focused on the segregation issue and the fate of the park system. From July to October 1963, the committee held fourteen meetings in towns and cities statewide to assess public sentiment about whether it would be better to have integrated state parks or no parks at all. Meanwhile, all units in the South Carolina state park system closed their gates indefinitely in September.

The public discussion revealed a range of white attitudes. Majorities in some communities, including Barnwell, Beaufort, and Edisto Beach, preferred to keep the parks closed.[120] The meeting in Barnwell County took place just after Barnwell State Park had shut its gates. The local newspaper reported that 99 percent of those present favored keeping the park closed "unless it could re-open on a segregated basis."[121] At the Greenville meeting in July, one resident declared that the Supreme Court had "committed treason" and its members should be imprisoned. He offered the often-expressed rationalization that African Americans' arrival as slaves had by now resulted in better lives than they would have had otherwise: "They are living a better life in America than any other country. I know that they could not live half as good a life as they can here." Advocating closure rather than integration, he declared that "the Bible teaches segregation."[122]

There was also significant support at the Greenville meeting for keeping the parks open. A ninth-grade schoolteacher expressed concern that more and more facilities were closing down and made unavailable over the segregation issue, including Greenville's skating rink, swimming pool, and tennis court. "I would take my family to the parks if they were integrated today," he stated, adding, "I don't have to associate with them ['Negroes'] if I don't want to." Another attendee was of the opinion that since perhaps few African Americans would seek access even if allowed, he "would hate very much to see the facilities close. The national parks are integrated, but I have never seen a Negro camp in a national park." One resident dismissed the fear of violence: "My grandfather said if the Negroes vote in the Primaries of South Carolina, blood will run in the streets. The court ruled; he said, 'The court have [sic] ruled, we will abide by it.' I have not known of any violence as a result. I have been to conventions, no violence. Lunch counters were integrated, have not paid any attention. There was no violence. God is moving. . . . Before the ball team was integrated, we said, 'It could not happen.' Not one of us get up and turn our TV off when they are having a game. It would be the same if parks were integrated."[123]

Five of those who spoke in Greenville advocated closure while at least twenty wanted to keep the parks open. Similar results were seen at most other meetings. Twenty-six out of twenty-seven at the meeting in York, including nine African Americans, expressed such support.[124] At Columbia, the final public meeting, twenty of twenty-three favored reopening the parks. As the process neared its end, Rep. Arrants summarized the public sentiment: "The great majority of persons appearing before the committee want the parks reopened on a desegregated basis, but are opposed to integrated swimming."[125]

The Arrants Committee issued its report on January 14, 1964. A bill to reopen the state park system was passed by the South Carolina House and Senate and was signed by the governor in April. The state parks, including Edisto, which had been closed since 1956, were officially reopened at 9:00 a.m. on June 1, 1964, although swimming and cabin camping facilities remained closed to the public.[126]

Like its Deep South neighbor, Georgia clung to segregation in its parks for as long as possi-

ble. Its journey toward desegregation began in 1962 with complaints by members of the local NAACP and the Georgia Council on Human Relations, an interracial group, over discrimination in the use of various facilities at Jekyll Island State Park, including its golf course.[127] Leaders of the council, including executive director Frances Pauley and associate director Rev. Oliver W. Holmes, had met with members of the Jekyll Island State Park Authority, assuring that their organization stressed biracial cooperation. As they put it, the council applied "reason instead of force . . . to solve racial problems." Pointing to legal precedent regarding the desegregation of public golf courses and the attorney general's stated reluctance to pursue such cases that would inevitably result in defeat, council stated, "We appeal to you to take the initiative and not delay the inevitable."[128]

In response, Ben Fortson, who served as both Georgia's secretary of state and chairman of the Authority, refused to consider a policy change. A news account described Fortson as stating that "desegregation would 'ruin' the resort," and predicting that integration "would cause white visitors to stay away." Claiming that the Authority "must do what is best for the majority of the people," Fortson declared, "a majority of the white people won't accept integration."[129] After the meeting, Pauley wrote to Fortson to reiterate the organization's preference for quietly negotiated desegregation rather than legal action. Fortson, however, refused to change his position, instead reassuring concerned white visitors—one of whom exclaimed that desegregation would "turn this delightful resort into a buzzards [sic] roost"—that the "Jekyll Island Authority will never do anything to destroy the Island." He declared, "We have no intention and will have no intention of changing the situation.[130]

The recalcitrance of the authority prompted a lawsuit filed in federal court on September 24, 1963, by NAACP attorneys on behalf of seven plaintiffs from Savannah. Naming Ben Fortson and the rest of the Jekyll Island State Park Authority as defendants, the attorneys asked the court for a permanent injunction against the park's segregated operation. The plaintiffs included W. W. Law, R. E. Parks, Risco Mobley, Horace W. Gordon Jr., Wilbert Williams, Julius C. Hope, and Helen Clements. They had attempted during the previous summer to access facilities that included the park's golf course, the pool facility called Aquarama, and private restaurants and motels that had been built on land leased from the authority. They were denied entry to all of them on the basis of race.[131]

In late July 1964, Judge Frank A. Hooper issued an injunction that barred the state from excluding African Americans from using the state park facilities. As the Associated Press reported, he also barred the state from selling, leasing, or otherwise disposing of property at Jekyll Island "unless the contracts explicitly prohibited racial discrimination."[132] The Civil Rights Act had gone into effect in the beginning of that month, and seeing no chance for victory, the Georgia attorney general declined to appeal the case. By the following summer season, state park desegregation in Georgia had, at least in some cases, become

a public event. On June 1, 1965, the *Chicago Daily Defender* reported that Stephens Memorial State Park in northeast Georgia had been desegregated by a "swim-in" attended by "100 young Negroes." The event took place "with the blessing of local and state officials" and capped a weekend of demonstrations in the nearby town of Crawfordsville, organized by the SCLC.[133]

Taking Stock of Progress

After Judge Martin ruled against the South Carolina Forestry Commission in July 1963, the Penn Center, the historic education and advocacy institution near Beaufort, issued a status report on desegregation of the South's public parks.[134] By then, the process was unfolding rapidly. The center's report counted twenty-six court cases between 1955 and 1963 aimed at park desegregation. Of those cases, twenty-five had resulted in a desegregation order, and an appeal was pending in a case in Jackson, Mississippi. Defendants complied with desegregation orders in twenty-one instances, while in four—three in South Carolina and one in Virginia (including Edisto and Seashore State Parks)—the facility in question had been closed. The Penn Center report emphasized that recreational desegregation in the vast majority of instances occurred with no legal action at all, a result likely influenced by federal court outcomes. The Center reported 509 instances in which public parks were voluntarily desegregated, in contrast with 19 that did so under court order. Municipalities had been at the forefront of the desegregation trend in public parks, golf courses, and even most swimming facilities, with the exception of those in Mississippi. The report also noted that by 1963 several states had opted to desegregate their entire state park systems and other recreational facilities.[135]

Beyond the border states and Oklahoma, which desegregated their state parks soon after the 1955 Supreme Court ruling, several other states were now moving forward with the process. Arkansas's policy was the most ambiguous. The report stated that with no state parks specifically available to African Americans, officials there adopted a case-by-case policy in reviewing requests to utilize facilities. North Carolina had considered closing its parks after the ruling, but by 1963 it was engaged in what officials called a gradual process unfolding over several years, assigning no specific date for system-wide desegregation but allowing managers to use their discretion on a park-by-park basis.[136]

Most states desegregated their parks in a more definitive manner, although typically without publicity, a deliberate strategy employed as a means of avoiding racial altercations.[137] In 1962, Tennessee's governor quietly desegregated the state's park system by executive order.[138] Texas had desegregated all but four or five of its state parks by 1963, reporting that there was "no incident of a racial nature in the process."[139] Virginia had also opened its parks to all users in 1963 with no public announcement regarding the policy change. Parks director Ben Bolen noted, "The superintendents were merely notified not to deny colored

use. Their use by Negroes were [sic] limited and without incident."[140]

In Florida, according to park officials, the desegregation of state parks had been quietly initiated in 1963, though the new policy was not clarified or publicized until the settlement of a 1964 lawsuit.[141] The suit was filed by the NAACP following an incident in May 1963 in which two African American faculty members at Florida A&M University, Dr. Clarence Owens and W. O. Mack, together with their families, tried to enter Killearn Gardens State Park in Tallahassee. They were refused entry and Dr. Owens was threatened with arrest when he protested. According to the account, "They were subsequently allowed use of the park but it was then closed one month ahead of schedule so as to thwart desegregation."[142] The NAACP sued the Florida Board of Parks and Historic Monuments in March 1964, asking for the desegregation of all state parks. The attorneys cited the Killearn State Park incident as well as a thwarted attempt that month by Quillie L. Jones, a plaintiff in the case, to use the white beach at Little Talbot Island State Park.[143] By September, the park agency agreed to integrate the parks, remove all signs indicating segregation, and notify all state employees of the new policy.[144] Florida Park Service director N. E. Miller noted in the immediate aftermath of state park desegregation that "Negroes have visited the white parks and nothing out of the way has developed." He added that "whites generally leave when Negroes arrive at a predominantly white park, and . . . there have been no reported cases of whites desegregating predominantly

Fig. 5.4. A mixed-race tour at Florida Caverns State Park in 1972. Courtesy State Archives of Florida.

Negro parks."[145] Despite long-standing official fears, the region-wide desegregation of state parks was free of violence. (Fig. 5.4)

One can presume that the 1964 Civil Rights Act ended the legal application of segregation policies, but there is no clear indication of a desegregation date or process for the Alabama, Mississippi, and Louisiana park systems. While making no clear declaration, Mississippi officials stopped referring to Carver Point State Park in press releases as its "colored" or "Negro" park by 1967, if not earlier.[146] Alabama park promotional materials in 1964 still referred to the "Negro park area" at Joe Wheeler State Park, although one account suggests the

site's integration into the larger park in 1965.[147] An account by Louisiana's Department of Culture, Recreation & Tourism ambiguously describes the "official progress of desegregation" as ending in 1962 but states that actual park integration was "a long, gradual procedure." As was the case elsewhere in the South, even after the Civil Rights Act, "the stigma of segregation lasted for many more years and African American use of facilities previously designated as 'white only' remained extremely low." It was a tendency described in Louisiana as lasting through the 1970s.[148]

Despite the demands of the Civil Rights Act, desegregation was a long process characterized by tenacious prejudice. In both Virginia and South Carolina, for example, white reluctance to allow race mixing in state park swimming pools and cabins remained an issue. In 1965, at the end of the first year of desegregated state park operation, South Carolina's Forestry Commission solicited reports from the various superintendents regarding the outcome of the desegregation process. It concluded that African Americans continued to utilize the facilities originally designated for their use at a rate of 98.1 percent. Only small numbers were reported visiting the former white-only park facilities.[149] Given this outcome, the majority of park superintendents expressed a desire to remove the camping and swimming restrictions. Without swimming, the state park system had forfeited a major attraction, evident in sharply curtailed park revenues. Such pressures finally led the South Carolina Legislature to authorize the unrestricted opening of the state park system on July 1, 1966.[150]

Virginia's decision to allow fully unrestricted access to its parks was delayed even longer. A full year after the Civil Rights Act became law, the cabins and beachfront facilities for swimming at Seashore State Park remained closed. In a response to retired naval commander Berry D. Willis of Norfolk, who implored the governor to open swimming facilities, the governor's office declared, "The Board [of the Department of Conservation and Development] has given earnest consideration to the operation of this park and has concluded that the best interests of all our citizens would be served by its operation as a camping facility."[151] Willis had written, "Thousands of our citizens are being denied the use of the fine beach, bathing, and swimming facilities at State Seashore Park [sic] because they are the continuing victims of Virginia's massive error—'massive resistance' or as I prefer to call it, 'massive indifference.'"[152] The facilities at Seashore State Park were finally reopened on a desegregated basis by the 1967 season, nearly three years after the Civil Rights Act was signed.[153] The Jim Crow era of southern state parks had finally come to an official end.

SIX

WHAT'S BECOME OF THE PARKS?

After tumultuous years of lawsuits, protest, and reaction associated with civil rights activism, state officials chose essentially to ignore what later came to be viewed, even in the South, as a shameful past. As a result, the Jim Crow foundations of southern state park systems were forgotten in the years that followed. Even though most of the landscapes retain traces of their segregated design, what remains of that past is all but invisible to contemporary visitors. For example, more than a decade after park system desegregation in North Carolina, a profile of Jones Lake State Park in *Wildlife in North Carolina* magazine never mentioned that it was one of the first exclusive state parks for African Americans in the South. The article focused instead on nature and the aesthetic experience, describing Jones Lake's location among the "Carolina Bays" and its opportunities for hiking, nature study, and wildlife viewing.[1] In Florida, the origin of Little Talbot Island State Park as a segregated facility was not even mentioned in the park's most recent management plans.[2] The topic was left unexplored in a book about the histories of southern park systems produced in 1977 by the Association of Southeastern State Park Directors, while books about Kentucky's and West Virginia's state park systems omitted reference to the lone park in each state—Cherokee and Booker T. Washington, respectively—that was constructed for exclusively African American access.[3]

Because of this silence, little of the architecture of state park segregation has been memorialized in any way, and the past remains obscured. Most remnants of segregated design are known only to those with local knowledge and memories of the era—often even park staff are unaware of them. The focus of historical and cultural interpretation is on topics such as

149

the archeological traces of Native Americans who occupied the sites centuries ago, recent land uses that preceded a park's existence, and the history of CCC work. Today only eight of the forty parks discussed in this book acknowledge that they were among the few state parks in the South that allowed access to African Americans.[4] With this erasure, it is easy to forget that such park spaces even existed.

The question of what happened to these facilities since the end of Jim Crow has multiple answers that fall into four categories. The first includes a handful of sites that no longer function as parks. The former Watson State Park in Pine Bluff, Arkansas, closed in 1944, is today controlled by logging interests. (Fig. 6.1)

West Virginia's Booker T. Washington park was eventually absorbed into the forest on the outer edge of Institute. Georgia's Yam Grandy State Park also reverted to secondary forest over the years after it was transferred to the city of Swainsboro in 1976—all that remains as visible evidence of the park are the weed-infested remnants of a basketball court and a neglected playground.[5]

In the second category are a significant number of parks that today operate under different management, having lost their state park status during the 1970s and 1980s. The State of Georgia, for instance, removed all of its formerly exclusive "state parks for Negroes" from its system in 1975 in a cost-saving move.[6] Today, Lincoln State Park in Millen is managed as a privately owned park, while Fairchild State

Fig 6.1. The former Watson State Park site, now owned by logging interests. Photo by the author, 2012.

Park on Lake Seminole is controlled by the Army Corps of Engineers as "Fairchilds Park," operating mainly as a boat launch. Others are managed by county governments. George Washington Carver State Park, north of Atlanta, is now "Bartow-Carver Park" (in Bartow County), while the former Keg Creek State Park is maintained by Columbia County under the name "Wildwood Park."[7] South Carolina's Pleasant Ridge State Park was transferred to Greenville County in 1988,[8] and Mill Creek State Park is operated by Sumter County. In Florida, parks now under county control include John C. Beasley State Park and Frank B. Butler State Park, added late in the Jim Crow era for exclusively African American use, today run by Okaloosa and St. John's counties, respectively. The National Park Service now controls the former Fort Pickens State Park at Pensacola Beach, which once contained dual-use facilities, as part of the Gulf Islands National Seashore. Magnolia Lake State Park—the last African American facility to be constructed in the state of Florida—is today contained within the Camp Blanding State Wildlife Management Area. In South Carolina, the former Campbell Lake State Park also remains in state hands, but as a minimally maintained recreation area in the Sand Hills State Forest.

The third category encompasses nearly all of the former dual-use parks and four of the exclusively African American sites, and illustrates the most common outcome of desegregation—the combination of Black and white facilities and removal of overt references to race.[9] Examples include Cherokee State Park, which was folded into neighboring Kentucky Lake State Park in 1964, and North Carolina's Reedy Creek State Park, absorbed into William B. Umstead State Park in 1966. In Mississippi, Carver Point was maintained as a separate facility until it was deemed financially nonviable in 1972 and became a group camping area in Hugh White State Park.[10]

Another case, Prince Edward State Park in Virginia, demonstrates how racialized patterns of visitation could continue for years after park desegregation. Separate use reportedly persisted even after Prince Edward and neighboring Goodwin Lake were combined as "Prince Edward/Goodwin Lake State Park." An interpretive display at the park describes the de facto segregation that persisted until the name was changed again: "The separate races continued to frequent the parks to which they had grown accustomed. Integration did not effectively occur at the park until 1986, when it was again renamed and became Twin Lakes State Park."[11]

That so few of the once-exclusive state parks for African Americans have survived with their original state park status reflects visitation patterns that followed desegregation. The decision to eliminate these parks was normally justified by relatively low usage and thus low revenue. While the Virginia case suggests reluctance by some to cross perceived racial lines, it was also the case that African Americans were no longer restricted to the former "Negro parks," which were poorer in size, scenic quality, and amenities. Instead, families could visit the larger and better equipped formerly white state parks that were now officially open to them. At the same time, it was also the case across the South that

Fig. 6.2. "Area 2" of Louisiana's Lake Bistineau State Park was constructed in 1956 as the state's first segregated facility for African American use.
Photo by the author, 2012.

white visitors normally avoided the state park facilities that were known as "Negro parks," despite their officially integrated status. Together these tendencies worked to undermine the viability of the former African American sites.

The former dual-use state parks removed signs of racial separation, but the footprints of segregated design remained. For instance, the north end of both Hunting Island and Huntington Beach in South Carolina had been the location of their respective African American beaches. The separate area at Hunting Island still exists, today as a popular tent and trailer camping area of the park, while Huntington's once-segregated North Beach is now a day-use picnic and swimming area. Such clues to the segregated past are visible at nearly all of the for-

mer dual-use locations. Most typically, a separate entrance leads to a park area of smaller size and limited facilities. In Louisiana, "Area 2" at Lake Bistineau State Park identifies a smaller, separate area of the contemporary park that includes picnic tables, a swimming pool, and a group camp. (Fig. 6.2) At Chicot State Park, a separate entrance (miles from the main one) takes visitors to its "East Landing," the remnants of the segregated area located across Lake Chicot from the former white areas. In Georgia, "Entrance B" at Fort Yargo State Park leads to a boat launch and picnic area in the relatively small southwest section of the park.[12]

The fourth category includes just a few parks, highlighting the degree to which memories of the segregated past have been erased from state park landscapes across the South.

Of the state parks constructed exclusively for African American use, only three continue to operate today as individual state parks under their original names: Tennessee's Booker T. Washington and T. O. Fuller State Parks, and North Carolina's Jones Lake State Park. With this unbroken link to their Jim Crow origins, these three parks are among the few that have chosen to acknowledge their racialized past as part of their interpretive programs. Focusing on the parks' namesakes, the Tennessee parks include displays and brochures in their visitor centers, although the discussion of the past remains more limited than one might expect. The information at Booker T. Washington focuses on the iconic status of the man but does not address the history of segregation that led to the construction of this separate park. Echoing Washington's emphasis on personal responsibility, a park brochure explains that after being born into slavery, he worked "with great determination, secured an education, and became one of America's best known and loved citizens."[13] A similar brochure at T. O. Fuller State Park provides only a little more context, calling the exclusively African American site, "the first state park east of the Mississippi River and only the second in the nation." The interpretation at Jones Lake State Park goes much further, including a prominently displayed series of photos with captions in the visitor center that depict the history of the park and emphasize its original racially segregated status.

In the former dual-use parks, where once-segregated facilities exist side-by-side on the same grounds, there remain numerous opportunities to interpret the past, but of the twenty former dual-use sites, only Lake Murray State Park has yet done so. The Oklahoma park is listed on the National Register of Historic Places, and its restored structures include the many cabins, dining hall, and other facilities in Camp No. 3—the organized group camp designated for African American youth in 1939. There is no signage at the site, but a pamphlet presents a self-guided "auto-walking tour" of Camp No. 3 and other historic structures designed by National Park Service architects and built by the CCC. The pamphlet acknowledges the camp's formerly segregated status, stating that "when Lake Murray State Park was built in the 1930s, racial segregation prevented African Americans from using most of the park's recreational facilities. In the 1930s it was the only complete, permanent camping facility for African Americans."[14] Although minimal, the statement goes further than any of the other dual-use parks, which have thus far avoided the segregation issue entirely.

Other once-exclusive parks that have made an effort at interpretation include William B. Umstead in North Carolina, which offers a visitor center display recounting its origin as the Crabtree Creek Recreational Demonstration Area constructed by the CCC. The exhibit acknowledges that Reedy Creek State Park, originally a segregated group camp within the RDA, had been administered separately as an exclusively African American park starting in 1950 and was reunited with the larger park in 1966. At Pleasant Ridge County Park in South Carolina, an interpretive sign titled "An Exceptional Leader" commemorates the long service of Leroy Smith, who was superintendent of the state park from 1951 until his death in 1979. It explains that the completion of Pleasant Ridge State Park by 1955 was "delayed by prejudice and funding." The store at Virginia's Twin Lakes State Park (once Prince Edward State Park) includes a display of photos and text that effectively juxtaposes images from the past of family fun and relaxation with a description of the circumstances of its origins in a lawsuit challenging racial exclusion from Virginia's park system.[15]

Of all the sites, the most elaborate interpretive effort thus far is at Kentucky's former Cherokee State Park (today part of Kenlake State Park) where staff have restored its main buildings to their original form and even rep-

licated the park's original entrance sign. (Fig. 6.3) Additionally the Kentucky Department of Highways has erected a historical marker at the entrance that describes Cherokee as "a product of 'Jim Crow' segregation" and aptly notes that it was "built when African Americans fought to integrate recreation facilities" in the state. Interest in the site for its historical value had grown in recent years, and in 2009 the park was added to the National Register of Historic Places and designated as a Kentucky Landmark by the Kentucky Heritage Council.[16] The full restoration of the park's restaurant was completed in 2010, when the site was officially reopened as "Historic Cherokee at Kenlake State Resort Park."

As these examples show, official remembrance of segregation and the struggles for civil

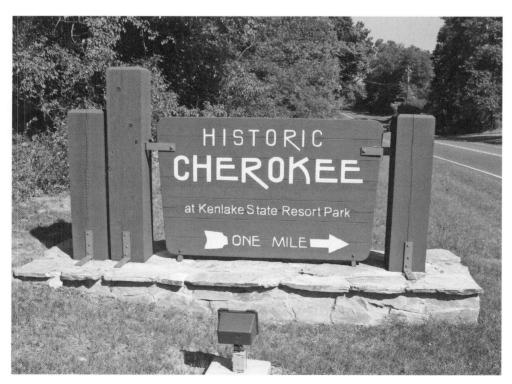

Fig. 6.3. A replica of the entrance sign commemorates the existence of Cherokee State Park, now part of Kenlake State Park. Photo by the author, 2012.

rights has become more common in recent decades. Street signs frequently bear the names of such icons as Martin Luther King Jr., Rosa Parks, and Malcolm X, while memorial markers increasingly commemorate sites of civil rights protest and even white retaliation and tragedy.[17] Even the vestiges of everyday practices of racial segregation are being increasingly preserved. Robert Weyeneth points out that by the early twenty-first century, nominations to the National Register of Historic Places in Georgia, Florida, and South Carolina included movie theaters, bus and rail stations, and beach parks containing visible features of their segregated pasts. Further recognition in the state parks may soon follow.

In *Shadowed Ground*, the geographer Kenneth Foote explores the trend toward commemoration through a broad range of examples in which communities, states, and the nation have marked sites of violence and tragedy, and his study demonstrates that memorialization is not a simple exercise.[18] Questions arise regarding who controls the message, what the message ought to be, and even whether remembrance is a good idea in the first place.[19] Many state park agencies, which normally regard nature interpretation and the protection of plant and animal communities as their primary tasks, may not see remembrance of the segregated past as part of their mission. On the other hand, marking this racialized history can be potentially advantageous as a way of drawing new visitors. Most important, such actions help to preserve the national memory of African American struggles for racial justice.

In northeastern Florida near Jacksonville,

the National Park Service restored slave quarters at Kingsley Plantation on Fort George Island after acquiring the property in 1991. In 2005 the office of Florida governor Jeb Bush issued a press release during Black History Month recognizing Bill Baggs Cape Florida State Park on Key Biscayne as an important location along the Underground Railroad. The press release noted that the site was "one of the state's first meeting sites for freedom seekers [and] . . . provided a gateway to liberty for slaves."[20] While significant, these forms of memorialization are perhaps easier to establish than that of segregated park spaces. In the Bill Baggs example, the governor and the Florida Park Service could proudly embrace the Underground Railroad as a celebrated aspect of American history. At Kingsley Plantation, the National Park Service could memorialize features of a shameful past while honoring the enslaved people who had lived and toiled there. Such interpretation marks a disturbing era, but one in which the agency itself is not implicated.

Circumstances are very different regarding the interpretation of segregated state parks. In these cases the southern park agencies are directly responsible for perpetuating and defending Jim Crow and designing and constructing racially segregated spaces. The construction of segregated state parks, particularly during the postwar years, was achieved as part of a resistance strategy, in opposition to the NAACP's push for desegregation. Memorialization can be a delicate issue in such circumstances of white resistance to civil rights activism, as Weyeneth points out. But he suggests that while some may find this "one frontier too far," it is also the case that "from the perspective of using material culture to understand the texture of race relations in the Jim Crow era, white resistance is an inextricable part of the fabric."[21] The passage of decades likely makes such memorialization more possible, and more park agencies will likely take up the challenge. Such stirrings are already evident in Florida, where a recent management plan for Tomoka State Park recommends the addition of interpretive signage acknowledging the segregated history of its Sunset Picnic Area; the plan for Florida Caverns State Park makes a similar recommendation for its former "Negro Picnic Area," today referred to as the Beech Picnic Area.[22]

In his contribution to the 1944 volume *What the Negro Wants*, Tuskegee Institute president Frederick D. Patterson began with a declaration: "Most American Negroes are not allowed to forget the fact of their racial identity during any but the briefest periods of their lives." This "enforced consciousness," as he put it, had been produced systematically and with a "connotation of inferiority" by depriving African Americans of the benefits of citizenship enjoyed by others. In the South in particular, Patterson linked such deprivation to the humiliations often faced in social encounters with whites, which, he stated, "makes life for the Negro in the South a daily depressing experience."[23] Largely barred from park spaces, African Americans were excluded from the enjoyment, stress relief, and mental rejuvenation that park access promised.[24]

The sociologist Gunnar Myrdal commented in the same year that the United States was probably more conscious of the importance of recreation than any other country in the world. Noting the trying and stressful circumstances that Patterson described, Myrdal suggested that if publicly funded park facilities were designed to relieve the stresses and challenges of modern life, then one ought to concede that, "on the average, Negroes have greater need for public recreational facilities than have whites."[25] But the history of parks presented in this book shows that African Americans, in the South and beyond, had to fight for this access. One legacy of this struggle is a sense of alienation from such experiences in what effectively remains defined as "white space."[26]

In her work *Black Faces, White Spaces*, the geographer Carolyn Finney points out that even today African Americans are not allowed to forget their racialized identities, including when contemplating places that we call "the environment," "nature," and "the Great Outdoors." While such perceptions are diverse and complex, similarities, as she states, "draw from a collective history and consciousness that is reinforced and remembered through media, textual representation, and experience." She notes that perceptions of exclusion in environmental matters continue to present barriers to African American participation, while accounts of park histories remain grounded in a "dominant environmental narrative" that "does not adequately address collective African American experiences in relation to natural landscapes." The unwillingness so far of most southern state parks to address these experiences exemplifies her point. Interpreting the Jim Crow history of these parks would be at least one step toward greater inclusiveness in these environmental narratives. Finney explains the significance of taking such steps:

> Recent history shows that African Americans are continually using the past as a way to represent themselves and say, "we were there" and "we are here now." Why should it be any different when talking about the environment? Specifically, for African Americans, memory, both collective and individual, provides a way to name and re-create a place, which gives or re-affirms the power to re-create ourselves and the places we live in. This allows us to construct *environmental spaces* in our own image.[27]

But this work remains difficult and still encounters resistance from some observers who believe that issues of "nature" and "race" have little or no connection. In spite of such obstacles, it is important to continue to demonstrate that the seemingly separate concerns of "nature" and "society" are, in fact, entangled, or, as Finney puts it, to reconcile "the seemingly separate but equal growth/creation of the Wilderness Act and the Civil Rights Act of 1964."[28]

In 1925, in the depths of Jim Crow racism in America, park advocate Stanley Coulter declared that the "life giving silences" provided by state parks would "give new values to life and effort and win a new courage for the work still before us."[29] The work still before us, in a new era, requires the courage to face the past. In visiting our state parks, may we gather courage from the silences and continue the work of coming to terms with the nation's fraught racial history.

NOTES

Introduction

1. Ollie Moore to John L. Gordon, August 1, 1968; Leonard E. Dawson to John L. Gordon, July 15, 1968; Amy Thompson to John L. Gordon, July 4, 1968; all in Parks and Historic Sites Collection, Georgia State Archives, Morrow.

2. The title of this book, *Landscapes of Exclusion*, was inspired by the geographer David Sibley's use of the phrase in his essay "Outsiders in Society and Space" in *Inventing Places: Studies in Cultural Geography*, ed. Kay Anderson and Fay Gale (New York: Wiley, 1992), 107–22.

3. "America's Best Idea" is the subtitle of a documentary film series on the national parks by Ken Burns. The sentiment is attributed to the writer Wallace Stegner.

4. Leon F. Litwack, *Trouble in Mind: Black Southerners in the Age of Jim Crow* (New York: Vintage, 1999), 218–19.

5. Ibid., 219.

6. Margaret Walls, *Parks and Recreation in the United States: State Park Systems* (Washington, D.C.: Resources for the Future, 2009).

7. Stanley Coulter, "Scenery—A Natural Resource," in *A State Park Anthology*, ed. Herbert Evison (Washington, D.C.: National Conference on State Parks, 1930), 13–17. Coulter was a longtime professor at Purdue University, where he served as dean of the School of Science and contributed important writings on botany and the need for parks.

8. Freeman Tilden, *The State Parks: Their Meaning in American Life* (New York: Knopf, 1962).

9. *The National Conference on State Parks, Number 5*, December 1926, box 2966, folder National Park Conference, State Parks 0-33, NPS Central Classified File 1933–1949, RG 79, Records of the National Park Service (RNPS), National Archives at College Park, Md. (NACP).

10. Tilden, *State Parks*, 4.

11. Robert Shankland, *Steve Mather of the National Parks*, 3rd ed., rev. and enl. (New York: Knopf, 1970); Ney C. Landrum, *The State Park Movement in America: A Critical Review* (Columbia: University of Missouri Press, 2004).

12. Tilden, *State Parks*, 3–4.

13. Linda Flint McClelland, *Presenting Nature: The Historic Landscape Design of the National Park Service, 1916 to 1942* (Washington, D.C.: U.S. Department of the Interior, 1993).

14. Workers of the Writers' Program, Works Progress Administration, *South Carolina State Parks* (South Carolina State Commission of Forestry, 1940), 3 (document available at South Caroliniana Library, University of South Carolina, Columbia).

15. Gunnar Myrdal, *An American Dilemma: The Negro Problem and Modern Democracy* (New York: Harper & Brothers, 1944), 347.

16. J. Austin Burkhart, "Yonder Sits the Rocking Chair," *The Crisis* 59 (1952): 619–25.

17. The *Plessy* case, named for the plaintiff, Homer Plessy, originated in 1892 in New Orleans, challenging a Louisiana law that required segregated rail travel. The

landmark U.S. Supreme Court decision in 1896 upheld the constitutionality of Jim Crow laws until the Court overturned the ruling in its 1954 decision in *Brown v. Board of Education*.

18. Robert R. Weyeneth, "The Architecture of Racial Segregation: The Challenges of Preserving the Problematical Past," *Public Historian* 27 (Fall 2005): 15.

19. H. Jay Wallace, *Civilian Conservation Corps Park Program, Muscle Shoals, Alabama, Accomplishments April 1, 1934, to April 1, 1936*, Muscle Shoals Office, Land Planning and Housing Division, TVA, Wilson Dam, Alabama, July 1, 1936, 7, box 11, folder 601-12 Recreational Survey Alabama, Entry P107, Classified Files 1936–1947, Recreational Area Study, RG 79, RNPS, NACP.

20. Nancy L. Grant, *TVA and Black Americans: Planning for the Status Quo* (Philadelphia: Temple University Press, 1990), 88.

21. Georgia Department of State Parks, *Interesting Facts about Georgia's State Parks* (n.d.), and *Georgia's State Parks and Their Progress in the 1960–61 Fiscal Year* (1961), Georgiana Collection, Hargrett Rare Book and Manuscript Library, University of Georgia, Athens.

22. *Journal and Guide* quoted in "State Parks for Negroes," *New South*, April–May 1954, 6.

23. "State Parks for Negroes," *New South*, 6.

24. Nathan Cole, *The Road to Hunting Island, South Carolina* (Dover, N.H.: Arcadia Publishing, 1997), 67.

25. Robert M. McKay, "Segregation and Public Recreation," *Virginia Law Review* 40 (1954): 703. A law professor at Emory University and from 1954 at New York University, McKay was named dean of NYU's Law School and was chair of the commission that investigated the 1971 riot at Attica Prison in New York.

26. "State Parks for Negroes," *New South*, 2. The study included data from Florida, Georgia, Kentucky, Louisiana, Mississippi, South Carolina, Tennessee, Texas, and Virginia. Information was not available from Alabama, Arkansas, Maryland, North Carolina, Oklahoma, and West Virginia.

27. Robert M. McKay, "States—Summary," December 16, 1953, Southern Regional Council Papers, Auburn Avenue Research Library on African American Culture and History, Atlanta, Ga. McKay listed 7,879 acres for the total land area of African American parks but stated that the figure did not include the acreage of African American sections in dual-use state parks in South Carolina and Florida. I added 1,000 acres to McKay's total as an approximation of the additional space.

28. Burkhart, "Yonder Sits the Rocking Chair," 621.

29. Steve Valocchi, "The Emergence of the Integrationist Ideology in the Civil Rights Movement," *Social Problems* 43 (February 1996): 116–30.

30. Numan V. Bartley, *The New South, 1945–1980: The Story of the South's Modernization* (Baton Rouge: Louisiana State University Press and the Littlefield Fund for Southern History, 1995); Michael J. Klarman, *From Jim Crow to Civil Rights: The Supreme Court and the Struggle for Racial Equality* (New York: Oxford University Press, 2004).

31. South Carolina ultimately constructed six of these facilities; Georgia included seven in its system; Florida opened ten state park areas for African Americans prior to park integration. North Carolina and Tennessee included two in their state park systems, while Oklahoma's share was reduced in 1951 from two to one facility when the "Negro Picnic Area" at Roman Nose State Park was closed.

32. Col. Richard Lieber quoted in Tilden, *State Parks*, 11–12.

33. Owen J. Dwyer and Derek H. Alderman, *Civil Rights Memorials and the Geography of Memory* (Chicago: Center for American Places at Columbia College Chicago, dist. by University of Georgia Press, 2008), 21–22.

I. Jim Crow Recreation

1. Yosemite Land Grant (Act of June 30, 1864), 13 Stat. 325.

2. Ethan Carr, *Wilderness by Design: Landscape Architecture and the National Park Service* (Lincoln: University of Nebraska Press, 1998), 27; Richard Grusin, *Culture, Technology, and the Creation of America's National Parks* (New York: Cambridge University Press, 2004).

3. Carr, *Wilderness by Design*, 27. Olmsted's design for Yosemite was never implemented. It was shelved by the other park commission members, who preferred to create a resort-type atmosphere in the park.

4. Ibid., 21.

5. Grusin, *Culture, Technology*, 22.

6. Ibid., 23–24.

7. The national park in 1890 included Yosemite's "high country"; Yosemite Valley remained in state hands until its incorporation into Yosemite National Park in 1906.

8. Ney C. Landrum points to the earliest use of the phrase in Wisconsin in 1878 with the short-lived creation of The State Park, which was eventually sold to logging interests in 1898. Landrum, *The State Park Movement in America: A Critical Review* (Columbia: University of Missouri Press, 2004), 37.

9. Thomas Cox, *The Park Builders: A History of State Parks in the Pacific Northwest* (Seattle: University of Washington Press, 1998).

10. Freeman Tilden, *The State Parks: Their Meaning in American Life* (New York: Knopf, 1962), 5.

11. Paul S. Sutter, *Driven Wild: How the Fight against Automobiles Launched the Modern Wilderness Movement* (Seattle: University of Washington Press, 2002).

12. Carr, *Wilderness by Design*, 52.

13. Tilden, *State Parks*; Landrum, *State Park Movement*.

14. Frederick Law Olmsted Jr., "Bases for the Selection of State Parks," in Herbert Evison, *A State Park Anthology* (Washington, D.C.: National Conference on State Parks, 1930), 67–68.

15. James L. Greenleaf, "The Study and Selection of Sites for State Parks," in Evison, *State Park Anthology*, 71, 74–75, 76.

16. Harold A. Caparn and Jay Downer, "Planning a State Park for Use," in Evison, *State Park Anthology*, 96.

17. Tilden, *State Parks*, 11.

18. The monument was maintained by the United Daughters of the Confederacy on state land until the Florida Board of Parks and Historic Memorials formally took administrative control in 1949. Today the site is called Olustee Battlefield Historic State Park. "History of Florida State Parks," in *Histories of Southeastern State Park Systems* (n.p.: Association of Southeastern Park Directors, 1977), 22.

19. James Wright Steely, *Parks for Texas: Enduring Landscapes of the New Deal* (Austin: University of Texas Press, 1999).

20. The forest reserve was renamed Patapsco State Park in the 1930s; Robert F. Bailey, *Maryland's Forests and Parks: A Century of Progress* (Charleston, S.C.: Arcadia Publishing, 2006), 40.

21. Landrum, *State Park Movement in America*, 69.

22. "Arkansas State Parks," in *Histories of Southeastern State Park Systems*, 17.

23. Cox, *Park Builders* 12.

24. Hersey, "Hints and Suggestions to Farmers: George Washington Carver and Rural Conservation in the South," *Environmental History* 11 (1998): 239–68.

25. Caroline Dormon, *Louisiana Landscape: State Parks for Louisiana* (n.p.: Louisiana State Parks Association, 1931), 1 (copy in Special Collections, Hill Memorial Library, Louisiana State University).

26. Texas created its park agency in 1920 to administer its historical parks. Florida and Tennessee each created a park agency in 1925, although neither undertook any state park development until into the next decade. Florida's first was Highlands Hammock State Park, completed in 1935, while state park construction in Tennessee did not commence until 1938. A similar time lag was evident in Virginia, where its General Assembly authorized a state park system in 1926, although no parks were opened until 1936.
See Steely, *Parks for Texas*; "History of Florida's State Park System," Florida Department of Environmental Protection (webpage no longer available); "History of Virginia State Parks," in *Histories of Southeastern State Park Systems*, 174.

27. West Virginia created a Division of State Parks in 1933, housed within its Conservation Commission. The state in 1925 had acquired the parcel that became Watoga State Park, but development commenced only with the establishment of CCC camps at the site in 1934. Also in 1934, Mississippi's legislature authorized the state's Forestry Commission to acquire state park lands, Louisiana established its State Parks Commission, and the South Carolina Commission of Forestry was given responsibility to develop and oversee state parks. Its efforts began that year with a 706-acre land donation from residents of Cheraw. See "History of Mississippi State Parks," in *Histories of Southeastern State Park Systems*, 111; "History of Mississippi State Parks," Mississippi Commission on Natural Resources, November 1985, Mississippi State Archives, Jackson; "Louisiana State Parks: The Problem and the Answer," First Annual Report to the Governor (New Orleans: State Parks Commission, 1935), 10; "History of South Carolina State Parks," in *Histories of Southeastern State Park Systems*; Stephen Lewis Cox, "The History of Negro State Parks in South Carolina: 1940–1963" (master's thesis, University of South Carolina, 1992).

28. "History of Alabama State Parks," in *Histories of Southeastern State Park Systems*, 8–9.

29. Ibid., 9.

30. Leon F. Litwack, *Trouble in Mind: Black Southerners in the Age of Jim Crow* (New York: Vintage, 1999), xiii.

31. Ibid., 233.

32. Barbara Young Welke, *Recasting American Liberty: Gender, Race, Law, and the Railroad Revolution, 1865–1940* (New York: Cambridge University Press, 2001), 279.

33. Edward L. Ayers, *The Promise of the New South: Life after Reconstruction* (New York: Oxford University Press, 1992), 144.

34. Grace Elizabeth Hale, *Making Whiteness: The Culture of Segregation in the South, 1890–1940* (New York: Pantheon Press, 1998), 53–54.

35. Jason Sokol, *There Goes My Everything: White Southerners in the Age of Civil Rights, 1945–1975* (New York: Vintage, 2007). The name Booker T. Washington came to be associated with acceptance of southern traditions, invoking among whites the affectionate image of the Old Negro. Whites in general would assure themselves that most of "their Negroes" were like Washington and supported the southern "tra-

dition" of racial segregation. Decades later southern park officials named two state parks for Booker T. Washington, one in southeastern Tennessee (1938) and the other in Institute, West Virginia (1949). Two state parks were named for his Tuskegee protégé, the botanist George Washington Carver, in northern Georgia (1952) and in north-central Mississippi (1954).

36. Litwack, *Trouble in Mind*, 201.

37. Ibid., 204.

38. Robert M. McKay, "Segregation and Public Recreation," *Virginia Law Review* 40 (1954): 697–731; Helen F. Schwartz, "Recreation and the 14th Amendment," *New South* (April 1955): 5–7.

39. McKay, "Segregation and Public Recreation, 702.

40. North Carolina Board of Conservation and Development, "Minutes of the July 1 and 2, 1957, Meeting," Florida State Archives, Tallahassee.

41. Writing about southern railways, Barbara Young Welke points out that even where there were formal segregation laws, their enforcement was not rigid: "Looking at the laws alone misleadingly suggests completeness and finality where it did not in fact exist." Welke, *Recasting American Liberty*, 271. Exceptions were made on trains for Black servants traveling with white employers and Black caretakers of white children, and similar exceptions were evident in state parks. Park managers, for instance, could potentially exercise discretion in permitting access for particular African Americans. On this basis, park coordinator A. H. Nall of the Mississippi's Park Service wrote in response to a park survey from the Southern Regional Council in 1952, "There are nine State Parks in Mississippi which are operated for the whites only, with the negroes being permitted to fish in the lakes in designated areas." A. H. Nall to Anna Holden, November 21, 1952, SRC Papers, Auburn Avenue Research Library on African American Culture and History, Atlanta.

42. McKay, "Segregation and Public Recreation," 701.

43. George B. Tindall, *The Emergence of the New South, 1913–1945* (Baton Rouge: LSU Press, 1992), 145.

44. John Muir, *Our National Parks* (1901; repr. Madison: University of Wisconsin Press, 1981), 1.

45. Roderick Frazier Nash, *Wilderness and the American Mind*, 4th ed. (New Haven: Yale University Press, 2001), 150.

46. Gary Gerstle, "Theodore Roosevelt and the Divided Character of American Nationalism," *Journal of American History* 86 (1999): 1285.

47. Carolyn Merchant, "Shades of Darkness: Race and Environmental History," *Environmental History* 8 (July 2003): 386.

48. Thomas G. Dyer, *Theodore Roosevelt and the Idea of Race* (Baton Rouge: LSU Press, 1992), 144.

49. Denis Cosgrove, "Habitable Earth: Wilderness, Empire, and Race in America," in *Wild Ideas*, ed. David Rothberg (Minneapolis: University of Minnesota Press, 1995), 34, 35.

50. Merchant, "Shades of Darkness," 385.

51. Stephen R. Fox, *The American Conservation Movement: John Muir and His Legacy* (New York: Little, Brown, 1981), 116–17.

52. Reginald Horsman, "Race and Manifest Destiny: The Origins of American Racial Anglo-Saxonism," in *Critical White Studies: Looking behind the Mirror*, ed. Richard Delgado and Jean Stefancic (Philadelphia: Temple University Press, 1997), 139–44.

53. Kimberley K. Smith, *African American Environmental Thought: Foundations* (Lawrence: University of Kansas Press, 2007), 107.

54. Ibid.

55. Ibid., 109.

56. Madison Grant, *The Passing of the Great Race; Or, the Racial Basis of European History* (New York: Charles Scribner's Sons, 1916).

57. Smith, *African American Environmental Thought*, 112.

58. William A. Stinchcomb, "State Parks Near Large Cities," in Evison, *A State Park Anthology*, 54, 55.

59. James Frederick Murphy, "Egalitarianism and Separatism: A History of Approaches in the Provision of Public Recreation and Leisure Services for Blacks, 1906–1972" (Ph.D. diss., Oregon State University, 1972).

60. Ibid., 3.

61. Ernest Attwell, "Playgrounds for Colored America," *The Playground* 15 (1921): 84. This essay was originally published in *Park International*, November 1920.

62. Ibid., 85.

63. Murphy, "Egalitarianism and Separatism," 3.

64. Robert Lassiter quoted in Thomas F. Parker, "Recreation for Colored Citizens," *The Playground* 19 (1926): 651–52.

65. Ernest Attwell, "Recreation for Colored America," *The American City* 35 (1926): 164.

66. J. L. Reddix, "State Parks and the Race Problem" (1950), Southern Regional Council Papers, Auburn Avenue Research Library on African American Culture and History, Atlanta.

67. Forest B. Washington, "Recreational Facilities for the Negro," *Annals of the American Academy of Political and Social Science* 140 (November 1928): 274, 275.

68. Ibid.

69. Charles S. Johnson, *The Negro in American Civilization: A Study of Negro Life and Race Relations in Light of Social Research* (New York: Routledge, 2005), 457, 310.

70. The perception among many African Americans of landscapes and "nature" as places of toil and danger

but also of potential freedom can be traced to slavery. The environmentalist and historian Dianne D. Glave explains that "wilderness was a place to roam and hide for a moment's peace from slaveholders, or it could be a means of permanent escape." However, such places "were also dangerous, not only because of predatory animals but also because of predatory whites." Glave, *Rooted in the Earth: Reclaiming the African American Environmental Heritage* (Chicago: Lawrence Hill Books, 2010), 8. For a book-length discussion of the topic of African American relationships to nature, see Carolyn Finney, *Black Faces, White Spaces: Reimagining the Relationship of African Americans to the Great Outdoors* (Chapel Hill: University of North Carolina Press, 2014).

71. Gunnar Myrdal, *An American Dilemma: The Negro Problem and Modern Democracy* (New York: Harper & Brothers, 1944), 335–36.

72. Jearold Winston Holland, *Black Recreation: A Historical Perspective* (Chicago: Burnham, 2002), 121.

73. Nancy L. Grant, *TVA and Black Americans: Planning for the Status Quo* (Philadelphia: Temple University Press, 1990),

74. Ibid., 86.

75. Ibid., 89.

76. Grant, *TVA and Black Americans*, 89. The quotation is from "The Proposed North Alabama State Park for Negroes," August 26, 1940, appendix D, TVA files, RG 142, National Archives.

77. Colin Fisher, "African Americans, Outdoor Recreation, and the 1919 Chicago Race Riot," in *"To Love the Wind and the Rain": African Americans in Environmental History*, ed. Dianne D. Glave and Mark Stoll (Pittsburgh: University of Pittsburgh Press, 2006), 69.

78. Williams quoted ibid.

79. W. E. B. Du Bois, *Darkwater: Voices from Within the Veil* (New York: Harcourt, Brace, and Howe, 1920), 226. (Created in 1919, Lafayette National Park was renamed Acadia National Park in 1929.)

80. Smith, *African American Environmental Thought*, 2.

81. Du Bois, *Darkwater*, 229.

82. Ibid., 228–29.

83. Patrick C. West, "The Tyranny of Metaphor: Interracial Relations, Minority Recreation, and the Wildland-Urban Interface," in *Culture, Conflict, and Communication in the Wildland-Urban Interface*, ed. Alan Ewert, Deborah Chavez, and Arthur Magill (Boulder, Colo.: Westview Press, 1993).

84. Washington, "Recreational Facilities for the Negro," 279.

85. Harris's plea was to the National Park Service, asking them to provide camps within the Recreational Demonstration Areas that were being constructed during the waning years of the New Deal. Stanley A. Harris to Julian H. Salomon, February 28, 1938, box 017, folder 901-01 Recreation Facilities for Negroes, Entry P100, Recreational Demonstration Area Program Files 1934–1947, RG 79, RNPS, NACP (hereafter cited as RDA Program Files).

2. The New Deal and Early State Parks in the South

1. William C. Everhart, *The National Park Service* (New York: Praeger, 1972), 14–15.

2. Robert Shankland, *Steve Mather of the National Parks* (New York: Knopf, 1951), 185, 187–88.

3. Raymond Wolters, *Negroes and the Great Depression: The Problem of Economic Recovery* (Westport, Conn.: Greenwood, 1970), ix.

4. The official name of the CCC was Emergency Conservation Work (ECW). The agency's popular name, Civilian Conservation Corps, became official in 1937.

5. Everhart, *National Park Service*, 32.

6. Harlan D. Unrau and G. Frank Williss, *Expansion of the National Park Service in the 1930s: An Administrative History* (Washington, D.C.: National Park Service, 1983), chap. 3, para. 1, available online at ParkNet: www.cr.nps.gov/history/online_books/unrau-williss/adhi.htm.

7. John C. Paige, *The Civilian Conservation Corps and the National Park Service, 1933–1942: An Administrative History* (Washington, D.C.: Department of the Interior, 1985), chap. 5.

8. Ethan Carr, *Wilderness by Design: Landscape Architecture and the National Park Service* (Lincoln: University of Nebraska Press, 1998), 266.

9. Oklahoma State Historic Preservation Office, *Final Survey Report: Intensive-Level Survey of New Deal-Era State Parks in Oklahoma* (Oklahoma City: Oklahoma Tourism and Recreation Department, 1993), 27.

10. There were a number of reasons for this gradual shift during the 1930s. The historian George Tindall points to improved education, new theories of race that centered on culture rather than biology, the changing southern economy, the rise of fascism in Europe, and the Great Migration of African Americans to the North, which enhanced political influence among African Americans. Such Black influence bolstered liberal concerns about inequality and discrimination, which influenced federal policies during the New Deal. George B. Tindall, *The Emergence of the New South, 1913–1945* (Baton Rouge: Louisiana State University Press, 1992), 565.

11. Gunnar Myrdal, *An American Dilemma: The Negro Problem and Modern Democracy* (New York: Harper & Brothers, 1944), 346–47.

12. Ibid., 347.

13. The African American group camp at Virginia's Swift Creek RDA would remain segregated after the site became Pocahontas State Park, but state officials did not count the location as an African American state park space.

14. Herbert Evison to W. Norman Watts, June 14, 1940, box 017, folder 901-01 Recreation Facilities for Negroes, Entry P100, RDA Program Files.

15. Arno Cammerer to A. E. Demaray and Conrad Wirth, September 30, 1936, ibid.

16. Raymond Wolters, "The Negro and the New Deal," in *The New Deal*, ed. John Braeman, Robert H. Bemner, and David Brody (Columbus: Ohio State University Press, 1975), 200.

17. Audrey Thomas, ed. *Mary McLeod Bethune: Building a Better World, Essays and Selected Documents* (Bloomington: Indiana University Press, 1999).

18. June Hopkins, *Harry Hopkins: Sudden Hero, Brash Reformer* (New York: St. Martin's Press, 1999).

19. Wolters, "The Negro and the New Deal," 188.

20. Roscoe Dunjee, "Cotton Picking and the New Deal," *Black Dispatch*, September 17, 1936.

21. Wolters, "The Negro and the New Deal," 176.

22. John A. Salmond, *The Civilian Conservation Corps, 1933–1942: A New Deal Case Study* (Durham: Duke University Press, 1967), 101; Owen Cole Jr., *The African-American Experience in the Civilian Conservation Corps* (Tallahassee: University Press of Florida, 1999), 25–26.

23. Cole, *African-American Experience*, 21; Salmond, *Civilian Conservation Corps*, 95; Michael S. Holmes, "The New Deal and Georgia's Black Youth," *Journal of Southern History* 38 (1972): 443–60. See also Allen F. Kifer, "The Negro under the New Deal" (Ph.D. diss., University of Wisconsin, 1961).

24. "Thousands of Race Boys Now Serving in National CCC Camps, Survey Reveals," *Chicago Defender*, March 16, 1935; "48,000 Negroes in CCC Camps," *New York Amsterdam News*, December 7, 1935; Dunjee, "Cotton Picking and the New Deal"; "CCC After 7 Years," *Chicago Defender*, April 6, 1940. Salmond also concludes that "the CCC, despite its obvious failures, did fulfill at least some of its obligations toward unemployed American Negro youth." Salmond, *Civilian Conservation Corps*, 101.

25. Regarding the NRA, for instance, John K. Kirby points to African American objections that policies regarding "Negroes . . . were frequently evaded through devices such as occupational and geographic job classifications, wage loopholes, or simply lack of NRA enforcement." Kirby, *Black Americans in the Roosevelt Era: Liberalism and Race* (Knoxville: University

of Tennessee Press, 1980), 41–42. See also Wolters, *Negroes and the Great Depression*, for a detailed discussion of both agencies.

26. Wolters, "The Negro and the New Deal."

27. Wolters, *Negroes and the Great Depression*, xi.

28. Kirby, *Black Americans in the Roosevelt Era*, 218.

29. *Pittsburgh Courier*, January 11, 1936, in Wolters, *Negroes and the Great Depression*, 210–11.

30. Kirby, *Black Americans in the Roosevelt Era*, 234.

31. Linda Flint McClelland, *Presenting Nature: The Historical Landscape Design of the National Park Service, 1916 to 1942* (Washington, D.C.: U.S. Department of the Interior, 1993), 232.

32. In reaction to this Park Service trend, other critics would collaborate to create the Wilderness Society, which pressed for the protection of what they perceived as truly wild places. See Paul S. Sutter, *Driven Wild: How the Fight against Automobiles Launched the Modern Wilderness Movement* (Seattle: University of Washington Press, 2002).

33. Richard Lieber, "Address to the National Conference on State Parks," June 12, 1935, Skyland, Virginia, 3, box 2966, folder National Park Conference, State Parks 0-33, NPS Central Classified File 1933–1949, RG 79, RNPS, NACP.

34. Richard Lieber, "The Task of Conservation," in *A State Park Anthology*, ed. Herbert Evison (Washington, D.C.: National Conference on State Parks, 1930), 9–12.

35. Lieber, "Address to the National Conference on State Parks," 4.

36. Oklahoma State Historic Preservation Office, *Final Survey Report*, 21; M. C. Weber, *Roman Nose: A History of the Park* (Okla.: Oak Haven Books, 1994). Both the report on New Deal–era structures and Weber's book indicate that its plan included a segregated section for African Americans, although neither is certain when it was opened. Oklahoma's Recreational Area Study confirms that the park contained an African American recreational area in its 1938 inventory of parks in the state. See Division of State Parks, *Parks and Recreation in Oklahoma: Progress Report*, appendix D, table 3.

37. Oklahoma State Historic Preservation Office, *Final Survey Report*, 20.

38. "Parks for Negroes, Parks for Whites," *Black Dispatch*, August 13, 1936.

39. "Negroes and Parks," *Oklahoma News*, reprinted in "What Other Editors Say," *Black Dispatch*, September 17, 1936.

40. "Parks for Negroes, Parks for Whites."

41. Frederick Law Olmsted Jr., "Bases for the Selection of State Parks," in Evison, *State Park Anthology*, 67–69.

42. Oklahoma State Planning Board, "Preliminary Report on State Planning: Facts and Findings Pertaining to Physical, Social, and Economic Conditions Which Are Essential to Comprehensive State Planning for Oklahoma" (Oklahoma City, 1936), 117.

43. Division of State Parks, *Parks and Recreation in Oklahoma*, 16–17.

44. Oklahoma State Historic Preservation Office, *Final Survey Report*, 27.

45. The regional designations for state park work under the New Deal changed several times during the 1930s. At the national level, state park development under Emergency Conservation Work (ECW) was initially divided into four districts but in 1935 was split into eight. The following year the districts were consolidated into four, and in 1937 the National Park Service reorganized its operations to conform to these four ECW regions. In this arrangement, Maier was first appointed to ECW District III, which then became District VII, and in 1937 he was appointed as director of the Southwest Region. See McClelland, *Presenting Nature*, 229–30, 234.

46. Steely, *Parks for Texas*. Within the revolving regional boundaries, Maier's influence extended to states including Arkansas, Colorado, Kansas, Louisiana, Montana, Nebraska, New Mexico, North Dakota, Oklahoma, South Dakota, Texas, Utah, and Wyoming. McClelland, *Presenting Nature*, 236.

47. McClelland, *Presenting Nature*, 236.

48. Oklahoma State Historic Preservation Office, *Final Survey Report*, 20.

49. Weber, *Roman Nose*, 14.

50. Oklahoma State Historic Preservation Office, *Final Survey Report*, 20–21.

51. Weber, *Roman Nose*, 19.

52. Ibid., 21. Weber notes that the land was leased to the state for a period of ninety years, ending in 2034.

53. Ibid., 24.

54. Oklahoma Planning and Resources Board, *First Annual Report of the Division of State Parks, Fiscal Year Ending June 30, 1938*, 28; copy in Oklahoma State Library.

55. Weber, *Roman Nose*, 44.

56. Ibid., 47.

57. Ibid.

58. Ibid., 39.

59. Plans for this African American resort are discussed in chapter 5.

60. Oklahoma State Historic Preservation Office, *Final Survey Report*, 15–16, 17, 33. Other sources place the initial date of consideration at 1931.

61. Ibid., 33

62. *History of Recreational Demonstration Projects and Development of Policies*, December 20, 1935, 6, box 002, folder 101 General History, Entry P100, RDA Program Files.

63. Herbert Maier to M. G. Huppuch, February 22, 1936, and Arthur R. Merkle, "Analysis of Survey of Camp Facility Needs, Lake Murray State Park Extension LB-09," n.d., both box 200, folder 601-12 Recreational Areas, Entry P100, RDA Program Files.

64. "Lake Murray Party to Be Held by National Park Service, Sunday, April 10," unidentified newspaper, April 2, 1938, box 198, folder 207-05 Camp Appraisal Reports 3, Entry P100, RDA Program Files.

65. "Administration of Lake Camps Discussed." *Daily Ardmorite*, March 20, 1938.

66. "Lake Murray Conference Sunday," unidentified newspaper, April 9, 1938, ibid.

67. Ibid.

68. Herbert Maier to M. G. Huppuch, February 22, 1936, RDA Program Files.

69. Milo Christiansen, "Report on Organized Camp Meetings (White and Negro), Lake Murray, Oklahoma, March 19 and April 10 1938," box 198, folder 207-05 Camp Appraisal Reports 3, Entry P100, RDA Program Files. Despite the prevailing pessimism, 150 people attended the African American meeting (the number at a separate white meeting was not tallied, although 175 invitations were sent).

70. Ibid.

71. Milton J. McColm to NPS Director, March 9, 1938, box 29, folder 601-12 Recreational Survey Oklahoma, Entry P107, Classified Files 1936–1947, Recreation Area Study, RG 79, RNPS, NACP. McColm indicates that the Park Service was contemplating this decision in early March and that the decision was influenced by concern that white groups would not use the site if it had previously been used by African Americans.

72. A. R. Reeves to L. M. Watkins, December 23, 1938, box 017, folder 901-01 Recreation Facilities for Negroes, Entry P100, RDA Program Files. This memo by Oklahoma's director of state parks states: "In the beginning during the early discussions of the development of this area it was the opinion of the State as well as the opinion of the Regional Office of Technicians that this organized camp would not need to be as elaborate as the other original camps in Lake Murray. This was necessary because of funds available with which to work and the time element since this organized camp is to be ready for occupancy this 1939 season."

73. Milo Christiansen, "Negro Organized Camp, Lake Murray State Park—Oklahoma, Report on Summer Use, 1939," box 198, folder 207-05 Camp Appraisal Reports 3, Entry P100, RDA Program Files.

74. Anne L. Caution to various local African American organizations, May 1, 1939, box 197, folder 207-25 Camp Appraisal Reports 1938–1940, Entry P100, RDA Program Files.

75. Christiansen, "Negro Organized Camp, Lake Murray State Park."

76. "By Staff of State Park Board," in Southern Oklahoma Boosters Club, *Beautiful Lake Murray Camp Site No. 3*, January 8, 1940, box 197, folder 207-25 Camp Appraisal Reports 1938–1940, Entry P100, RDA Program Files.

77. "Tucker Tower and This Year's Visitors Will See It," ibid.

78. "By Staff of State Park Board."

79. "How to Get to the Camp," ibid. The success of the 1940 season remains unclear, but the African American camp continued to be maintained as a segregated section of Lake Murray State Park. See Oklahoma Planning and Resources Board, "Your State Playgrounds: Lake Murray State Park," April 13, 1953, information sheet, copy in Oklahoma State Library.

80. Today it is known as the University of Arkansas at Pine Bluff.

81. "Dr. J. B. Watson Buried After Campus Rites," *Chicago Defender*, December 19, 1942; "John Brown Watson (1869–1942)," *The Encyclopedia of Arkansas History & Culture*, www.encyclopediaofarkansas.net/encyclopedia/entry-detail.aspx?entryID=333.

82. C. F. Clayton to Conrad L. Wirth, May 13, 1935, and C. F. Clayton to M. C. Huppuch, July 15, 1935, both box 002, folder 0-32 General Preliminary Proposals, Entry P100, RDA Program Files.

83. J. Milton McColm, "Statement: Development of State Parks and Recreational Areas in Arkansas by National Park Service," May 22, 1947, box 2969, folder Arkansas General, State Parks 0-33, NPS Central Classified File 1933–1949, RG 79, RNPS, NACP.

84. Herbert Maier to M. C. Huppuch, March 1, 1935, box 195, folder Pine Bluff Negro Park Ark Entirety, Entry P100, RDA Program Files.

85. Conrad L. Wirth to Director of the Land Program, May 8, 1935, and Mr. Croft to Mr. DeGelleke, April 23, 1935, both ibid.

86. John Brown Watson to Ed L. Campbell, May 26, 1937, John Brown Watson Collection, Brown University Library; Wirth to Director of the Land Program, May 8, 1935.

87. B. M. Gile to C. F. Clayton, June 13, 1935, box 195, folder Pine Bluff Negro Park Ark Entirety, Entry P100, RDA Program Files.

88. Mr. Stockton to Mr. DeGelleke, "Comment on Proposed Recreational Development for Negroes, Pine Bluff, Arkansas," n.d., ibid.

89. Ibid.

90. L. C. Gray to Lawrence C. Merriam, September 9, 1935, ibid.

91. Herbert Maier to B. M. Gile, June 10, 1935, ibid.

92. J. B. Watson to L. C. Gray, September 25, 1935, ibid.

93. Ibid.

94. "State Park for Colored Looms as a Certainty," *Atlanta Daily World*, June 26, 1937.

95. "All-Colored Park Ok'd in Ark.," *Atlanta Daily World*, June 15, 1937.

96. John Brown Watson to Ed L. Campbell, May 26, 1937; "State Park for Colored Looms as a Certainty."

97. Watson to Campbell, May 26, 1937.

98. Ibid.

99. "Begin Work on $30,000 Park," *Pittsburgh Courier*, May 21, 1938.

100. Arkansas State Parks Commission, *Third Annual Report*, December 5, 1939, 11.

101. *Hattie M. Watson v. Arkansas State Parks Commission*, Pulaski Chancery Court, November 22, 1944, copy in John Brown Watson Collection, Brown University Library.

102. Arkansas State Parks Commission, *Third Annual Report*; "Recreation for All Is Found at State's Public Parks," *Arkansas Gazette*, January 12, 1941.

103. "Recreation for All Is Found at State's Public Parks."

104. "History of North Carolina State Parks," in *Histories of Southeastern State Park Systems* (n.p.: Association of Southeastern State Park Directors, 1977), 128.

105. Division of Parks and Recreation, *Jones Lake State Park General Management Plan*, North Carolina Department of Environment and Natural Resources, March 2006, I-4, 5, 8.

106. The property was granted to the state by the federal government in 1954. Ibid., I-9.

107. Ibid., I-7, 8.

108. "North Carolina Sponsors First State Park for Race in South." *Journal and Guide*, August 5, 1939.

109. Branch of State Parks, *Report on State Parks, State Lakes, and Other Recreational Areas, January 1, 1939 to July 1, 1939*. North Carolina Department of Conservation and Development, Forestry Division. By that time, two group camps for whites had already been completed.

110. "Camp Whispering Pines," 1, 2, 6, box 069, folder 207-25 Camp Appraisal Reports, Entry P100, RDA Program Files.

111. "A Rough Park History of William B. Umstead State Park," July 17, 1999 (park brochure). The white park was renamed William B. Umstead State Park in 1955, for the recently deceased governor.

112. "Park Development Underway," *Raleigh News & Observer*, April 26, 1950.

113. "State's Parks Continue to Attract Throngs Each Year to Various Parts of North State," *Rocky Mount Sunday Telegram*, September 14, 1952.

114. Bevley Coleman, "A History of State Parks in Tennessee" (Ph.D. diss., George Peabody College for Teachers, 1963), 6–9.

115. Ibid., 248.

116. "TVA to Form State Park for Negroes," *Winchester (Tenn.) Truth and Herald*, January 12, 1939.

117. Coleman, "A History of State Parks in Tennessee," 263.

118. Hamilton County Regional Planning Commission, "Proposed Negro State Park Near Chattanooga, May 1938, Tennessee Division of State Parks" (unpublished), in Coleman, "A History of State Parks in Tennessee," 264.

119. Coleman, "A History of State Parks in Tennessee," 264.

120. Ibid.

121. Grant, *TVA and Black Americans*, 88.

122. Ken Wynn, "Bell Tolls for Booker T.," unidentified newspaper, [n.d.], 1968, Department of Conservation Papers, Tennessee State Library and Archives, Nashville.

123. "State to Improve Negro Park Here," *Chattanooga Times*, March 7, 1948.

124. W. M. Hay, "Report to Accompany Master Plan for Shelby Negro State Park," August 19, 1941, box 420, folder 601-03 Camp Sites, Entry P90, State Park Files 1934–1947, RNPS, NACP. In 1938 the African American population was estimated at around 290,000 within a fifty-mile radius of the site.

125. NAACP Memphis Branch to National Park Service, May 10, 1937, box 017, folder 901-01 Recreation Facilities for Negroes, Entry P100, RDA Program Files.

126. Conrad L. Wirth to Charles H. Houston, June 16, 1937, ibid.

127. E. W. Hale to Mrs. Franklin D. Roosevelt, November 25, 1937, and Malvina T. Schneider to Sec. Harold Ickes, November 27, 1937, both ibid.

128. Harold L. Ickes to Mrs. Franklin D. Roosevelt, December 10, 1937, ibid.

129. E. W. Hale to Harold L. Ickes, December 17, 1937, ibid.

130. Arno B. Cammerer to E. W. Hale, January 6, 1938, ibid.; "Many Facilities Being Provided in New Shelby Park for Negroes," *Atlanta Daily World*, April 25, 1939.

131. "Many Facilities Being Provided in New Shelby Park for Negroes."

132. Hay, "Report to Accompany Master Plan for Shelby Negro State Park," 3; "Work on Negro Park Pushed by CCC Crew," *Memphis Commercial Appeal*, April 25, 1939.

133. "Many Facilities Being Provided in New Shelby Park for Negroes."

134. Coleman, "A History of State Parks in Tennessee," 375.

135. Ibid., 366. It was originally called Shelby Archaeological Park. The site was assessed in 1957 for possible inclusion in the National Park system, though ultimately it would be designated in 1959 as a fully separate state park unit named Chucalissa Archeological State Park. "National Park at Memphis? It's Possible," *Memphis Press-Scimitar*, May 28, 1957.

136. "Dream of Years for Negro Recreation Spot Nears Reality—Shelby Negro State Park," *Memphis Press Scimitar*, June 17, 1941.

137. "Work on Negro Park Pushed by CCC Crew."

138. J. Charles Poe to Conrad L. Wirth, November 24, 1942, box 420, folder 601-03 Camp Sites, Entry P90, State Park Files 1934–1947, RNPS, NACP.

139. Ernie Hoberecht, "Shelby Bluffs Dedicated to Spirit of Democracy," *Memphis Press-Scimitar*, June 15, 1942.

140. Poe to Wirth, November 24, 1942.

141. "No Immediate Plans to Build Swimming Pool for Negroes," *Atlanta Daily World*, May 31, 1953; Coleman, "A History of State Parks in Tennessee," 363.

142. "Fuller Golf Course Officially Opened," *Memphis Commercial Appeal*, November 11, 1957. The course was closed in 2011.

143. For a discussion of New Deal–era state parks in South Carolina, see Tara Mitchell Mielnik, *New Deal, New Landscape: The Civilian Conservation Corps and South Carolina's State Parks* (Columbia: University of South Carolina Press, 2011).

3. Park Service Planning Meets Resistance

1. Freeman Tilden, *The State Parks: Their Meaning in American Life* (New York: Knopf, 1962), 4.

2. Ney C. Landrum points out that as late as 1937 the membership (of several hundred) included sixty-six Park Service professional staff in contrast with only fourteen directors of state park agencies. See Landrum, *The State Park Movement in America: A Critical Review* (Columbia: University of Missouri Press, 2004), 122, 170.

3. Horace Albright, quoted ibid., 115.

4. Landrum, *State Park Movement in America*, 133.

5. Conrad Wirth, *Parks, Politics, and the People* (Norman: University of Oklahoma Press, 1980), chap. 7 (n.p.), available at www.nps.gov/parkhistory/online_books/wirth2/chap7c.htm.

6. Linda Flint McClelland, *Presenting Nature: The Historical Landscape Design of the National Park Service 1916 to 1942* (Washington, D.C.: U.S. Department of the Interior, 1993), 249.

7. Ibid., 249.
8. Landrum, *State Park Movement in America*, 153.
9. Ibid., 131.
10. Harlan D. Unrau and G. Frank Williss, *Expansion of the National Park Service in the 1930s: An Administrative History* (Washington, D.C.: National Park Service, 1983), chap. 3, available online at ParkNet: www.cr.nps.gov/history/online_books/unrau-williss/adhi.htm.
11. Landrum, *State Park Movement in America*, 129.
12. Ibid., 131.
13. W. J. Faulkner to Sam Brewster, August 26, 1937, RFN, RDA Program Files.
14. "Revised List of Recreational Demonstration Projects, Waysides and National Park Area Extensions, Embracing Lands Acquired and Optioned by the Resettlement Administration for the National Park Service," October 15, 1936, RFN, RDA Program Files.
15. Faulkner to Brewster, August 26, 1937.
16. W. J. Faulkner to Arnold Cammerer, August 26, 1937, RFN, RDA Program Files.
17. A. E. Demaray to W. J. Faulkner, September 29, 1937, ibid.
18. Report on the National Conference on the Problems of the Negro and Negro Youth, January 22, 1937, p. 3, Central Classified Files 1937–1956, RG 48, Records of the Office of the Secretary of the Interior, 1826–2009, NACP.
19. Ibid., 30.
20. Fred Z. Johnston to NPS Director, October 14, 1937, RFN, RDA Program Files.
21. Bevley Coleman, "A History of State Parks in Tennessee" (Ph.D. diss., George Peabody College for Teachers, 1963), 243–53.
22. "List of Recreational Demonstration Projects, Waysides and National Park Area Extensions, Embracing Lands Acquired and Optioned by the Resettlement Administration for the National Park Service," October 15, 1936, RFN, RDA Program Files.
23. "Projects of the Land Utilization Division, Resettlement Administration, Department of Agriculture, on Which Plans Have Been Made for Negro Recreational Facilities," July 1937, RFN, RDA Program Files.
24. Herbert Evison to NPS Director, August 6, 1937, RFN, RDA Program Files.
25. Region I of the Park Service at the time included the states of the Northeast as well as southeastern states east of the Mississippi River.
26. R. C. Robinson to Herbert Evison, August 5, 1937, RFN, RDA Program Files.
27. Four of the projects on the list would eventually be completed as state parks for African American use, although very little progress had been made by the time of Robinson's report. As mentioned in chapter 2, the Jones and Salters Lakes Land Use Project near Elizabethtown, North Carolina, was opened in 1939 as the popular Jones Lake State Park. Two South Carolina projects on the list, near the towns of Sumner and Cheraw, would eventually be opened as Mill Creek State Park in 1941 and Campbell Lake State Park in 1946, administered from nearby (white-only) Poinsett State Park and Cheraw State Park, respectively. Discussions about the opening of Campbell Lake State Park took place in 1937, but its status remained on hold until after World War II. A fourth project near Farmville, Virginia, would see only modest development until a postwar lawsuit led to the transformation of the lakeshore site into Prince Edward State Park by 1950.
28. Robinson to Evison, August 5, 1937.
29. Ibid.
30. R. C. Robinson to Herbert Evison, May 4, 1937, RFN, RDA Program Files.
31. Kenneth B. Simmons to Conrad Wirth, September 22, 1936, RFN, RDA Program Files.
32. Arno Cammerer to A. E. Demaray and Conrad Wirth, September 30, 1936, RFN, RDA Program Files.
33. A. E. Demaray to Arno Cammerer, October 1, 1936, RFN, RDA Program Files.
34. Ibid.
35. The presidential retreat site at Catoctin RDA was selected by FDR in 1940 and was originally called Shangri-La. The name was changed by President Dwight Eisenhower to Camp David, in honor of his son.
36. Conrad Wirth to Stanley A. Harris, March 18, 1938, RFN, RDA Program Files.
37. W. J. Trent Jr. to Harold Ickes, June 21, 1939, RFN, RDA Program Files.
38. For an extensive profile of Trent's work, see Terence Young, "A Contradiction in Democratic Government: W. J. Trent, Jr., and the Struggle to Desegregate National Park Campgrounds," *Environmental History* 14 (October 2009): 651–82.
39. Trent Jr. to Ickes, June 21, 1939.
40. Arthur Demaray to Harold Ickes, June 30, 1939, RFN, RDA Program Files.
41. Harold Ickes to W. J. Trent Jr., July 6, 1939, RFN, RDA Program Files.
42. Director Arno Cammerer faced health problems toward the end of his tenure and suffered a heart attack in 1939, which prompted Demaray to step in to fill the role. Cammerer stepped down the following year, to be replaced as director by Newton B. Drury, and died in 1941 from another heart attack while serving as director of the eastern region of the Park Service.
43. A. E. Demaray to Harold Ickes, July 21 1939, RFN, RDA Program Files.

44. McClelland, *Presenting Nature*, 252.
45. The study was completed in 1941 but was not released until early 1942.
46. R. C. Robinson and A. P. Bursley, "Technical Report: Recreational Area Planning Division. Subject: Supplementary Report for the South Carolina Park, Parkway, and Recreational Area Study on Camping, Swimming, and Golf, August 14, 1939," box 19, folder 0-027 South Carolina R S Reports, Entry P107, Classified Files 1936–1947 Recreation Area Study, RG79, RNPS, NACP.
47. "Rough Draft of Notes and Comments: Park, Parkway and Recreational-Area Study, North Carolina Report," March 4, 1941, box 17, folder 207 North Carolina R S Reports, Entry P107, Classified File, 1936–1947 Recreation Area Study, RG 79, RNPS, NACP. The state would ultimately fail to expand beyond the two facilities already available to African Americans at Jones Lake State Park and Crabtree Creek RDA.
48. Russell H. Lyons, "A Study of the Needs and Facilities for Recreation among the Negroes of Louisiana" (master's thesis, Louisiana State University, 1940), 31. Lyons's master's thesis was based on work on Louisiana's Recreational Area Study.
49. Ibid., 46.
50. Report of the meeting of the Florida Planning Board, July 25, 1940, box 11, folder 0-207 Florida Reports, Entry P107, Classified Files 1936–1947 Recreation Area Study, RG 79, RNPS, NACP.
51. [Unknown] to Acting Director of Region, July 5, 1940, ibid.
52. James B. Williams to Conrad Wirth, June 10, 1940, ibid.
53. R. C. Robinson and A. P. Bursley, "Technical Comment: Recreational Planning Division, Subject: Florida Park, Parkway and Recreational-Area Study Report," May 6, 1940, ibid.
54. Mississippi State Planning Commission, "Tentative Final Report of the Park, Parkway and Recreational-Area Study: Mississippi, January 1, 1938," p. 84, box 15, folder 207 Mississippi R S Reports, Entry P107, Classified Files 1936–1947 Recreation Area Study, RG 79, RNPS, NACP.
55. Ibid., 70.
56. Ibid., 26.
57. Ibid.
58. R. C. Robinson to Evison, October 23, 1937, RFN, RDA Program Files.
59. J. Lee Brown, "Comment on Mississippi Report for the Recreation Study," February 16, 1938, box 15, folder 207 Mississippi R S Reports.
60. Mississippi State Planning Commission, "Tentative Final Report," 69.
61. Ibid., 96
62. Robinson to Evison, October 22, 1937.
63. Andrew W. Karhl, *The Land Was Ours: African American Beaches from Jim Crow to the Sunbelt South* (Cambridge: Harvard University Press, 2012), 52.
64. Cleveland G. Allen, "Bishop Jones Establishes Negro Chautauqua at Waveland, Miss.," *New York Amsterdam News*, April 7, 1926.
65. Robinson to Evison, October 22, 1937.
66. "Gulfside Popularity Increasing as Constructive Recreational Center," *Pittsburgh Courier*, July 14, 1934.
67. Karhl, *The Land Was Ours*, 79.
68. Robinson to Evison, October 22, 1937.
69. Ibid.
70. Ibid.
71. A definitive explanation for this outcome remains unclear from the preserved record.
72. A state park would finally be established at the Gulfside location in 1972. Named Buccaneer State Park, it was created on the state-owned portion of land that had been leased by the Gulfside Association when the state park project was being considered. As for the Gulfside Association, after 1939 Bishop Jones would manage to reestablish its financial standing, along with the success of the resort. The coastal facility was destroyed by Hurricane Katrina in 2005; however, the association continues to pursue its educational mission.
73. The Park Service had approved a mixed-race group to use a white-only organized group camp at the Chopawamsic RDA in the 1941 season. Details of the incident are related by Susan Strickland in *Prince William Forest Park: An Administrative History* (Washington, D.C.: U.S. Department of the Interior, 1986).
74. Herbert Evison to NPS Branch of Recreational Planning and State Cooperation, May 26, 1937, RFN, RDA Program Files.
75. Stanley Hawkins to Regional Director, December 23, 1937, ibid.
76. Ibid. The reference to different watersheds is obscure in this source. In chapter 4 the issue of water drainage in and around proposed African American park sites appears as a significant concern in South Carolina. Planners there sought to reassure local white residents that water bodies in such sites, where African Americans would swim, did not drain through white park areas or communities. It is possible, though not verified, that the reference in this Virginia case may be related to that same concern expressed among the Swift Creek Camp Advisory Committee or others in the area.
77. Hawkins to Regional Director, December 23, 1937.
78. Ibid.

79. "Camp Advisory Committee Resolutions," attached to Hawkins to Regional Director, December 23, 1937.

80. Herbert Evison to Conrad Wirth, January 10, 1938, RFN, RDA Program Files.

81. Ibid.

82. Wirth to Region One Director, January 21, 1938, ibid.

83. Fern Babcock to Harold Ickes, August 13, 1940, box 197, folder 203 Complaints, Entry P100 (hereafter cited as Complaints), RDA Program Files.

84. While the RDA Camp Advisory Committees controlled decisions for longer-term use by groups during the camping season, decisions regarding short-term stays were made by the RDA managers, who were federal employees.

85. George H. Quarterman to Josh Lee, October 29, 1940, Complaints, RDA Program Files.

86. A. E. Demaray to Fern Babcock, August 24, 1940, ibid.

87. Requests for long-term use at RDAs by organized groups were addressed by the advisory boards, which oversaw the camps. Decisions on short-term requests were made by RDA managers.

88. Region III Director to NPS Director, November 29, 1940, Complaints, RDA Program Files.

89. Quarterman to Lee, October 29, 1940.

90. Harold Ickes to Wilburn Cartwright, November 27, 1940, Complaints, RDA Program Files.

91. Ibid.

92. Region III Director to NPS Director, November 29, 1940.

93. E. K. Burlew, First Assistant Secretary, to Newton Drury, Director of the National Park Service, Racial Discrimination General 1937–1942, RG 48, Records of the Office of the Secretary of the Interior, 1826–2009, NACP.

94. Susan Strickland, *Prince William Forest Park: An Administrative History* (Washington, D.C.: U.S. Department of the Interior, 1986).

95. Landrum, *State Park Movement in America*, 132.

96. Harold Ickes, "Supplemental Foreword," *A Study of the Park and Recreation Problem in the United States* (Washington, D.C.: National Park Service, 1942).

97. Unrau and Williss, *Expansion of the National Park Service in the 1930s*.

98. "End of Intolerance for U.S. Minorities Demanded by Ickes," *The Star*, June 6, 1944; copy in box A319, folder Ickes, Harold 1941–1948, Records of the NAACP II, Collections of the Manuscript Division, Library of Congress, Washington, D.C.

99. See Rawn James Jr., *Root and Branch: Charles Hamilton Houston, Thurgood Marshall, and the Struggle to End Segregation* (New York: Bloomsbury Press, 2010).

4. Pursuing "Separate but Equal" after World War II

1. Numan V. Bartley, *The New South, 1945–1980: The Story of the South's Modernization* (Baton Rouge: Louisiana State University Press and the Littlefield Fund for Southern History, 1995), 174–76.

2. For more on this issue, see William E. O'Brien, "State Parks and Jim Crow in the Decade before *Brown v. Board of Education*," *Geographical Review* 102 (April 2012): 166–79.

3. Educational institutions were among the NAACP's most visible targets in its courtroom campaign, but its actions over state park exclusion were also effective. These actions commenced soon after the war. A 1947 lawsuit filed in Kentucky to make public municipal parks accessible helped usher in the 1951 opening of Cherokee State Park, located on the western shore of Kentucky Lake. In 1948, a lawsuit in Virginia would press the state park agency to improve facilities at an existing public park for African Americans in Farmville, which reopened in 1950 as Prince Edward State Park. Another suit filed in Austin, Texas, in 1949 led to the opening of a section for African Americans in Tyler State Park in 1951. A suit filed in 1951 to gain African American access to Seashore State Park in Virginia preceded additional important lawsuits in Maryland and South Carolina. All of these legal actions attracted the close attention of the southern park agencies, which understood the constitutional implications and wanted to get ahead of the trend.

4. Minutes of the Thirteenth Annual Meeting of the Association of Southeastern State Park Directors, 12, Directors Subject File, Georgia State Archives, Morrow.

5. Mississippi State Board of Park Supervisors, *Ninth Biennial Report of the State Board of Park Supervisors for the Years July 1, 1953, through June 30, 1955*, 7, State Documents collection, Mississippi Department of Archives and History, Jackson (hereafter cited as MDAH).

6. Roy Wilkins, "The Negro Wants Full Equality," in *What the Negro Wants*, ed. Rayford W. Logan (1944; repr., Notre Dame, Ind.: University of Notre Dame Press, 2001), 117, 113.

7. Jerrold Packard, *American Nightmare: The History of Jim Crow* (New York: St. Martin's Press, 2002), 212.

8. Bartley, *The New South*, 9.

9. George B. Tindall, *The Emergence of the New South, 1913–1945* (Baton Rouge: Louisiana State University Press, 1992), 716.

10. Wilkins, "The Negro Wants Full Equality," 116.

11. Harlean James, ed., *American Planning and Civic Annual* (Washington, D.C.: American Planning and Civic Association, 1955), 68; Louisiana Department

of Culture, Recreation & Tourism, "The History of Louisiana's State Parks," Office of State Parks, 2009; Louisiana State Parks and Recreation Commission, *Eleventh Report, 61–64: Modern Recreation and Historic Romance* (Baton Rouge: Louisiana State Parks, 1964). The report indicates the allocation of $10,000 for the development of "Fontainebleau Negro Park" for the 1961–62 year.

12. Billy Townsend, "History of the Georgia State Parks and Historic Sites Division," http://gastateparks.org/content/georgia/parks/75th_Anniv/parks_history.pdf. For a detailed look at Carver's conservation work, see Mark D. Hersey, *My Work Is That of Conservation: An Environmental Biography of George Washington Carver* (Athens: University of Georgia Press, 2011).

13. Ney C. Landrum, *The State Park Movement in America: A Critical Review* (Columbia: University of Missouri Press, 2004), 167.

14. Townsend, "History of the Georgia State Parks.".

15. Polly Claiborne to Charles Collier, April 13, 1962, Parks and Historic Sites, Georgia State Archives, Morrow; Townsend, "History of the Georgia State Parks."

16. Yam Grandy State Park expanded to eleven acres after six acres were granted to it by the city of Swainsboro in 1967. See Horace Caldwell to Asa D. Kelley, May 4, 1967, Parks and Historic Sites, Georgia State Archives, Morrow.

17. Townsend, "History of the Georgia State Parks."

18. "First Negro State Park to Be Opened in March," *Constitution State News Service*, February 22, 1952. The headline says "first," but it is apparent that George Washington Carver State Park was constructed earlier. See Townsend, "Histories of the Georgia State Parks."

19. Department of the State Parks, *Georgia's State Parks and Their Progress in the 1960–61 Fiscal Year*, December 1961, Georgiana Collection, Hargrett Rare Book & Manuscript Library, University of Georgia, Athens.

20. For a more detailed look at this park, see William E. O'Brien, "The Strange Career of a Florida State Park: Uncovering a Jim Crow Past," *Historical Geography* 35 (2007): 160–84.

21. J. L. Beardsley, "St. Andrews State Park Is on Peninsula," *Clearwater Sun*, April 19, 1959; Governor Collins—Radio, "State Parks," August 20, 1955, Series 1945, Florida State Archives, Tallahassee (hereafter cited as FSA); Emmet L. Hill to E. M. Lisle, April 8, 1954, Series 1943, FSA; Walter A. Coldwell, "Report to the Florida Board of Parks and Historic Memorials," October 6, 1952; Florida Board of Parks and Historic Memorials to Sidney S. Kennedy, May 27, 1954, Series 1943, FSA; memo to James Cook, November

10, 1955, Series 1353, FSA; R. S. Hager to H. E. Tooks, May 7, 1962, Series 1945, FSA.

22. A historical account of Florida's state parks counted 55 units in the system in 1963, with 42 of them operating and open to the public. Florida Department of Environmental Protection, "History of Florida's State Park System," www.floridastate parks.org (no longer available).

23. Elbert Cox to Lewis G. Scoggin, November 28, 1949, Series 1945, FSA; A. T. Edmunds and W. T. Ammerman to NPS Regional Director, "Analysis of Major Problems Involved in Setting Up Capital Improvement Programs for Florida State Parks" (attached to Cox to Scoggin letter), 7, Series 1945, FSA; Florida Department of Environmental Protection, Division of Recreation and Parks, *Big Talbot Island State Park and Little Talbot Island State Park Unit Management Plan*, June 1998, 92; "Funds Increased as Talbot Isle Added to Park System," *Florida Times-Union*, June 8, 1951.

24. Elizabeth Towers to Lewis Scoggin (n.d., December 1950), Series 1945, FSA.

25. Eileen Butts to Karl Bickel, July 10 1951, Series 1944, FSA.

26. Martin G. Williams to J. Kenneth Ballinger, June 22, 1951, Series 1944, FSA.

27. "Facilities and Use of Florida State Parks" (Table), July 1, 1950 to June 30, 1951, Series 1951, FSA.

28. "Little Talbot Island Park Opening Set Saturday," *Florida Times-Union*, August 31, 1951.

29. Walter A. Coldwell, "Report to the Florida Board of Parks and Historic Memorials," October 6, 1952, box 2198, folder L7019 Florida part 2, Entry P11, Administrative Files 1949–1971, RG 79, RNPS, NACP.

30. Stan Cohen, *Where People and Nature Meet: A History of West Virginia's State Parks* (Charleston, W.Va.: Pictorial Histories Publishing Co., 1988), 8–9; "History of West Virginia State Parks" in *Histories of Southeastern State Park Systems* (n.p.: Association of Southeastern State Park Directors, 1977), 177–205.

31. U.S. Department of the Interior, Heritage Conservation and Recreation Service, National Register of Historic Places Inventory—Nomination Form, West Virginia 4-H Camp for Negroes, Camp Washington-Carver, 1980, copy in West Virginia Archives and History, Charleston.

32. Geneva K. Valentine to West Virginia Conservation Commission Division of Parks, September 19, 1940, and response from Linn Wilson, September 23, 1940, Papers of the NAACP, Part 15, Series B, Reel 14, copy in Hargrett Rare Book and Manuscript Library, University of Georgia, Athens.

33. Kermit McKeever, "State Parks," *Annual Report*

1951–52, October 1952, 26, West Virginia Conservation Commission Annual Reports, West Virginia Archives & History Library, Charleston.

34. J. Howard Myers, ed., *West Virginia Blue Book 1949*, State of West Virginia, Charleston, 760; "Division of State Parks 1949–1950," *Annual Report of the Conservation Commission of West Virginia, July 1, 1949 to June 30, 1950*, 31–47; "State Parks," *Annual Report 1951–1952*, 28; "Park Named for Negro Educator," *Charleston Daily Mail*, August 5, 1949.

35. "State Parks," *Annual Report 1951–52*, 28.

36. Kermit McKeever, "History of West Virginia State Parks, 1934–1972," n.d., West Virginia Archives & History Library, Charleston; Cohen, *Where People and Nature Meet*. Booker T. Washington State Park was desegregated by 1955 and quickly faded into obscurity. By 1956 the Conservation Commission's annual reports no longer listed the park among its units.

37. "Conclusions and Recommendations," Kentucky Park, Parkway, and Recreational Study 1938, attached to Elbert Cox to Russell Dyche, August 22, 1946, Central Classified File 1933–1949, RG 79, RNPS, NACP.

38. As an alternative, it might seem that the most logical location for such a facility was at the former Otter Creek RDA, which added an organized group camp for African Americans in 1939. While most RDAs around the country were destined to become state parks, the Otter Creek property was instead deeded in 1947 to the city of Louisville to operate as a municipal (albeit rural) park. "Conferees Okay $112,000 Boost for Park Fund," *Middlesboro (Ky.) Daily News*, June 4, 1955.

39. Hugh Morris, "All-Negro State Park of 300 Acres Is Proposed," *Louisville Courier Journal*, May 11, 1946; Harry Bolser, "State Opens Negro Park in Lake Area," *Louisville Courier Journal*, May 31, 1951; "Kentucky Plans State Park—Strictly Jim Crow," *Chicago Defender*, May 18, 1946.

40. *In Kentucky: Abraham Lincoln Sesquicentennial Year*, n.d., vol. 21, Department of Public Relations, KY—Cherokee State Park file, Kentucky Department for Libraries and Archives, Frankfort, Ky.

41. Bolser, "State Opens Negro Park in Lake Area."

42. "Cherokee State Park," *In Kentucky* 17 (Summer 1953), 42, KY—Cherokee State Park file, Kentucky Department for Libraries and Archives.

43. Ibid.; Joe Creason, "A Honey of a Park for Negro Citizens," ibid.

44. Creason, "A Honey of a Park for Negro Citizens."

45. "Parks, Diversified," *Louisville Courier Journal*, April 27, 1952.

46. Bolser, "State Opens Negro Park in Lake Area."

47. Ibid.

48. Mississippi State Board of Park Supervisors, *Ninth Biennial Report*, 7.

49. Ibid.

50. Mississippi Park Commission, *Biennial Report of the Mississippi Park Commission for the Years July 1, 1955 through June 30, 1957*, 7, MDAH. The Mississippi Park Commission was created in 1956.

51. "Booker Park Pool Ready to Use Soon," *Chattanooga Times*, April 17, 1950.

52. "Thousands Expected at Ceremonies Today Dedicating Two State Parks." *Chattanooga Times*, July 2, 1950.

53. Harold Knox, "Shelby's State Park Growing to Meet Negroes' Need," *Memphis Press-Scimitar*, June 21, 1950.

54. Bevley Coleman, "A History of State Parks in Tennessee" (Ph.D. diss., George Peabody College for Teachers, 1963), 363; "Fuller Golf Course Officially Opened," *Memphis Commercial Appeal*, November 11, 1957.

55. "State Park for Negroes Being Planned," *Nashville Banner*, September 30, 1949.

56. Coleman, "A History of State Parks in Tennessee," 244.

57. Ibid., 247.

58. "Negro Park Damaged," *Chattanooga Times*, October 8, 1948.

59. W. M. Litchford to Glenn Nicely, January 29, 1953, in Coleman, "A History of State Parks in Tennessee," 249.

60. W. J. Faulkner to Sam Brewster, August 26, 1937, RG 79, RNPS, NACP; H. L. Hermann to C. S. Swan, June 30, 1949, Department of Conservation Papers, Tennessee State Library and Archives, Nashville (hereafter cited as TSLA).

61. State Planning Division and Division of State Parks, *Operation '66: A Proposed State Parks and Recreation Program for Tennessee* (Nashville: Tennessee State Planning Commission and the Tennessee Department of Conservation, 1956), Department of Conservation Papers, TSLA.

62. "State Considering Negro State Park," *Nashville Tennessean*, August 28, 1960.

63. J. Brents McBride to Governor Buford Ellington, August 22, 1960, Department of Conservation Papers, TSLA.

64. Ibid.

65. "State Considering Negro State Park," *Nashville Tennessean*, August 28, 1960.

66. McBride to Ellington, September 2, 1960, Department of Conservation Papers, TSLA.

67. Coleman, "A History of Tennessee State Parks," 252.

68. James Segrest to Ben Morgan, November 28, 1945, Department of Conservation files, Alabama Department of Archives and History, Montgomery (ADAH).

69. M. R. Tillotson to Walter B. Jones, May 1, 1940, 6, RG 79, RNPS, NACP.

70. C. A. Gaston to Ben Morgan, August 5, 1946, Department of Conservation files, ADAH.

71. For a thorough historical account of this project, see Robert G. Pasquill Jr., *Planting Hope on Worn-Out Land: The History of the Tuskegee Land Utilization Project, Macon County, Alabama, 1935–1959* (Montgomery, Ala.: New South Books, 2009).

72. Ibid., 54.

73. Ibid., 75–76.

74. Segrest to Morgan, November 28, 1945.

75. Ibid.

76. "Slate State Park for Race in Alabama," *Chicago Defender*, March 31, 1951.

77. Allen T. Edmunds to Region I Director, July 2, 1953, Administrative Files 1949–1971, RG 79, RNPS, NACP.

78. Earl M. McGowin to Senator Joe S. Foster, Rep. R. L. Eslick, and Rep. N. L. Reynolds, May 29, 1951, Department of Conservation files, ADAH.

79. James L. Segrest to Earl M. McGowin, October 23, 1951, Department of Conservation files, ADAH.

80. "State Is Taking 2,200 TVA Acres," *Dothan Eagle*, October 20, 1949.

81. "Joe Wheeler Park Is Located in Heart of Tennessee Valley," *Birmingham News*, April 16, 1950. The TVA's Wheeler site is described in detail in *The Wheeler Project: A Comprehensive Report on the Planning, Design, Construction, and Initial Operations of the Wheeler Project*, Technical Report no. 2 (Washington, D.C.: GPO, 1940).

82. "Alabama Park Facilities: Joe Wheeler Park," *Alabama Conservation* 30 (June–July 1958): 6.

83. "State Is Taking 2,200 TVA Acres."

84. C. H. Jackson, member of the Conservation Advisory Board, quoted in James L. Segrest to Earl M. McGowin, August 20, 1952, Department of Conservation files, ADAH.

85. Ibid.

86. Ibid.

87. Alabama Department of Conservation, "Report for the Fiscal Year October 1, 1952–September 30, 1953," 151, Department of Conservation files, ADAH.

88. Stephen Lewis Cox, "The History of Negro State Parks in South Carolina: 1940–1963" (master's thesis, University of South Carolina, 1992).

89. C. H. Flory to James H. Hammond, November 6, 1948, State Forestry Commission Papers, South Carolina Department of Archives and History, Columbia (hereafter cited as SCDAH). At Clarks Hill Lake, the Forestry Commission had planned to construct a relatively high quality 1,183-acre state park for African Americans at Hickory Knob, but the legislature declined to allocate funds. The site was developed as a state park after the end of segregation. As Stephen Cox remarked, "Hickory Knob, originally planned as the premier Negro state Park in the state, is today the 'flagship' of the South Carolina State Park System and the state's only resort park." Cox, "The History of Negro State Parks in South Carolina," 28.

90. C. West Jacocks to Adele Minihan, August 25, 1952, SRC Papers, Auburn Avenue Research Library on African American Culture and History, Atlanta.

91. Adele Minihan to George S. Mitchell, August 25, 1952, ibid.

92. C. H. Schaeffer to Senator J. H. Hammond, July 22, 1948, State Forestry Commission Papers, SCDAH.

93. Ibid.

94. Cox, "The History of Negro State Parks in South Carolina," 26.

95. C. H. Flory to C. H. Schaeffer, July 16, 1948, State Forestry Commission Papers, SCDAH.

96. C. West Jacocks to Files, September 21, 1949, ibid.

97. Jacocks to Files, September 21, 1949; A. Schellenberg to C. West Jacocks, September 1, 1949, ibid.

98. G. G. Blackmon to the South Carolina State Commission on Forestry, August 15, 1947, ibid.

99. C. H. Flory to John L. Hawkins, October 22, 1947, ibid.

100. Petition attached to Ray R. Williams to C. H. Flory, November 13, 1947, ibid.

101. C. H. Flory to Senator Ray R. Williams, November 17, 1947, ibid.

102. P. R. Plumer to C. H. Flory, May 13, 1948, ibid.

103. Ibid.

104. C. H. Flory to P. R. Plumer and T. D. Ravenel, June 17, 1948, ibid.

105. Editorial from Greenville newspaper (date and source unknown), ibid.

106. G. M. Hubbard to the South Carolina Park Commission, July 10, 1948, ibid.

107. Ibid.

108. C. H. Flory to P. R. Plumer, June 30, 1948, ibid.

109. C. H. Flory to Files, August 2, 1948, ibid.

110. Ibid.

111. Schaeffer to C. H. Flory, August 4, 1948, ibid.

112. A. Schellenberg to Files, October 3, 1949, SCDAH.

113. Ibid.

114. Cox, "The History of Negro State Parks in South Carolina," 53.

115. Chad Prosser, *Beautiful Places: The Timeless Beauty of South Carolina State Parks* (Columbia: State Department of Parks Recreation and Tourism, 2009), 17.

116. Cox, "The History of Negro State Parks in South Carolina," 53.

117. Ibid., 55, 57.

118. Walter T. Ahearn to Kenneth R. Huff, December 11, 1962, and "Huntington Beach State Park Negro Area" (from a report, n.d.), 33, both State Forestry Commission Papers, SCDAH.

5. Going to Court

1. Gilbert Jonas, *Freedom's Sword: The NAACP and the Struggle against Racism in America, 1909–1969* (New York: Routledge, 2005), 45. Originating in the NAACP's legal department, which was led by Charles Houston during the 1930s, the Legal Defense and Educational Fund, as it is formally called, was created as legally separate entity in 1940 under the leadership of Thurgood Marshall.

2. Michael J. Klarman, *From Jim Crow to Civil Rights: The Supreme Court and the Struggle for Racial Equality* (New York: Oxford University Press, 2004), 173; Jonas, *Freedom's Sword*, chap. 2.

3. "A Court Rules That Parks Are for All," *New South* 10 (April 1955): 1. The Southern Regional Council was formed in 1944 by white and Black educators, journalists, and religious leaders as a moderate voice for southern reform. Prior to its 1951 decision to promote desegregation, the SRC was "the most traditional of mainstream liberal organizations. It sought to improve race relations within a segregated society." Numan V. Bartley, *The New South, 1945–1980: The Story of the South's Modernization* (Baton Rouge: Louisiana State University Press and the Littlefield Fund for Southern History, 1995), 30.

4. "A Court Rules That Parks Are for All."

5. "Negro Enters Suit to Force Park Equities," *Richmond Times-Dispatch*, July 10, 1948.

6. The department's "Fiscal and Operational Report to the Association of Southeastern State Park Directors for 1957–59" listed Prince Edward as the only state park area for African Americans in the commonwealth. *Proceedings of the 17th Annual Meeting of the Association of Southeastern State Park Directors*, Montgomery Bell State Park, Burns, Tenn., November 3–6, 1958, RG 79, RNPS, NACP.

7. "Section in Pocahontas Held Deplorable," *Richmond News Leader*, September 14, 1960.

8. "Va. State Park Near Farmville," *Atlanta Daily World*, January 30, 1949. A memo to Governor W. M. Tuck, which outlined the Virginia Conservation Department activities in fall 1947, did not mention the possible construction of African American state park facilities. This omission suggests that the 1948 lawsuit was the main motivator in creating Prince Edward State Park. W. A. Wright to W. M. Tuck, September 23, 1947, Governor Tuck Papers, Library of Virginia, Richmond.

9. Marian Wynn Perry to Moses White and Dorothy Goodwin, March 9, 1948, Legal File, Discrimination, box II-B63, Papers of the NAACP, Library of Congress, Washington, D.C. (hereafter cited as NAACP Papers).

10. "Oklahoma Negro Resort Area First of Its Kind," *Resourceful Oklahoma* 3 (November 1952): 7.

11. Ibid.; "The Lookout," *Indian Journal* (Eufaula, Okla.), November 20, 1952.

12. "Oklahoma Negro Resort Area First of Its Kind."

13. "State Parks, Muskogee, Okla.," January 1953, Discrimination: Parks and Playgrounds 1952–55, box 238, NAACP Papers.

14. "NAACP Polling State Officials on State Lodge," *Ada Evening News*, May 28, 1954; "State Parks, Muskogee, Okla.," January 1953, NAACP Papers.

15. "Lodge at Tenkiller Reservoir Studied," *Ada Evening News*, November 15, 1956; "Board Shelves Tenkiller Deal," *Miami Daily News-Record*, November 21, 1958.

16. Texas State Parks Board, *Guide to State Parks of Texas*, July 1947, box 1991/50-17, Attorney General Litigation File, Texas State Library and Archives, Austin (hereafter cited as AGLF, TSLA).

17. The ban on discrimination against Latin Americans in parks was an outcome of a "good neighbor" policy, initiated in 1943 by Texas governor Coke Stevenson and the Texas Legislature, which was designed to improve relations between Texas and Mexico.

18. T. R. Register to Gordon K. Shearer, April 19, 1949, box 1991/50-17, AGLF, TSLA.

19. Dee Frederick, "'Impossible' to Admit Negroes, Says Texas Park Official; Suit Expected," *Chicago Defender*, May 28, 1949; Gordon K. Shearer to T. R. Register, April 22, 1949, box 1991/50-17, AGLF, TSLA.

20. Shearer to Register, April 22, 1949.

21. U. Simpson Tate to Gordon Shearer, May 11, 1949, AGLF, TSLA.

22. Thurgood Marshall to U. Simpson Tate, June 10, 1949, Legal File: Discrimination, box II-B63, NAACP Papers.

23. William L. McGill to Governor Shivers, November or December 1949, box 1977/81-305, Shivers Papers, TSLA.

24. Although African Americans were officially excluded from all parks, in preparing its defense, the Parks Board found that a number of state park managers were allowing African American access on an ad hoc basis. Board executive director Gordon Shearer had mailed an informal survey that asked two questions of each of the system's managers: Have any Negroes ever requested admission to your park? And if so, what was the response from park staff? The replies revealed an inconsistent application of the official exclusion policy. A few individual managers were even allowing

open access to all facilities, including toilets. At Monument Hill State Park near La Grange, manager V. H. Sladczyk responded, "This park has had Negroes asking to visit the park and were admitted. In no instance have I questioned them as to their right to enter, nor have I discriminated against them in any manner whatsoever . . . ; they have had all the privileges which are granted to others." V. H. Sladczyk to Gordon K. Shearer, 22 June, 1950, box 1991/50-17, AGLF, TSLA. Ethel Harris, manager of San Jose Mission in San Antonio, responded similarly: "We have here no policy, practice or tradition which would allow any one to show discrimination to any one. We have one set of toilet facilities and never to my knowledge has there been any incident which would embarrass a Negro visitor to San Jose Mission." Ethel W. Harris to Gordon Shearer, 24 April, 1950, box 1991/50-17, AGLF, TSLA. Likewise, John L. McCarty, manager of Palo Duro Canyon State Park near Amarillo, said that no one was turned away from entering the park and that they received from two to five carloads of Negroes per week. He stated, "We have handled them just as we would any other group of people, letting them pay their admission charges and selling them souvenirs, sandwiches and drinks at our concession stands." John L. McCarty to Gordon K. Shearer, 21 June 1950, box 1991/50-17, AGLF, TSLA. The survey and responses from the park managers are also discussed by Sharon Morris Toney, "The Texas State Parks System: An Administrative History, 1923–1984" (Ph.D. diss., Texas Tech University, 1995), 118–20.

25. William L. McGill to Governor Shivers, December 30, 1949, box 1977/81-305, Shivers Papers, TSLA.

26. Resolution, State Parks Board—State of Texas. Minutes of the Meeting of the Texas State Parks Board, January 21, 1950, box 1991/50-17, AGLF, TSLA, TSLA.

27. "Negro Suit for Park Use," *Dallas Morning News*, January 1950, Shivers Papers, TSLA.

28. "Negro Parks Fund Request Gets No Hope," *Dallas Morning News*, January 26, 1951.

29. Notes from legislative testimony, Texas Parks Board Executive Secretary Sandefer, April 5, 1951, box 1988/81-427, Shivers Papers, TSLA.

30. Ibid.

31. Ibid.

32. Senate Committee Recommendation, Texas Legislature, February 8, 1951, box 1977/81-427, Shivers Papers, TSLA.

33. "State Park Opens for the Season, Manager Reports," *Tyler Courier-Times-Telegraph*, July 8, 1951; "Court Ruling May Soon Open State Parks to All Citizens," *Longview News*, November 9, 1955.

34. Ben H. Rice Jr., *Register v. Sandefer*, Civil Action 492, U.S. District Court Western District of Texas, Austin Division, January 28, 1960; The plaintiffs had agreed to the dismissal of the case during the previous year, after the death of Mr. Register. W. J. Durham to Honorable Joe Steiner, April 16, 1959, box 1991/50-17, AGLF, TSLA, TSLA.

35. Frank D. Quinn to Senator Ottis E. Lock, April 10, 1951, box 1977/81-427, Shivers Papers, TSLA.

36. Quinn to Lock, April 10, 1951. Similar letters were mailed to other senators.

37. Walter F. Murphy, *Congress and the Court, Chicago, 1962* (University of Chicago Press, 1962), 104.

38. Seashore State Park, the site of the first landing of English colonists in the Americas, was renamed First Landing State Park in 1997.

39. "Governor Spurns Bid to Explain Jim Crow Stand," *Chicago Defender*, September 8, 1951. His views were expressed originally in John S. Battle to M. E. Diggs, August 20, 1951, Governor John S. Battle Papers, Library of Virginia.

40. "Won't Drop Suit to End Segregation," *Chicago Defender*, August 25, 1951; Raymond V. Long to J. Lindsay Almond Jr., December 31, 1954, Department of Conservation Papers, Library of Virginia.

41. Plaintiffs in the case included Milton Lonesome, Marion Downes, Karleen Downes, Alvin Graham, Beatrice Martin, Bowen Jackson, Christine Jackson, and Lily Mae Jackson. The defendants, including R. Brooke Maxwell, were state officials with the Maryland Forest and Parks Commission. "U.S. Appeals Court Ends State, City, Beach Segregation," *Afro-American*, March 26, 1955.

42. "Federal Court Bans Bias on Maryland Beach," *Atlanta Daily World*, June 9, 1953.

43. Walter White to Harry S. Truman, July 11, 1952, Discrimination: Parks and Playgrounds 1952–55, box 238, NAACP Papers.

44. In 1949 Judge Chestnut had also ruled to uphold segregation in *Boyer v. Garrett*, stating that public park segregation in Maryland was allowed as long as substantially equal facilities were available. See "Opinion on Defendants' Motion to Dismiss," Judge Calvin Chestnut, *Boyer v. Garrett*, December 30, 1949, Civil Action 4152, U.S. District Court, Maryland. That decision was upheld on appeal in the following year. In 1950 *Beal v. Holcombe*, filed in district court in Houston, Texas, was also decided in favor of the defendants. The plaintiffs had claimed a constitutional violation since the City of Houston offered seventeen parks for whites but only four for African Americans. Furthermore the arrangement included three municipal golf courses in the public parks for whites but none in any of the African

American parks. Citing *Plessy* and subsequent rulings as precedent, Judge T. M. Kennerly ruled in favor of the city in December 1950, despite the significant disparity. He argued that while they lacked golf courses, the four parks available to African Americans contained "substantially the same facilities and equipment of the seventeen Parks used exclusively by white people." Judge Kennerly also reasoned that the plaintiffs' focus on the denial of golfing as an activity was "not meritorious" since all the city's parks excluded a whole range of possible games. Like the white parks, he asserted that the African American parks did contain facilities for various games (e.g., tennis, baseball, and playgrounds), suggesting to him that "it does appear that the City with wholesome care has provided for the present day activities of both races." Findings of Fact and Conclusions of Law, Judge T. M. Kennerly, *Beal v. Holcombe*, Civil Action 5407, U.S. District Court, Southern District of Texas, Houston Division, December 4, 1950.

45. James O. Eastland, *The Supreme Court, Segregation, and the South, Speech of Hon. James O. Eastland of Mississippi in the Senate of the United States, Thursday, May 27, 1954* (Washington, D.C.: GPO, 1954), 15, 3.

46. Ibid., 3.

47. Frederick Sullens, *Jackson Daily News*, May 23, 1954, quoted in Eastland, *The Supreme Court, Segregation, and the South*, 5.

48. "Now It's the South's Move," *Richmond News-Leader*, June 1, 1955.

49. Bettye Collier-Thomas and V. P. Franklin, *My Soul Is a Witness: A Chronology of the Civil Rights Era, 1954–1965* (New York: Henry Holt, 1999), 48.

50. Minutes of the Thirteenth Annual Meeting of the Association of Southeastern State Park Directors, 12. Directors Subject File, Georgia State Archives, Morrow.

51. Ibid.

52. Raymond V. Long to Governor Thomas B. Stanley, January 20, 1955, Department of Conservation Papers, Library of Virginia.

53. "Bill for Segregated Va. Parks Introduced," *Chicago Defender*, February 16, 1952.

54. "Virginia Gov. Wants to Stick to Bias Policy," *Atlanta Daily World*, March 22, 1955; "Judge Forbids Virginia to Lease Parks," *Chicago Defender*, March 26, 1955.

55. Fourth Circuit Court of Appeals ruling, cited in "A Court Rules That Parks Are for All," *New South* 10 (April 1955): 1.

56. "Judge Refuses Decision in Virginia Park Issue," *Atlanta Daily World*, May 4, 1955.

57. "Jim Crow Parks in Va. Outlawed," *Chicago Defender*, July 16, 1955.

58. Mary Lou Werner, "Virginia Loses Move to Segregate Parks," *Wilmington Journal*, October 9, 1956.

59. Lewis J. Roop to Governor Thomas B. Stanley, March 18, 1955, Department of Conservation Papers, Library of Virginia.

60. "May Demand Court to Open S.C. Beaches," *Chicago Defender*, December 13, 1952.

61. Cooler noted that the letters were identical but did not know who organized the effort. The letters all requested use of the park specifically at 11:30 a.m. on May 25, 1955. Stephen Lewis Cox, "The History of Negro State Parks in South Carolina: 1940–1963" (master's thesis, University of South Carolina, 1992), 64.

62. Donald B. Cooler to Charles Mason, May 21, 1955, State Parks Desegregation Files, South Carolina Department of Archives & History, Columbia (hereafter cited as SCDAH).

63. "File Suit to End Bias in S.C. Parks," *Chicago Defender*, August 6. 1955.

64. "Some Parks Would Revert if Integrated," *The State* (Columbia, S.C.), August 6, 1955.

65. W. D. Workman Jr., "S.C. May Eliminate State Parks as Result of Negro Court Action," *Charleston News and Courier*, July 26, 1955.

66. "Suit of Destruction," *The State* (Columbia, S.C.), August 6, 1955.

67. "Judge Quotes Frank Graham in Urging Negroes to Go Slowly on Integration," *Greenville News*, August 24, 1955.

68. Francis B. Taylor, "Edisto Park Case Referred to S.C. Courts," *Greenville News*, August 23, 1955.

69. "Judge Quotes Frank Graham in Urging Negroes to Go Slowly on Integration," *Greenville News*, August 24, 1955.

70. "Dixie Fumes Over New Supreme Court Ruling," *Chicago Defender*, November 19, 1955.

71. "Segregation Ban in Parks Decried," *New York Times*, November 9, 1955.

72. "Georgia Leasing Its State Parks," *New York Times*, April 22, 1956; "State Parks Being Leased," *Sumter (S.C.) Daily Item*, April 19, 1956.

73. "Dixie Fumes Over New Supreme Court Ruling."

74. Ibid.

75. Ibid.

76. "End Negro Park Curb," *New York Herald-Tribune*, May 26, 1954; "Public-Owned Negro Park in Charleston Opened to Whites," *Chicago Defender*, June 12, 1954.

77. Enoc P. Waters Jr., "Dilemma in the South: Kentucky Integration Pace," *Chicago Daily Defender*, March 25, 1959.

78. "Threatened Suit Opens Okla. Parks to Negroes," *Jet*, January 10, 1957, 10.

79. "Court Ruling May Soon Open State Parks to All Citizens," *Longview News*, November 9, 1955.

80. "Texas Park and Recreation Facilities Soon Open to

All," *Sweetwater News*, November 10, 1955. On November 8, 1955, the *Big Spring Herald* carried the headline "Texas Parks May Soon Open to All," while the *Marshall News-Messenger* read, "Ruling May Open Texas Parks to All."

81. Richard Morehead, "Negroes Ask Right to Use State Parks," *Dallas Morning News*, February 4, 1956.

82. "Parks Board Asks Report on Tourist Lodges," *Austin Statesman*, February 21, 1956; "Board Denies Plans for Hotels to be 'Put on Ice,'" *Houston Post*, February 21, 1956.

83. "Integration in Texas Schools Swift in Many Parts of State," *Corpus Christi Caller-Times*, March 1, 1956.

84. "Dixie Fumes Over New Supreme Court Ruling."

85. Cox, "The History of Negro State Parks in South Carolina,"70.

86. "Edisto Beach State Park, Complaint Filed in U.S. District Court," OB-3, State Parks Desegregation Files, SCDAH.

87. Cox, "The History of Negro State Parks in South Carolina," 75.

88. Ibid., 71; "Text of Order in Edisto Case," *Charleston News and Courier*, April 20, 1956.

89. "Racial Issue Won't Block 'The Breaks' Park Opening," *Richmond News-Leader*, July 21, 1955.

90. "Enjoying Nature Is One Thing," *Richmond News-Leader*, July 21, 1955.

91. T. D. Ravenel to C. West Jacocks, August 11, 1956, State Parks Desegregation Files, SCDAH.

92. Chas. H. Flory to All Park Superintendents, June 14, 1956, State Parks Desegregation Files, SCDAH.

93. "Ga. Park Denies Pakistanian on Race Fear Plea," *Atlanta Daily World*, August 13, 1960.

94. "'No Reaction' to Park Integration," *Kingsport Times*, December 8, 1955.

95. Michael J. Klarman, *From Jim Crow to Civil Rights: The Supreme Court and the Struggle for Racial Equality* (New York: Oxford University Press, 2004), 321.

96. Organized sit-ins at lunch counters in the South had actually begun in the 1950s, although the Greensboro effort was considered to have the greatest inspirational impact on the movement. See Jonas, *Freedom's Sword*, 173–74.

97. The Congress of Racial Equality (CORE), another influential civil rights organization, had been created in 1942 and was the main organizing force behind the Freedom Rides.

98. Steve Valocchi, "The Emergence of the Integrationist Ideology in the Civil Rights Movement," *Social Problems* 43 (February 1996): 116–30.

99. The Secretary to NAACP Branch and Youth Officers in Southern States, May 13, 1960, Discrimination: Parks and Playgrounds 1956–65, box A110, NAACP

Papers. The title "executive secretary" was changed in 1964 to "executive director."

100. "Racial Clash Is Averted at Federal Park in Mississippi," *Lake Charles American Press*, July 5, 1960.

101. "Negro Youths Taunt White Swimmers," *Hutchinson News*, July 5, 1960.

102. "State Park Is Closed," *News Tribune*, July 14, 1960.

103. "Park Board Meets Aug. 15 on Reopening Tomoka," *Florida Times-Union* (Jacksonville), July 28, 1960.

104. "State Park Is Closed," *News Tribune*, 14 July 1960.

105. The girls were Addie Mae Collins, Denise McNair, Carole Robertson, and Cynthia Wesley.

106. The activists were James Chaney, Andrew Goodman, and Michael Schwerner.

107. M. M. Sutherland to Eugene G. Wyatt Jr., November 14, 1960, Governor Lindsay Almond Papers, Library of Virginia, Richmond; "Truth and Seashore State Park," *Ledger-Star* (Norfolk), August 19, 1963.

108. "Close Park 7 Years to Bar Negroes; Finally Give Up," *Chicago Defender*, August 20, 1962.

109. Robert L. Hueston to Governor Albertis S. Harrison Jr., July 27, 1962, Governor A. Harrison Papers, Library of Virginia.

110. Margaret Hales to Governor Albertis S. Harrison, July 25, 1962, Harrison Papers.

111. "Truth and Seashore State Park."

112. "Seashore State Park to Host 18,700 Campers in 1963," Bureau of Business Research, Old Dominion College, October 1963, Harrison Papers.

113. "NAACP Attacks Segregated Parks in South Carolina," *Chicago Daily Defender*, July 26, 1961. The suit was filed on June 15, 1961.

114. Opinion and Order, *Brown v. South Carolina State Forestry Commission*, Civil Action AC-774, U.S. District Court for the Eastern District of South Carolina, Columbia Division, July 10, 1963.

115. Justice Arthur Goldberg quoted ibid.

116. Daniel R. McLeod to Fulton B. Creech, August 19, 1963, State Forestry Commission Desegregation Files, SCDAH.

117. "S. Carolina May Order All State Parks Closed," *Chicago Daily Defender*, July 22, 1963.

118. "News Release 12 – 1963–64," S.C. State Commission of Forestry, August 20, 1963, State Forestry Commission Desegregation Files, SCDAH.

119. Richard G. Coker to Governor Donald Russell, July 19, 1963, State Forestry Commission Desegregation Files, SCDAH.

120. Chad Prosser, *Beautiful Places: The Timeless Beauty of South Carolina State Parks* (Columbia: State Department of Parks, Recreation, and Tourism, 2009), 18.

121. "County Citizens Are Against Integrated SC State Parks," *Williston Way*, September 12, 1963.

122. Paul B. Kohlbaugh to Arrants Committee, July 19, 1963, "The Arrants Legislative Committee on Parks," State Forestry Commission State Parks File, SCDAH.

123. Joe Garrett, Bentley Hines, and M. B. Tolbert to Arrants Committee, ibid., 10, 12.

124. "Reopening of State Parks Gets Almost Complete OK," *The State* (Columbia, S.C.), October 2, 1963.

125. "Majority Want Parks Reopened," ibid.

126. Cox, "The History of Negro State Parks in South Carolina," 106. Additional restrictions were applied at two parks: family camping remained restricted at Myrtle Beach State Park, and at Santee State Park any activity other than fishing and nature trail use was prohibited. See State Forestry Commission, "State Parks: Summary," n.d., 4, State Parks Desegregation Files, SCDAH; "Restricted Parks Are Peaceful But Poor," *Charlotte Observer*, 9 July 1964.

127. Oliver W. Holmes to Ben W. Fortson Jr., October 19, 1962, and Julius C. Hope to Ben W. Fortson, July 24, 1962, both Georgia Archives, Morrow.

128. Georgia Council on Human Relations, Statement to the Jekyll Island State Park Authority Annual Meeting, March 11, 1963, Georgia Archives.

129. Charles Moore, "Integrate Jekyll, Group Here Urges," unidentified newspaper clipping, Georgia Archives.

130. Redden W. Adams to Ben Fortson Jr., March 12, 1963, and Ben W. Fortson Jr. to Redden W. Adams, March 22, 1963, both Georgia Archives.

131. "Suit Seeks End of Jekyll Island Bias," *Atlanta Daily World*, September 25, 1963.

132. "Georgia Island Told to Lift Color Bars," *New York Times*, July 28, 1964.

133. "Desegregate Ga. State Park," *Chicago Daily Defender*, June 1, 1965. While the state park desegregation process was itself reportedly nonviolent, the *New York Times* reported a clash between Black and white visitors in June 1966 at Georgia Veterans State Park, where two people were injured ("Negroes and Whites Clash at State Park in Georgia," June 27, 1966). A week later, the paper reported that a group of about one hundred Black and white visitors arrived at the park and found "the desegregated swimming pool mysteriously drained" ("Integrated Pool in Georgia Found Mysteriously Drained," July 4, 1966).

134. The historic Penn Center, home of one of the first schools for freed slaves in the United States, is located on St. Helena Island.

135. Penn Community Service, Inc., *Public Parks and Recreational Facilities: A Study in Transition* (Frogmore, S.C.: 1963), 3, State Forestry Commission Desegregation Files, box 2, folder, Park Study Data, SCDAH.

136. Ibid.

137. "Brief of Superintendents Remarks of Non-segregated Park Use—1964–65 Season," December 7, 1964, 3, State Forestry Commission, Desegregation State Parks, box 2, folder State Park Operation Data for Study Comm., SCDAH; Coleman, *A History of State Parks in Tennessee*, 252.

138. Coleman, *A History of State Parks in Tennessee*, 252.

139. Penn Community Service, *Public Parks and Recreational Facilities*, 4.

140. "Brief of Superintendents Remarks of Non-segregated Park Use—1964–65 Season," 3. Virginia declared that its parks had been desegregated, although the cabins and swimming facilities at Seashore State Park remained closed to all visitors. This superintendents' report, while focused on South Carolina parks, also included observations from park staff in some other states of the South, including Virginia, that fears of violence were unfounded. With twenty-three units in South Carolina responding, none reported any violent incidents.

141. "Now Integrated: Fla. State Park Board Asked to Air New Rules," *Pittsburgh Courier*, October 3, 1964, 11.

142. Ibid.

143. *NAACP v. Florida Bd. of Parks*, Civil Action 551, U.S. District Court for the Northern District of Florida, Tallahassee Division, 1, November 1964, copy in NAACP III 1956–65, box J8, NAACP Papers.

144. Ibid.

145. "Florida Parks Desegregate," *Pittsburgh Courier*, April 7, 1964, 18.

146. "Mississippi's Parks Offer Recreation," *Laurel Leader-Call*, April 25, 1967.

147. Alabama Department of Conservation, *Alabama State Parks*, brochure, 1964, Department of Conservation files, Alabama Department of Archives and History, Montgomery; Donna Harden, "Joe Wheeler State Park for the Colored," *Heritage of Lauderdale County, Alabama* (Canton, Ala.: Heritage Publishing Consultants, 1999), 69. Harden recollects: "In the year 1965 during the movement of Civil Rights, the park's name was changed to Joe Wheeler State Park. The park was open to all shades of people."

148. Louisiana Department of Culture, Recreation & Tourism, Office of State Parks, "The History of Louisiana's State Parks," 2009, no longer available online.

149. "Brief of Superintendents Remarks of Non-segregated Park Use."

150. Cox, "The History of Negro State Parks in South Carolina," 108.

151. Unsigned letter to Commander Berry D. Willis Jr., June 29, 1965, Harrison Papers, Virginia Archives.

152. Berry D. Willis Jr. to Governor Albertis S. Harrison Jr., June 24, 1965, Harrison Papers.

153. "Virginia News in Brief," *Register* (Danville), August

23, 1966. The article specifically refers to the cabins, but the swimming areas were probably also opened about this time.

6. What's Become of the Parks?

1. Marcia Constantino, "Jones Lake State Park," *Wildlife in North Carolina* (August 1977): 10–11.
2. Florida Department of Environmental Protection, Division of Recreation and Parks, *Big Talbot Island State Park and Little Talbot Island State Park Unit Management Plan*, Tallahassee, June 1998, and *Amelia Island State Park, Big Talbot Island State Park, Little Talbot Island State Park, George Crady Bridge Fishing Pier State Park Unit Management Plan*, June 2008.
3. *Histories of Southeastern State Park Systems* (n.p.: Association of Southeastern State Park Directors, 1977). Of the thirteen entries in this volume, only South Carolina's and Georgia's refer in passing to this segregated past (in the case of South Carolina, the racial history would be difficult to avoid since the state had closed the entire park system for the better part of a year to avoid court-ordered integration). The Mississippi entry mentions the name Carver Point but provides no information about the park; Kermit McKeever, "History of West Virginia State Parks 1934–1972," unpublished manuscript, n.d., West Virginia Archives & History Library, Charleston; Stan Cohen, *Where People and Nature Meet: A History of the West Virginia State Parks* (Charleston, W.Va.: Pictorial History Publishing Co., 1988); Clara Wootton, *The History of the Kentucky State Parks* (n.p.: Bluegrass Press, 1975); J. M. Wells, *Kentucky Parks* (Nashville, Tenn.: Benson Printing Company, 1966).
4. All description of interpretation at the parks is based on observations during site visits in 2012 and 2013.
5. Prentice Palmer, "State Relinquishes 13 Parks," *Atlanta Constitution*, May 27, 1976.
6. Claudia Townsend, "More State Confederate Sites Will Lose Funds," *Atlanta Constitution*, August 14, 1975. The list of about two dozen closures included the aforementioned Yam Grandy State Park and some sites commemorating the Confederacy, including Jefferson Davis State Park. This number of closed African American state parks does not count the two former dual-use sites, Georgia Veterans State Park and Fort Yargo State Park. There, the former African American park areas were absorbed into the larger park, as was the case at nearly all of the former dual-use sites in the South.
7. "Wildwood Empty, But Wait," *Augusta Chronicle*, April 11, 1975. In 2004 the site received a major upgrade to its camping and boating facilities, making it arguably the best developed of any of the former African American parks in the South. The site also houses the international headquarters of the Professional Disc Golf Association (PDGA).
8. Lynne Lucas, "Cabin Fever?," *Greenville News*, February 6, 1989.
9. Two exceptions in the dual-use category are the former Fort Pickens State Park, now a National Park Service site, and Roman Nose State Park, which closed its picnic area for African Americans in 1951.
10. Annual reports at the end of the 1960s documented the continuing lag in attendance at Carver Point relative to other Mississippi parks. In 1968–69, the park attracted only 423 visitors, while nearby Hugh White State Park, once for whites only, attracted 6,131 visitors. The report pointed to that park's "abundance of recreational facilities" that "dazzle the Park's guests." Mississippi Park System, *Annual Report July 1, 1968– June 20, 1969*, 5, State Documents collection, Mississippi Department of Archives and History, Jackson. By 2011 the state had leased the Carver Point site to a private operator, who rents the grounds for family reunions and other events.
11. Interpretative display at the Twin Lakes State Park store, 2012.
12. Perhaps the most dramatic transformation of a dual-use site is at the former African American section of Alabama's Joe Wheeler State Park. The segregated space was isolated from the park's main area on the south shore of Wheeler Lake. During the 1970s, however, the remote location was transformed by new development. A surge in state spending led to the construction of "superparks" in Alabama, expanding the dimensions and range of recreational amenities at particular sites, including Wheeler. With the construction of a lodge, golf course, boat launch, and later a camping area, most activity moved to previously undeveloped park land on the north side of the lake. The former entry road to the African American section became the main park entrance, and the former caretaker's residence for that area became the park office (which has since moved into the lodge). Visible remnants of the "Negro Recreational Area" today include an unmarked and unpaved boat launch area and the caretaker's cabin, today called "Fisherman's Cabin." The former TVA "Wheeler Village" area of the park on the south shore of the lake remains open for cabin rentals.
13. Tennessee Department of Environment and Conservation brochure (2005) available at Booker T. Washington State Park.
14. Oklahoma State Parks pamphlet for the "Auto-Walking Tour of Lake Murray State Park's Historic Structures," n.d.

15. In another example, Butler Park, a county facility near St. Augustine, Florida, has made available an audio tour of the beachfront site. The account emphasizes its origin as part of the Black community known as Butler Beach, but makes no mention of its existence in the Florida park system as Frank B. Butler State Park starting in 1959. Because of this omission, I have not included it among the sites that interpret their former status as segregated state parks.

16. Cherokee State Park is also listed as an African American Heritage Site by the Kentucky Heritage Council.

17. Owen J. Dwyer and Derek H. Alderman, *Civil Rights Memorials and the Geography of Memory* (Chicago: Center for American Places at Columbia College Chicago, dist. by University of Georgia Press, 2008).

18. Kenneth E. Foote, *Shadowed Ground: America's Landscapes of Violence and Tragedy*, rev. ed. (Austin: University of Texas Press, 2003).

19. Dwyer and Alderman make this point specifically in the context of civil rights commemoration in their *Civil Rights Memorials and the Geography of Memory*, 12–15.

20. Office of Governor Jeb Bush, "Bill Baggs Cape Florida State Park Honored as Network to Freedom Site," *MyFlorida.com*, February 22, 2005, no longer available.

21. Robert R. Weyeneth, "The Architecture of Racial Segregation: The Challenges of Preserving a Problematical Past," *Public Historian* 27 (Fall 2005): 42–43.

22. Florida Department of Environmental Protection, Division of Recreation and Parks, *Tomoka Basin State Parks Unit Management Plan*, August 2012, 141; Florida Department of Environmental Protection, Division of Recreation and Parks, *Florida Caverns State Park Unit Management Plan*, June 2006, 25.

23. Frederick D. Patterson, "The Negro Wants Full Participation in American Democracy," in *What the Negro Wants*, ed. Rayford W. Logan (1944; repr., Notre Dame, Ind.: University of Notre Dame Press, 2001), 259. Patterson was also cofounder of the United Negro College Fund, established in 1944.

24. At the same time, Carolyn Finney points out that African American perceptions of "relaxing" outdoor experience had long been complicated by experience both in slavery and under Jim Crow, which had shaped a legacy of wilderness perception in both positive and negative terms. See Finney, *Black Faces, White Spaces: Reimagining the Relationship of African Americans to the Great Outdoors* (Chapel Hill: University of North Carolina Press, 2014), 116–21; see also Dianne D. Glave, *Rooted in the Earth: Reclaiming the African American Environmental Heritage* (Chicago: Lawrence Hill Books, 2010).

25. Gunnar Myrdal, *An American Dilemma: The Negro Problem and Modern Democracy* (New York: Harper & Brothers, 1944), 346.

26. A growing body of contemporary research into racialized park visitation patterns confirms that race impacts park visitation. See Weber and Sultana, "Why Do So Few Minority People Visit National Parks? Visitation and the Accessibility of 'America's Best Idea,'" *Annals of the Association of American Geographers* 103 (2013): 437–64, and Patricia A. Taylor, Burke D. Grandjean, and James H. Gramann, *National Park Service Comprehensive Survey of the American Public, 2008–2009: Racial and Ethnic Diversity of the National Park System Visitors and Non-visitors*, Natural Resource Report (National Park Service, U.S. Department of the Interior, 2011). Since the late 1970s, academic and government-sponsored research, supported by the National Park Service and other concerned agencies, has presented general explanations for persistent relatively low rates of African American visitation. These include the relative poverty of African Americans, which constrains travel choice, cultural differences and ethnic preferences that create apparent distinctions between white versus minority recreational choices, and traveler experiences and expectations of discrimination when visiting parks. For a useful critique of this framework, see Patrick C. West, "The Tyranny of Metaphor: Interracial Relations, Minority Recreation, and the Wildland-Urban Interface," in *Culture, Conflict, and Communication in the Wildland-Urban Interface*, ed. Alan Ewert, Deborah Chavez, and Arthur Magill (Boulder, Colo.: Westview Press, 1993).

27. Finney, *Black Faces, White Spaces*, 99, 65–66.

28. Ibid., 92–115, 130.

29. Stanley Coulter, "Scenery—A Natural Resource," in *A State Park Anthology*, ed. Herbert Evison (Washington, D.C.: National Conference on State Parks, 1930), 13–17.

INDEX

Page references in *italics* refer to illustrations.